Praise for *In 27 Days*

"An emotional, heartfelt story. Vivid characters instantly draw the reader in, and the life-or-death suspense never lets up as the chapters count down from twenty-seven days to none. I couldn't turn the pages fast enough!"

A.V. GEIGER, author of
Follow Me Back

"Alison Gervais' smart twist on the second-chance plot makes *In 27 Days* a must-have for your bookshelf."

PATTY BLOUNT, award-winning
author of *Some Boys*

"An addictive, fast-paced read … this paranormal tale will have readers turning the pages to see if Hadley stops Archer from making a tragic mistake."

YA BOOKS CENTRAL, four-star review

"Heartwarming and authentic, *In 27 Days* is an emotionally gripping novel about second chances, falling in love, and the lengths we will go to in order to save the ones we care about."

TRISHA LEAVER, author of
The Secrets We Keep

"*In 27 Days* is a fully compelling, readable novel that reminds us of the power in kindness and compassion. Gervais skillfully shows how we never really know what someone else might be going through unless we ask. And how making a connection just might save a life."

CHRISTINA JUNE, author of
It Started with Goodbye

"Totally addictive! Hadley Jamison only has twenty-seven days to save enigmatic Archer Morales from death—and every second counts. A suspenseful adventure that you won't want to put down."

MARNI BATES, author of
Dial M for Murder

"*In 27 Days* is filled with love, pain, and suspense. I found myself unable to put the book down."

ASHLEY ROYER, author of
Remember to Forget

IN 27
DAYS

ALISON GERVAIS

BLINK

HarperCollins
PUBLISHERS
Since 1817

BLINK

The Day Of

There was something *off*. I couldn't put my finger on what exactly it was, but it was definitely there.

Yes, something was out of balance, I decided as I stepped off the bus and onto the sidewalk outside John F. Kennedy Prep. The place looked like it did almost every other day, with its red bricks, bright-colored banners strung up everywhere, and the jumble of students lingering around outside the front doors. The school had been around for more than a century, and it had that Old New York feel. Nothing was ever out of the ordinary.

Yet the gray clouds rolling in across the sky felt smothering, bringing with them a feeling of suspicion and . . . sadness. An almost suffocating sadness. New York was the city that never slept, the place that had a thousand different attitudes. But I'd never felt one like this before.

"C'mon, Hadley, you're in the way."

I quickly moved to the side as Taylor Lewis, my best friend, sauntered off the bus.

I first met Taylor during freshman orientation, when I'd been wandering the halls alone while looking for my classes. From that moment onward, she'd decided to take me under her wing because we were both wearing the same shirt from

American Apparel, and decided to teach me everything she already knew about the social scene at JFK. Without her, I would have been totally lost—literally, figuratively, and most certainly socially. Now, more than two years later, we were still best friends, and I was still content to hang out in Taylor's social-butterfly shadow.

"Why do you have that weird look on your face?" Taylor asked as we followed the throng of people through the front doors.

I glanced away from a group of teachers huddled together in the hallway by the front office, their heads together, whispering, and frowned at Taylor. "What look?"

She rolled her eyes and gave me a nudge with her elbow. "Never mind. Are you ready for that test in American Government today? I can barely understand what Monroe's talking about half the time, and I swear, it's totally pointless that we even know how many cabinet members there are or whatever, and I— Hadley, are you even listening to me?"

My focus was drawn to the pair of uniformed police officers located down the hallway from my locker, standing with the principal, Ms. Greene. By the stiff, grim expressions on their faces, I guessed they must have been talking about something highly unpleasant. But what would have brought the police to our high school?

"I'm sorry, Taylor, I'm just . . ." I couldn't come up with a word to describe how off I felt. "I don't know, just worried about the test too, I guess."

Taylor snorted out a laugh as I rummaged around in my locker for my chemistry textbook. "Why are you worried, Hadley? You're, like, the only one who actually manages to stay awake in Monroe's class."

"Guess I'm just lucky." That, or I had a lawyer for a dad who would flip if I didn't keep a decent grade in Government.

I left Taylor and made for homeroom, now feeling as though someone was following close behind me, breathing down my neck. I dropped into a seat toward the front of the class and focused on keeping my breathing in a steady pattern, succeeding until the first bell rang and our teacher didn't appear.

Mrs. Anderson, the German teacher who ran our homeroom, was probably the nicest person I'd ever met. She was almost always humming under her breath, and had a thousand-watt smile for every person who just happened to look her way. I didn't have the patience to learn German—I'd barely made it through my two required years of Spanish—but Mrs. Anderson seemed like a hoot, and she made homeroom bearable despite it being so ridiculously early in the morning.

The fact that Mrs. Anderson was late just added to my increasing unease. My friend Chelsea was convinced the teacher lived at JFK because she was always somewhere in the building with coffee and a sprinkled doughnut and attended every school function and football game. So where was she? It wasn't like Mrs. Anderson to be tardy.

More than five minutes passed before the door swung open and Mrs. Anderson came walking in. There was a coffee stain on the front of her sweater, and her glasses were slightly askew as she dumped a stack of folders on her desk, saying, "Sorry I'm late, class, sorry, there was a bit of a . . ." Her voice trailed off as she bit her lip, scrubbing at the stain on her sweater with a napkin. "Something rather . . . unfortunate happened."

In the seconds between her words, my heart picked up pace and beat an unsteady rhythm against my chest. I had no way of knowing what "unfortunate" thing happened, but a gut-wrenching feeling told me that whatever it was, it was *bad*.

Mrs. Anderson sighed as she tossed the napkin into the trash and leaned against her desk, crossing her arms over her chest. "Last night, one of our students here at JFK Prep committed suicide."

I sat back in my seat, feeling deflated as I let out a sharp gasp. *What?*

I'd known the moment I stepped off the bus not twenty minutes ago that something was wrong. But *this?* I wanted to ask who had so abruptly ended their life, but I found that I couldn't force myself to speak. My mouth was suddenly as dry as the Sahara Desert, and my tongue felt like sandpaper.

"Who was it?" a kid sitting a few rows behind me asked after the first few moments of tense silence.

Mrs. Anderson fiddled with the edge of her sweater. "Archer Morales."

That name was . . . very familiar. I'd heard it before, but I couldn't put a face to a name.

Wait a minute, a small voice in my mind reminded me. *Freshman English.*

That's right. Freshman English with Mrs. Casey. Archer Morales was the boy I'd sat next to first semester. I didn't make the instant connection when Mrs. Anderson had said his name because Archer had only spoken about three words the entire year.

Mrs. Anderson's voice faded into the background as she mentioned that school counselors would be available for the rest of the week at any time to talk about what happened. Soon, I couldn't hear her at all, too preoccupied with trying to remember anything I could about Archer Morales.

He'd been very quiet and kept his head down most of the time, diligently following along in whatever text we happened to be reading. The one and only time I'd really gotten a good look at his face was when we'd been forced to answer a set of questions on *Frankenstein*.

It might have been easy to forget a guy who rarely ever spoke, but this guy happened to be the most distracting person I'd ever met. I'd become tongue-tied almost the second he'd looked at me with these bright hazel eyes that made me feel like I was being X-rayed.

Looking back on that class now, I realized I'd done my best to forget the whole experience because of the annoyed expression on that attractive face the entire time we'd worked together. What girl wanted to remember the moment a guy made it clear he'd rather be doing anything else *but* look at you?

Come to think of it, that had seemed to be Archer Morales's attitude toward everything. JFK Prep was a big school, but I'd seen him in the hallways from time to time, easy to spot because of his height and tousled dark hair, but he'd always managed to be on his own, and everyone had always given him a wide berth.

Archer Morales was—*had been*—one of JFK Prep's outcasts. And now he was gone.

I bolted upright in my seat when the first period bell rang overhead, pulling me out of my reverie. The rest of the class was already on their feet and filing from the room, talking quietly with one another instead of chatting and laughing like normal. It was even more obvious now, the change in the atmosphere. I trudged my way through the halls to chemistry class in a daze, unable to wrap my mind around the fact that one of my classmates was dead.

It wasn't as if I'd really known Archer Morales. We couldn't even have been called friends on any sort of level. He'd been all but a perfect stranger to me. So why did I feel like I was about to fall apart?

By the time school let out, the temperature had dropped outside, making the air chilly and uncomfortable as I headed for one of the buses at the curb. What I really needed was to curl up in bed and forget this day ever happened.

I took an empty seat toward the back and leaned my head against the window, closing my eyes, for once thankful Taylor had decided to ditch early to spend time with her latest beau-du jour. None of the other girls we hung out with rode the same bus, so I was able to think in silence. The rocking of the vehicle was soothing, almost providing a distraction from the thoughts swarming around my brain like hurricane, but all too soon, the ride was over.

I pulled up the collar of my coat and crossed my arms over my chest, beginning the walk to the apartment building I'd lived in for almost my entire life. The complex was right on the edge of the Upper East Side, so it was a little more ostentatious than other buildings in Manhattan.

I often thought it was lonely, being shut up in the apartment while my parents worked impossible business hours, but I couldn't have been more thrilled I was going home to an empty apartment that afternoon. The familiarity of my messy bedroom and the comfy sheets on my bed had never seemed so appealing.

"Evening, Hadley," Hanson, the doorman, said as I approached the gray glass building. "Good day at school?"

I briefly considered telling Hanson what had happened. He was a nice man, and always seemed to be genuinely interested in how my day went. But I didn't want to say the words aloud, that one of my classmates had killed himself, because I still didn't want to believe that it had actually happened.

"Fantastic," I finally said as he held open the door for me.

"I remember what high school was like," Hanson said as I passed over the threshold. "As soon as you get out of there, the world's a much better place."

I had my doubts, but it was nice to hear Hanson say so anyway.

I crossed the marble-tiled, fountain-decked lobby to the elevators and rode up to the seventh floor. Heading down the lavishly decorated hallway, I pulled my set of keys out of my bag and unlocked the door to 7E.

My parents had never been what you could exactly call *humble*.

Our apartment was filled with pristine leather furniture, cream-colored carpets, and tasteful photos of the city hanging on the walls, which complemented the floor-to-ceiling windows that lined the living room and dining room. And the state-of-the-art, chrome appliance kitchen was almost another art piece in itself. My mother spent so little time here, it was amazing she'd even found the time to decorate the place to begin with.

A lawyer and an assistant CFO, my parents had intense work schedules, and they rarely gave me a second thought when they left the city on work trips leaving me behind for sometimes a week or longer. When that happened, my eighty-seven-year-old neighbor Mrs. Ellis would check in on me every other day or so to make sure I was doing all right, but that wasn't exactly the same thing as having a mom or dad around.

I knew I was extremely lucky to live in such a nice place and have so much money at my disposal, but the whole "rich" thing honestly made me a little uncomfortable, even if it was something I'd known for most of my life. My parents hadn't always made stellar paychecks. Sometimes I missed the simple little townhouse we'd lived in over in Chelsea before my mom was promoted and my dad took over his firm. At least then we'd actually spent time as a family and had dinner together every night.

I breathed a sigh of relief once I shut the door to my bedroom and locked it.

My bedroom was my happy place. The Christmas lights strung up above the balcony window, the Broadway playbills and pictures of Taylor and our group tacked up on the corkboard above my desk, the rows and rows of DVDs and CDs I'd collected over the years—all of it was the perfect escape from the stuffy leather furniture and the professional photographs of the city from some art gallery in SoHo that hung in the living room.

I half-heartedly attempted to memorize some formulas for chemistry, but five minutes later I gave up, chucked my textbook at the wall, and flopped facedown on my bed.

It felt as if there was some part of myself that was missing, now that Archer Morales wasn't alive and walking this earth anymore. It made me desperately wish that he were still here, despite the fact that he and I had only exchanged a few words.

Somehow I couldn't make sense of the fact that he was here yesterday, and now he was gone . . . permanently. Then again, I wasn't all that familiar with death. I'd gone to my great-grandma Louise's funeral when I was six, but that was the only time I'd ever experienced someone I knew, at least a little, passing away. But I didn't like seeing her body in a casket then, and I didn't like the idea of Archer's body lying cold somewhere now.

Burrowing underneath the covers, I shoved my face into a pillow and I finally started to cry.

Two Days After

Two days, one small news report, and an obituary in a local newspaper later, there was no denying the fact that Archer Morales was dead. As much as I hated the thought of one of my classmates feeling so much despair that they believed ending their life was the only way out, it was the truth. More than once, I found myself standing on my tiptoes in the hallway at school, trying to catch any small glimpse of Archer, but it was pointless. He'd always been there, somewhere in the background, but now he never would be again.

I stood in front of the floor-length mirror in my bedroom, tugging at the ends of the lacy black dress I'd found shoved in my closet. I felt awkward and uncomfortable wearing a dress when I normally stuck to jeans and a T-shirt, but I wanted to wear something nice to Archer's funeral. In homeroom the day before, Mrs. Anderson had announced that students were welcome to attend Archer's funeral to pay their respects, but it still didn't feel like a proper invitation. The hope that tonight would help me find some sense of closure, make sense of why I couldn't stop thinking about him, far outweighed any nerves.

After I decided I looked presentable enough, I slipped into my jacket, grabbed my purse, and left my room. The cab I'd called for was set to arrive any minute. I figured I should at least attempt to eat something small before leaving.

As I headed down the hallway toward the living room, I heard the sounds of a smooth, polite voice speaking. When I rounded the corner, I was shocked to find my father lounging on the couch, iPhone in hand, merrily chatting away.

What was the great Kenneth Jamison doing home so early? It was barely a quarter past six in the evening. This was unprecedented. The earliest I could remember him being home in the past three years was eight o'clock.

"Hey, Rick, I gotta go," he said, looking at me as I passed by. "Hadley's getting ready to leave."

He disconnected and tossed his phone onto the coffee table, getting to his feet while stretching his arms behind his head with a yawn.

"What are you doing home, Dad?" I asked. "You're never home this early."

"I know," my dad said, following me toward the kitchen. "But Rick and I closed the Blanchard-Emilie case today, so we took the rest of the night off to celebrate."

"Oh. That's nice."

An awkward silence that I so could have done without at that point fell as I pulled open the refrigerator, rummaging around for a snack.

It was always like this whenever I happened to see my dad.

He was my father, yes, but he was usually so engrossed in his work that we didn't really get the chance to spend much time together. An evening at home was a secondary concern for one of the city's most celebrated lawyers.

"So."

I came up from the fridge with a handful of grapes and a bottle of water, looking to my dad with a confused frown. "Yeah?"

"So." He cleared his throat, leaning up against the counter, crossing his arms. "You're going to that boy's funeral."

"Um . . . yeah," I said. "Archer Morales's."

His brows furrowed in thought for a moment. "Morales . . . Why does that name sound so familiar?"

I shrugged, popping a couple of grapes into my mouth. "No idea. There are probably hundreds of people with that name in the city."

"Maybe."

I munched on a few more grapes, silently hoping that the intercom by the door would ring at any moment, signaling the arrival of my cab, and I could make my escape from this unpleasant conversation.

I didn't want to talk to my father about Archer Morales.

What I really wanted to do was to muster up the courage to say good-bye to a boy I'd barely known, find a way to let go of him and not feel so unusually guilty. To apologize for not paying more attention, for not being there in some way for him.

"Is Taylor going with you to the funeral?" my dad asked after a moment.

"No, I'm going by myself," I said. "Taylor's busy."

My dad frowned again, looking unhappy at the prospect of my going out into the city alone. "Are you sure? I'm not really . . . comfortable with the idea of you going out in the city at night," he said. "I could always, um . . . go with—"

I was quick to stop him before he could get any further with that very unnecessary sentence. "Dad. Please. I know the rules about being out in the city at night. I'll be fine. I promise."

"All right. Just keep your phone on you, okay? And don't stay out too late."

Thankfully, the intercom buzzed loudly right at that moment, preventing the conversation from continuing any longer.

"That's my cab," I announced, finishing the rest of my water bottle. "I've gotta go."

"Er, right."

I gave my dad a quick hug and muttered out a good-bye, then walked swiftly from the kitchen, thoroughly grateful to be leaving.

The air was frigidly cold, biting at my skin as I stepped out into the early December night. Hanson offered me a smile and a wink as he held open the door of the cab idling at the curb.

"Going somewhere?"

"A . . . funeral," I admitted. "One of my classmates, um, committed suicide."

Hanson was silent for a moment. He didn't say he was sorry to hear that, and instead reached out to squeeze my shoulder. That, I think, was exactly what I needed.

I slid into the overstuffed seat, tightly clutching the seat belt as Hanson swung the door shut.

"Where to?" the driver grunted from up front in a gruff Brooklyn accent.

I gave the driver the address to the church Mrs. Anderson had mentioned. The cab pulled away from the curb and slid into traffic much too quickly for my liking. I leaned my head back against the seat and squeezed my eyes shut, breathing in through my nose and out through my mouth.

I had no idea what to expect once I arrived. The last

funeral I went to, I could barely remember. Would everyone be wearing black and crying? Would there be sad music playing? Would a fight break out among Archer's family members if someone spoke out of turn and said the wrong thing? Things like that seemed to happen at every funeral I'd ever seen on TV, but I didn't think that meant anything in the real world.

When the cab pulled up to the curb outside of the church, I grabbed a few bills from my purse to pay the fare, then stepped out onto the sidewalk before I could convince myself that this was a terrible idea and beg to be taken home.

I wrapped my arms around myself as a breeze whipped down the street, raising the hair on the back of my neck. I was expecting there to be people crowded around outside, sharing in their grief, but the place was as barren as the shelves in a store after Black Friday. But that same feeling of being watched crept over me as I walked up the front steps of the church.

As I stepped inside, the smell of incense used during mass immediately hit my nose. It had been a while since I'd been to church—we'd stopped going once my parents' careers had taken off—but the familiarity was comforting on some small level.

The lobby I was now standing in was just as empty as the steps outside, raising yet another alarm. Where was everyone? I slipped my phone out of my bag to make sure I hadn't gotten the time wrong.

6:58.

I couldn't just leave now.

I took a deep breath, dipped my fingers into the bowl of holy water on my left, crossed myself, and then walked into the inner portion of the church. The front altar was decorated with bouquets of white flowers and cloths, almost like a Christmas mass but with a much more somber air. Set on a stand in front of the altar was a modest casket covered in a display of more white flowers.

The church itself was beautiful, with stained glass windows and marble pillars, but it seemed even larger than it actually was due to the rows and rows of empty pews. Only the first two pews were occupied. I made out a few teachers—Mr. Gage, a math teacher, and Ms. Keller, who taught literature—and then a small number of people who went to JFK Prep that I knew only by face and not by name.

A part of me had expected the church to be packed. It was heartbreaking to see more people hadn't shown up to pay their respects to Archer Morales and his family. I kept my eyes fixed on the front of the church as I quickly made my way down the center aisle, determined not to meet anyone's gaze. Not wanting to draw attention to myself, realizing I'd shown up exactly two minutes before the start of the service, I took a seat in an empty pew a few rows back, folded my hands tightly in my lap, and waited for the ceremony to begin.

The funeral service officially started right as scheduled. The congregation rose to their feet while the small choir beside the altar started singing a soft, melodic tune. A priest accompanied by two deacons and an altar boy made his way up the aisle toward the altar. The priest had only been speaking for a few moments about losing a life so young when the crying began.

It didn't seem like anyone near me was crying, but after a moment of peering around on my tiptoes, I saw a woman in the front row being supported by the man beside her, and she was very clearly sobbing into his shoulder. I couldn't see her face, and I had no way of knowing who she was, but it didn't take much on my part to realize that the woman must have been Archer Morales's mother.

I decided then that very few things in the world could break your heart quite like a mother mourning the loss of her child. A boy was dead when he didn't have to be. After that, I figured it was okay for me to cry too.

The tears started falling fast and furiously as Mr. Gage walked up to the pulpit to say a few words about Archer and what an exemplary student he had been. I was crying while a boy with the same eyes as Archer's stood next and gave a kind, heartfelt eulogy. And I was sobbing when I was given a white rose and then stumbled my way up to the altar to lay the flower on Archer's casket.

Maybe I stood there longer than necessary, but what was I supposed to say? I'm sorry I didn't ever speak to you? I'm sorry you felt like you had to end your life? I wish you were still here?

"Archer, I'm—"

"Do you know my big brother?"

I quickly turned around and saw a little girl standing in front of me, with pretty dark curls and bright blue eyes, blinking up at me in confusion. The girl couldn't have been any older than five, and that somehow made it all the worse, learning that Archer had a little sister so young.

"Um . . . yeah," I said, wiping at my eyes. "I went to school with your brother."

The little girl gave a toothy grin. "He's pretty cool, huh?"

I felt another wave of sadness at the girl's words.

She hadn't said *was*. She said *is*. She spoke as if her brother were still alive. I didn't know how old she actually was, but she looked young enough to not fully understand the concept of death. I didn't envy the person who would have to explain to her that her brother would never be coming home again.

I did my best to give a small laugh at her enthusiasm. "Definitely."

"I'm Rosie," the little girl said, offering out a hand for me to shake in a rather adult-like manner.

"Hi, Rosie," I said, shaking her hand. "I'm Hadley."

"Mommy says I'm not supposed to talk to strangers, but since you know Archer and you're pretty, I think it's okay," Rosie said in a rush.

"Oh," I said, unsure of what to say. "Thank you?"

"C'mon, you should come meet my mommy!"

Rosie grabbed at my hand and tugged me back toward the pews, where a group of people had congregated, speaking with one another.

"Mom! Mom!" Rosie chirped, shoving through people's legs. "Have you met Hadley?"

A woman with long, dark hair tinged with a few streaks of gray and wide hazel eyes broke away from the elderly woman she'd been speaking with and turned to Rosie with a disapproving look. "Rosie, how many times have I told you not to run off?" she scolded, hand on hip. "You scare the living daylights out of me when you do that!"

Rosie seemed to brush this off and gestured up at me. "Mommy, have you met Hadley?"

The woman turned to me in surprise, and she looked vaguely familiar, even though I was positive I'd never seen her before. She really was rather pretty, but the dark circles underneath her bloodshot eyes and the pinched look about her face made it seem as if she hadn't slept a wink in days.

"Hadley, is it?" She gave a small smile as she reached out shake my hand. "Thank you for rounding up my daughter."

"It's no problem," I said quickly. "None at all. I was just . . ."

"Did you go to school with Archer?"

"Um. Yes." I nervously cleared my throat as the woman stared at me, an unusually kind look on her face, despite how exhausted she appeared to be. "We had English together freshman year."

"That's nice," she said softly. "I'm Regina, Archer's . . . m-mother."

Her voice cracked on that last word, and her eyes filled with tears, but she sucked in a deep breath as she scooped Rosie up into her arms and kissed her cheek, obviously trying to distract herself. Of course she looked familiar. Her eyes. It was hard to forget eyes like those.

Regina Morales had to be the strongest woman I'd ever seen. Her son had just died, and yet she was still trying to smile for her daughter. I was at a loss as to what to say to her. Any words of condolence I could possibly offer her wouldn't make an ounce of difference. So even though I was a total stranger, I hugged her. She didn't seem to mind.

Fifteen minutes later, I made my way out of the cathedral. It was now cold enough that I could see my breath make clouds in front of me as I exhaled. I stepped off the curb and waved a hand, trying to flag down a cab. Cars kept whizzing past, not showing any signs of slowing down.

"A young girl like yourself shouldn't be out and about in the city at this time of night, don't you think?"

I whipped toward the sound of the deep, husky voice that had just spoken behind me.

The light from the streetlamp a few feet away wasn't bright enough to illuminate the cathedral steps, but I could make out what looked to be the figure of a man sitting on the bottom step, legs sprawled out in front of him.

How could I have possibly not seen him? Had he even been there as I walked down the steps?

My words came out as a stammer. "Who . . . w-what do you want?"

"Not much."

I stumbled backward as the man rose to his feet, sauntering forward into the glow of the streetlamp.

Looking up at him made me wish I'd never stepped out of my apartment tonight. He was tall with slick, dark hair, and wore a black leather jacket, jeans, and scuffed-up boots. I couldn't make out any distinctive facial features, but with his sunken eyes and hollow cheekbones, he looked as if he had never eaten a scrap of food in his life.

That wasn't the creepiest thing about him, though. His eyes were. Those black, depthless eyes staring down at me made it feel as if he knew every thought that had ever crossed my mind before.

"I . . . I'm not looking for trouble," I said, unable to keep my voice from trembling. "I think you—"

"Oh, I'm not here to bring you any trouble, Hadley Jamison," the man said, cracking a smirk that sent a sliver of fear down my spine.

Who *was* this guy?

"How do you—"

"Know your name? I know everything, Hadley. It kind of comes with the job description."

I may not have been a genius, but I knew enough of what was really out in the world to tell that there was something wrong with this man. Something *very* wrong with this man.

"Look, I don't know who you are," I said uneasily, "but you better stay away from me."

The man rummaged around in his pockets and came up with a cigarette, which he immediately lit and then took a long drag. I couldn't help but gag when the acrid smoke hit my nose.

"Or you'll what?" he said, raising an eyebrow. "Scream?"

My heart was pounding so fast, I thought I might keel over in a dead faint. I quickly calculated my chances of making a run for it, or at least jumping into the first cab I could find, but since I was wearing heels, the odds were not in my favor. I doubted I would be able to get my shoes off fast enough to start running without being easily overtaken.

What was I supposed to do?

"Who are you?" I demanded.

Another wide, eerie smirk curled the man's mouth as he took a second drag on his cigarette. He shrugged a shoulder. "I'm known by a lot of names, actually. The Grim Reaper. The angel Azrael. Mephistopheles. But I suppose for simplicity's sake, you can just call me Death."

CHAPTER 3

The Deal

When I was four years old, I had the not-so-bright idea to jump into my aunt Theresa's pool even though I had absolutely no clue how to swim. The shock of the cold water biting at my skin had frozen me to the core. When I'd finally been pulled out, I couldn't hold back the shivers that wracked through me, and I'd spent several minutes gasping for air.

The same unpleasant, frightening sensation washed over me as I stood on the sidewalk outside the church, staring up into the depthless black eyes of the man who claimed to be Death.

"Er . . ." I snapped my mouth shut to keep my teeth from chattering. "Umm . . . I think . . . I-I . . ."

Every fiber of my being was screaming at me to *move*, to start running and to not look back, but I couldn't force myself into motion.

An almost amused expression crossed Death's face. "You must be made of much stronger stuff than I thought, Hadley Jamison. I was expecting you to have already taken off running and screaming by now."

"Give me another second and I will be," I managed to say, unable to keep back a shiver.

"Oh, I don't think you really mean that," Death mused with a shake of his head. He dropped his cigarette onto the ground and snubbed it out with the toe of his boot. "I think you're interested in what I have to say."

"I-I . . . I'm not—"

"Let's take a little walk, shall we?"

Death had a sudden vise-like grip on my arm and began pulling me right into the middle of oncoming traffic.

"What, are you crazy?" I shrieked, trying to yank my arm out of his iron grasp. "You're going to get us killed!"

Death let out an annoyed sigh, sinking his nails into my arm. "Oh, do be quiet, will you? I know when you're going to die, and I can assure you, it's not going to be tonight."

Somehow, that wasn't reassuring.

Death stepped up onto the sidewalk across the street and set off walking at a brisk pace, all but dragging me along behind him. I tried digging my heels into the ground, relentlessly tugging at my arm, but I was afraid that if I struggled any further I would end up breaking a bone. I thought about screaming at the top of my lungs, maybe making a grab at someone walking by, but not one person on the sidewalk would even meet my eyes. It was as if they were completely oblivious to the teenage girl being dragged down the street by some man who looked like an extra from *Interview with the Vampire*.

We made it two blocks before Death abruptly stopped and bent down to mutter in my ear, "You and I both know I'll just catch you and drag you back by your hair if you try to make a run for it. So I suggest you play along for now, hmm?"

I swallowed hard, fighting back the bile rising in my throat. I did not consider myself a wimp. I was a New Yorker; I could look after myself. But right at that moment? I wasn't sure if I had ever been so frightened in my entire life.

"Fine," I said, my voice more like a squeak.

"Good girl."

I stopped trying to bolt, even though the urge had now become overwhelming.

By the time Death finally stopped walking, my feet ached inside my heels. "Here we are," Death said, pulling the door to a Starbucks open with a little flourish.

I stumbled my way into the coffee shop, holding my arms tightly around myself. This had to be some strange, terrifying nightmare; had a guy claiming to be Death really just shown up at my classmate's funeral to escort me all the way to a Starbucks? Death's hands descended on my shoulders and forcefully steered me up to the front counter. The girl at the register looked up with a cheery smile that was immediately wiped clean once she laid eyes on Death.

"Erh . . ."

"Good evening," Death said, his tone suddenly formal. "We'd like two black coffees, please."

The girl nodded robotically, fumbling around for the cups with shaking hands. Death slid a crisp ten-dollar bill across the counter, smiling kindly. "No change."

"Erhm . . . thank you."

From the way the girl stumbled around, not meeting our eyes, it was obvious my plan of mouthing *help me* was not going to work. I grabbed the two coffee cups when the girl handed them over, and Death steered me over to a table by the window that sat beneath a row of paper snowflakes. My stomach did a little flip-flop when Death took a seat, the fluorescent lighting above casting his face into brighter light.

It was like looking at someone terminally ill; his skin was

the color of parchment, which stretched taut across his sharp cheekbones, and his eyes were sunken in. No wonder he went by Death. He *looked* like it. Even stranger were the black markings crisscrossing every inch of his hands, slipping up the sleeves of his jacket, and creeping under the collar of his shirt. It took me a second to realize that the markings were actually small, crudely shaped clocks.

Death's lips twisted into a grim smile as he stared up at me, gesturing to the seat across the small table from him. As he moved his arm, I could've sworn I saw the tiny hands on each of the clocks *moving.* "Have a seat."

I carefully lowered myself into the seat, clutching my cup of coffee. "Right." I cleared my throat, hoping to muster up even the smallest amount of courage to get through whatever this was. "What is this about?"

Death set his coffee cup down and clasped his hands together, leaning across the table toward me. "I thought we could have little chat about Archer Morales."

I downed a swallow of coffee, the hot liquid scalding my throat, and shuddered at the bitter taste. "I'm not . . ." I grasped the coffee cup compulsively. "I think you're . . ." I wasn't sure if I was tongue-tied because of this situation with Death, or because Death wanted to talk about Archer Morales. "I . . . I really think I should be—"

Death's hand was on my shoulder, forcing me back into my chair before I'd even gotten to my feet.

"Listen closely, Hadley, because I'm only going to say this once. I am going to offer you the chance to go back in time twenty-seven days to prevent Archer Morales from ending his life."

It was quite possible that my heart stopped beating in the silence that fell after Death's words. He wanted me to do *what*?

"Sorry, what did you just say?"

"I told you I was only going to say it once."

"Is this some kind of joke to you?" Somehow, I'd gotten up, and I was leaning across the table, getting right into Death's face. "Do you think it's funny that one of my classmates killed himself?"

Death stared at me with a blank look before suddenly bursting into laughter.

It was all I could do to keep from grabbing my coffee and throwing it in his face.

"On the contrary, Hadley," he said after a moment, still chuckling. "I find this to be a very serious matter."

He snapped his fingers.

What followed had to be the strangest thing I'd ever seen before. The effect was slow moving, like rolling fog, but one by one, every last person in Starbucks froze right in the middle of whatever they had been doing. The stream of liquid pouring from an espresso maker remained suspended in midair. A woman in the process of blowing her nose was stuck with her face screwed up in an awkward expression. A man and a woman stepping into the shop, wih a little boy in between them clutching at their hands, were stopped right in the middle of the doorway, and a cold breeze was wafting in from outside.

"What . . ."

"I assure you, I'm quite serious about this," Death said, resting his chin on his clasped hands. "Now, would you mind sitting down so we can have a calm, rational discussion?"

I dropped into my chair, my legs unable to keep supporting

me. Pinching myself seemed like a good idea, but I couldn't get my arm and hand to cooperate.

"How . . ." I swallowed again, trying to think of what to say.

"How do I stop time?" Death finished for me. "Well, that's just part of the job description." He shrugged, sipping at his coffee. "It's such a shame, isn't it? Archer Morales was really a very good kid. Came from a nice family. Mama's boy. Loved his little sister. And you, Hadley Jamison, don't want him dead."

"Of course I don't," I snapped.

"The gift of life is valuable, something to be treasured," Death continued. "And it's a travesty when something like that is snatched away too early. I've been around for thousands of years, seen thousands of things, but I have never seen something as terrible as a soul being taken away when it didn't need to be. So, tell me, Hadley. If you had the chance to prevent something bad from happening, despite everything you were afraid of and what might happen . . . would you do it?"

I thought of Archer Morales and everything he'd lost. He was never going to get to go to prom or graduate high school or go to college, or to meet the love of his life, get married, maybe have kids, see the world or *change* the world.

I thought of Regina, Archer's mother, and his little sister Rosie and how she didn't yet understand her brother was gone. Just how badly he was going to be missed.

How could I *not* do this? Even if I was simply playing along with some madman who had the power to freeze time.

"Okay."

Death gave me a curious look. "Okay . . . what?"

"I'll . . . I'll do it. Whatever it is I need to do to . . . to save Archer."

"Is that right?"

I nodded, not trusting my ability to speak.

Death kept his eyes fixed on me for several moments as I simply sat there, trying to convince myself that this was real, and that maybe, just maybe, I really was being given the opportunity to save Archer.

"I'm not going to promise you this is going to be easy."

"I'm not stupid enough to think that."

"Smart girl."

He reached into his leather jacket and came up with a stack of tightly furled papers, which he dropped onto the table in front of me.

"A contract?" That small bit of movie cliché seemed so utterly ludicrous in the midst of this more-than-serious situation. "But I thought—"

"Humor me."

I slid the stack of papers toward me and glanced down at the first page. "Just how, exactly, am I supposed to read this contract if I can't even read what it's written in?" I pointed out, tapping my finger on the paper. "All these weird black symbols weren't something they taught us to read in kindergarten."

"English isn't the only language in the world. This whole contract is just a formality as it is," Death assured me. "Trust me."

"And why should I trust you?"

He reached a hand inside his jacket again and came up with a pen. he held it out for me to take. "Just another leap of faith."

I was beginning to get the feeling I would be doing a fair few leaps of faith if I signed my name on the contract Death was offering.

"My father is a lawyer, you know," I said. "I'm not stupid enough to just sign away on the dotted line without knowing what the catch is."

"There is no catch," Death said, eyebrows raised, a shocked expression on his face, like he couldn't believe I would even think about suggesting he was messing with me. "I would never lie."

That was obviously sarcasm, and I decided not to comment on it. And I knew nothing about Death, but it was obvious the man was anything *but* human. His attempt at trying to convince me he was one was laughable.

"The longer you drag this out, the more difficult it'll be to send you back. Archer's already been gone two days."

The mention of Archer was enough to make me snatch the pen and flip to the last page. I spent a tense moment of hesitation before I scribbled my name down on the appropriate line, then shoved the stack of papers back across the table at Death.

"Now what's supposed to happen?" I demanded. "And why do I only have twenty-seven days?"

Twenty-seven days didn't seem like it would be enough time to convince someone they didn't need to end their life. It didn't seem like there would ever be enough time in the world to convince someone they didn't need to end their life.

"The time allotted in each contract is never the same," Death told me as he reached over to grab the papers and shove them back into his jacket. "In this case, twenty-seven days is the amount of time it took Archer Morales to first consider taking his own life and then to finally go through with it."

My heart lurched in my chest, and it took a moment of deep breathing to not feel like I was about to burst into tears again. I didn't want to think of what that must have felt like for Archer.

"But I should warn you," Death said, drawing me away from my painful thoughts.

Of course there had to be that little afterthought, something he'd failed to mention until *after* I'd already signed the contract.

"Warn me about what?" I asked hesitantly.

"There are things in this world that have a . . . set order," Death said carefully, as if choosing his words. "And sometimes there are . . . *things* that aren't too happy when that order is disrupted. Sometimes they don't like it."

It was obvious that Death was barely scratching the surface of his warning, and it was not comforting. If Death was one of those *things* out there in the world, what else might there be? "You could've mentioned that *before* I signed the contract, you know."

"Yes, well, I wouldn't worry your pretty little head about it *too* much," Death answered. "Good luck, kid."

He snapped his fingers again before I could protest, and everything went black.

CHAPTER 4

Let the Games Begin— 27 Days Until

E xcuse me, Miss Jamison? Miss Jamison? *Miss Jamison!*"
I jerked awake with a shout, nearly tumbling out of my seat and onto the floor.

Mr. Monroe, my annoying, balding American Government teacher, was hovering over me, disapproval written all over his face.

"Thank you for choosing to wake up and join the rest of the class, Miss Jamison," he said disparagingly

"I'm sorry, Mr. Monroe, I didn't mean to fall asleep, I—"

My voice broke off as I took in my surroundings, realizing that I was sitting in the middle of my American Government classroom, surrounded by my snickering classmates, the date on the whiteboard boldly displayed in green marker for all to see.

November 11.

Everything came to a screeching halt and began to crash down around me. November 11. What? The last time I'd checked, it had been December 9th. I had just gone to Archer

Morales's funeral because he had committed suicide, and then I'd—made a deal with Death.

I'd made a deal with Death. Archer Morales had killed himself, and I'd made a deal with Death in order to stop him. Was I truly sitting in my American Government class twenty-seven days in the past?

"E-Excuse me, Mr. Monroe? I need to . . ." I stood, grabbed at my coat and bag, and stumbled my way toward the door. "I've got to . . ."

Make a run for it? Throw up? Pass out? Anything sounded better than staying in this classroom any longer.

I dashed down an empty hallway lined with lockers and banged my way into the girls' restroom. I checked the stalls to make sure that the place really was empty, then collapsed against the counter, my breath coming out in sharp gasps.

I twisted the faucet on and splashed cold water in my face, thankful I wasn't wearing makeup. Then, with another deep breath, I started at my reflection in the grimy mirror, hoping I would at least recognize myself.

It was a relief to see that I still looked like me; still a brunette with the same plain brown eyes and straight nose, but my cheeks were as pale as a sheet and the expression on my face was one of pure shock. I was even wearing a pair of jeans and a blouse I remembered wearing weeks ago and had last seen on the floor of my closet.

I distinctly remembered the air of depression hanging over the school the day we found out Archer killed himself, how empty and sad his funeral had been, and I definitely knew that I had met Archer's mother, Regina, and his little sister, Rosie.

And there was no way, even in my worst nightmares, I

could have imagined somebody like Death. I wouldn't ever be able to forget his gaunt face or his unsettling smirk, the way he stared at me with those unnatural black eyes, or even those pages full of those weird, looping symbols that I'd been forced to sign—the contract.

"All right, Hadley," I said to my reflection. "Either you just had some crazy dream, or this is all actually real and you've just time traveled."

I felt ridiculous just saying those words aloud to myself. Good thing no one else was around to hear me talking to my reflection. I left the restroom and leaned against the wall outside, squeezing my eyes shut. I needed to come up with a plan, except my mind had gone spectacularly blank. I wasn't a science fiction buff, and for all I knew there could be some set of time travel laws I was supposed to follow. I could've already broken a handful of them in the five minutes since I opened my eyes.

Was I supposed to go back to the church? Go back to that Starbucks, see if Death was still there, and try to contact him in some way?

And then the answer occurred to me so abruptly, I felt stupid for not having thought of it right away.

Look for Archer.

Even if this was all a dream—and I suddenly hoped it wasn't and Archer was alive—I had to find him. Before I could really organize my thoughts into actions, I took off walking down the hallway, around a few corners, until I was breezing through into the library. Google had been invented for a reason, and I was going to take advantage of it.

I found an empty computer at one of the stations near

the Nonfiction section and took a seat, using my school ID to log in.

Pulling up Google, I did a cursory glance to make sure no one was really paying attention to me, then typed in *Manhattan, Archer Morales, obituary.*

Hundreds of results popped up.

I scrolled through the first few links, but none of the articles or obituaries had any information I was looking for. No headlines saying *Tragic Story of Local Teenager's Suicide* or *Funeral Service Held for Young High School Student* or anything. I spent a good ten minutes searching for any scrap of information that might prove useful, and when it turned out to be pointless, I logged off the computer.

What next, then? Wander the halls and peek into every classroom in the hope Archer might be in one of them? The bell rang loudly overhead, signaling the end of the class period. I checked the time on the wall clock beside me and realized that my lunch hour had just begun.

I left the library and followed the throng of students filing down the staircase and into the cafeteria. I jumped in the food line behind a gaggle of freshmen girls and snatched at the first batch of fries I could get my hands on.

"HADLEY! There you are!"

I turned at the voice and saw Taylor barreling her way through the line to my side.

"Where were you last night?" Taylor demanded, eyes narrowed at me. "I called your phone and texted you, like, a hundred times, and you didn't answer! Did you forget we were supposed to go hang out at the Javabean?"

"You did?" I slipped my phone out of my pocket and

checked my messages. I had three missed phone calls and nineteen unread text messages. "Oh. Sorry. I got caught up with my homework and I fell asleep early."

Taylor's eyebrows shot up her forehead. "What's up with you? You didn't even ride the bus this morning."

"Err . . . yeah. I woke up late and had to take a cab. I missed first period."

I was such a pitiful liar. I was surprised Taylor hadn't called me out on it.

"Uh-huh." Taylor grabbed a salad and followed me as I made for the cash register. "Because you wake up late so often."

"Look, it was an accident," I said. "I promise, everything is okay. I'm fine."

It would be a relief to blurt out the truth to Taylor and tell her everything that just occurred, but there was no way on earth she'd ever believe me. Nobody would ever believe a story as crazy as mine. I wasn't even sure I believed it entirely myself. I needed to see Archer with my own eyes, see for myself that he was alive and breathing, before I could consider this my newly altered reality.

Taylor stared me down for another moment with a perplexed look before she finally relented, giving a heavy sigh. "Fine."

She then launched into a story about her current beau, a football player named Noah Parker, as I handed some change to the lady at the cash register and went to scope out a table to sit at. Everything was back to normal for Taylor. Too bad I couldn't say the same.

Lunch passed in a blur spent tuning out Taylor and the rest of the girls as I scarfed down my french fries. I discreetly tried to examine every person who strolled by the table, and those sitting around me, hoping I would be lucky enough to catch sight of a pair of hazel eyes or dark hair belonging to Archer. No such luck.

As soon as lunch ended, I dashed off to my locker to swap books for my next class. Continuing on like everything was normal and nothing completely life altering had just happened was the last thing I wanted to do, but my best chance at finding even a small glimpse of Archer was by staying at school. So I made it through the day, and by that I really meant I managed to behave normally enough for people not to notice that there was something seriously wrong with me.

I walked unsteadily from my seventh-period class toward my locker so I could grab my things and head home. I had a date with my bed, a couple of Tylenol to deal with the sharp throbbing above my left eye, and a cup of tea. I hoped that after a nice long sleep, I would be able to think more clearly and come up with a plan to find Archer. Assuming this wasn't all a dream, of course. I'd never realized before just how fine the line between dream and reality was. It really wasn't all that difficult to confuse the two if you weren't in your right mind—which, clearly, I wasn't.

I dumped all of my things into my bag when I reached my locker, and turned to make for the bus when I smacked right into someone and went tumbling to the floor.

"Oomph!"

"My bad."

Letting out a huff of air, I brushed my hair out of my eyes and looked up at the person I'd accidentally walked into. I was staring up at Archer Morales.

"You!" I gasped, scrambling upright. "What are *you* doing here?"

Archer Morales raised an eyebrow, a confused look crossing his face. "The answer to that would be because I go to school here. What are you doing here, Hadley?"

It was as if my brain had suddenly gone into overdrive, and I couldn't come up with any words or actions that wouldn't make it seem as if I were completely insane. The expression on Archer's face as he stared down at me clearly said it was already too late for that.

He gave me a small, polite nod and set off down the hallway at a brisk pace. Only thirty seconds of interaction and already he was walking off? Definitely not a good sign.

"Hey, wait a second!" I practically had to sprint to keep up with him. "How do you know my name?"

I didn't think I'd left that much of an impression on him, let alone enough to remember me from one class two years ago.

Archer stopped at the head of the staircase and turned back to stare at me. "You're Hadley Jamison, daughter of that hotshot lawyer and his businesswoman wife. We had English together freshman year. You turned the color of a lobster whenever I looked at you."

Good to see he remembers that, I thought with an eye roll. Just great. "Well, I guess I just— Hang on, where are you going?"

I stumbled my way down the stairs after Archer as he kept walking with lengthy strides. I may have had little experience with boys, but I wasn't stupid; it was obvious Archer was trying to put as much distance between us as possible. Unfortunately for him, leaving him alone wasn't an option for me.

"Away from you," he finally called over his shoulder.

That definitely confirmed my suspicions. "That's not— I mean, I just . . ."

It was impossible for me to formulate a coherent thought. My feet seemed to be moving faster than my brain was, and it wasn't proving helpful in making a good first impression with Archer.

"I mean, I meant to say, how are you doing?" I said, fumbling for words. "It's been a while since I've seen you. I wanted to talk to you."

"Because girls like you so often talk to guys like me," Archer said with a snort that might have been a laugh.

I caught the door before it could swing shut in my face as he strolled outside. "What do you mean, girls like me?"

"Rich girls who don't know a thing about anything," he deadpanned—something he was obviously used to saying, if not thinking.

I would have laughed if that comment hadn't stung so much.

"Hey! You don't even know me!" I shouted after him.

"Don't need to," he called back. He slipped into a crowd of people milling about on the sidewalk and disappeared from sight within a few seconds.

I watched him go, a feeling of utter defeat washing over me. That had not gone well.

Because I was desperate and I seemed to be only marginally hanging on to what sanity I had left, I took the train across town to the church where Archer's funeral had been held in the hopes of finding at least one small trace of Death to prove that this wasn't all just one very frightening dream.

The doors of the church were locked and there wasn't a single person in sight, so after snooping around for a few minutes and feeling utterly stupid, I decided to backtrack to that Starbucks.

The coffee shop was packed with the late afternoon rush, but I knew the second I leaned up on my tiptoes to peer around the place that Death was not among this mix of people. I would have let out a frustrated scream if doing so wouldn't have guaranteed my getting kicked out of the store. Instead, I settled for buying a mocha and trudging my way back to the subway.

It took another hour or so before I finally reached home. I managed to drag myself to my bedroom, where I flopped face down on the bed and immediately fell asleep. I dreamt of nothing, and when I finally woke, it was pitch black outside, I was stiff all over, and I wasn't too surprised that the date displayed on my phone was still November 11.

I rolled out of bed and walked into the bathroom, stripped off my clothes, and stood underneath the hot flow of water in the shower for half an hour. The shower did nothing to help me feel relaxed, like it normally would have. I stepped out, and after wrapping myself in a towel felt more tense and anxious than I had before.

I went to the sink to brush my teeth, and a startled gasp flew past my lips when I caught sight of the black streaks on my arm.

Bringing my arm up closer to my face, I took note of the crude little numbers etched on the skin of my wrist. 27.

You have twenty-seven days to stop Archer Morales from committing suicide.

I scrubbed at the numbers on my wrist with hot water and soap and a washcloth for several minutes, but the numbers were practically tattooed on. I wrenched open the bathroom drawer where I kept my odd assortment of jewelry and rummaged around until I found the rope of Navajo ghost beads my friend Chelsea had brought back for me from one of her trips visiting family in New Mexico. I wrapped the beads around my wrist several times, making an impromptu bracelet that was big enough to hide the numbers on my skin. The less I had to look at them, the better. According to legend, the ghost beads warded off bad spirits and nightmares and brought protection to the wearer—something I would probably need for the next twenty-seven days.

I pulled on my pajamas once I left the bathroom and slipped back underneath the covers on my bed. I didn't fall asleep until well after midnight, too afraid to close my eyes and face what I might see while dreaming.

CHAPTER 5

A Dream Can Be Reality— 26 Days Until

I had been asleep for what felt like five minutes when I flew awake at the sharp, burning pain centered in my wrist. I sunk my teeth into my lip to keep from crying out; it was that painful. I rolled over and turned on the lamp set on my nightstand, tugging at the ghost beads still wrapped around my wrist. The skin on my wrist felt tender as I carefully slid off the bracelet. The number 27 previously etched in black on my wrist had been replaced with the number 26.

This was how Death was going to remind me of how little time I had to stop Archer from committing suicide?

"That's just sick," I muttered to myself, cradling my arm against my chest.

I glanced over at my alarm clock as I carefully slid the ghost beads back over my wrist, and saw that it was 2:49 in the morning. It only took a moment to connect the dots. If I lost a day at this time in the morning, that must mean that was the moment Archer killed himself.

It took a while to fall back asleep after that revelation.

Rain was pelting down outside when I opened my eyes again. There was a sharp throbbing in my forehead, and I'd managed to become tangled in my blankets sometime during the night. I rolled over and slapped a hand around on the nightstand for my cell phone, shrieking when I saw the time.

It was a quarter to seven, which meant that I had exactly fifteen minutes to get my act together if I wanted to catch the bus around the corner to school. A small part of me had hoped that yesterday really had been a dream, but the date on my cell phone clearly said it was November 12th.

"What *is* this?" I shouted up at the ceiling. The ceiling didn't answer.

I rolled out of bed with a groan and quickly pulled on the first articles of clean clothing I could get my hands on. After I shoved all of my school things into my bag, I made for the bath-room to brush my hair, and put on the smallest bit of makeup to look somewhat presentable. I scarfed down a granola bar and tossed back some orange juice, and then I was out the door, in the elevator, and sprinting through the lobby to catch the bus outside as soon as the elevator doors slid open.

I'd forgotten to grab an umbrella from the hall closet, so I was soaked by the time I thundered up the steps of the bus.

"Geez." Taylor let out a low whistle as I collapsed into the seat beside her. "You look like you just crawled your way out of a swamp."

"Thanks," I said. "I needed that."

When we arrived at school, I dodged my friends, focused

on finding Archer. I could figure out what I was going to say to him once I knew where he was—clearly, I did not do so well when it came to making first impressions on the fly. I did not need a repeat of our less-than-friendly conversation yesterday. It was time to get to work and figure out the best way to approach him.

I didn't catch sight of Archer all morning, and when the bell rang for lunch hour, I bypassed the cafeteria and went to the library instead. I'd been so exhausted last night that I'd gone to bed without doing any of my homework, and now I had to finish up a short essay on *The Great Gatsby* before fifth-period English. I took a seat at one of the tables near the back of the library, in the quiet, and got to work explaining why F. Scott Fitzgerald's novel was one of the greatest of the 20th century, all the while thinking about how writing this paper was not nearly as important as what I should be doing—finding Archer.

Twenty-five minutes passed and I'd just about finished my essay. I leaned back in my seat, stretching and shaking out the cramp in my hand, then almost fell over onto the floor. Archer Morales was sitting in an armchair pushed up into the corner, past the Fiction "Q–S" shelves, beside a small side table with his things on it.

This was real. This was unbelievably, frighteningly real. Yesterday hadn't been a dream, and Archer Morales really was alive.

I gathered up my homework, shoved it back into my bag, and approached Archer without a second thought. He looked up from the book he'd had his head buried in and immediately rolled his eyes. I could have sworn he muttered *you again.*

I fought back a blush and spoke while I still had some small amount of dignity left. "I feel as if we got off on the wrong foot yesterday. I wanted to introduce myself properly. I'm Hadley Jamison."

He stared at the hand I held out for him to shake as if it were covered in leeches and gave a snort of laughter. "Really unnecessary, Hadley." The way he said my name made it seem as if it were the punch line to some joke. "I told you yesterday—I already know who you are."

"I, well, I just thought it might be nice if we got to know each other," I said. "You seem like a nice guy, and—"

"Let me just stop you right there," Archer said, rising to his feet. I had to tilt my head back to keep our eyes locked, he was that tall. "I don't know what game you think you're playing, but if I were you, I'd quit while you're ahead. I'm not a fan of it."

"What?" I was momentarily stunned. "I'm not playing a game. I really just . . . want to be friends, you know?" I inwardly cringed at how ridiculous that had sounded. I wished I could've come up with a better line.

"Well, then, save yourself the trouble," Archer told me as he dumped his things into his backpack. "I'm not a nice guy. You don't want to get to know me."

I didn't honestly believe Archer wasn't a nice guy, and I also didn't think that was just his personality. His level of standoffish behavior had to be by choice. So why would he continuously push people away? Did he act this way with everyone, or only those who happened to say more than five words to him?

The bell rang overhead, signaling the end of lunch and the start of fifth period. Archer took that opportunity to make a break for it, walking swiftly through the library.

"Won't you please hear me out for just a second, Archer?" I said, rushing after him, catching his arm.

"You've never spoken to me before, Hadley," Archer said, glaring down at me. I quickly let go of his arm and took a step back. "What changed your mind, huh? Some sort of bet? Is it the cool new thing to be friends with JFK's social outcast?"

"No! It's not!"

Death told me this wasn't going to be easy, but I had no idea Archer could be so . . . so *rude*.

"Leave me alone," Archer said bluntly. "I'm getting a little tired of you wasting time I don't have."

Buddy, you have no *idea about how little you have,* I thought.

"All I'm asking," I began, taking a deep breath, "is that we at least have the chance to get to know each other. Maybe even hang out once or twice. I mean, you never know, do you? We could have a lot in common or something."

By the inquisitive expression on Archer's face, it seemed he was actually debating my request. "Why?" he finally asked a moment later.

"Why, what?"

"Why do you even *care*?"

For half a second, I was about to tell Archer the truth. That I knew somewhere deep down inside of him he felt enough hurt and despair that he would want to end his life, and I wanted to help him because of it. Nobody deserved to go through something like that alone.

"Because . . . because I . . ." I bit my lip, my stomach churning uncomfortably. "Well, nobody should have to be alone. Everybody needs a friend, don't they?"

I realized the mistake I'd made as soon as those words left

my mouth. Archer's expression hardened, his lips thinning into a tight line.

"Did I say I was alone?" he said, eyebrow raised. "Tell me, Hadley, has it ever occurred to you that I enjoy being by myself? Has it ever occurred to you that I really just don't like people?"

The thought *had* occurred to me more than once since our interlude yesterday, but I'd sort of been hoping he was just kidding.

"No, but . . . you've got it written all over your face," I said.

It was childish, but we embarked on an epic stare down for several moments. The intensity of his glare nearly made my knees start knocking. If he went around like that all the time, I could see why people avoided him like the plague.

"Honestly, I don't think you're as big and tough as people think you are," I blurted. "You could do with a friend."

His eyes narrowed and his surly expression deepened. "Looks like I'll have to start being more of a jerk from now on. Can't have people thinking I'm not all that *big and tough*."

I mentally filed that comment away. It was something about Archer I needed to look into further, and it was the perfect place to start figuring him out. Either he was joking—and I highly doubted that—or he really did intentionally push people away from him.

"Archer, I—"

"Look, I don't need your pity," Archer said flatly. "Save yourself the Good Samaritan act and just leave me alone."

He walked away, not once looking back.

I simply stood there, knowing I was going to be late for class and wondering what I was supposed to do next.

CHAPTER 6

Third Time's the Charm— 25 Days Until

It was a relief to escape from American Government class for lunch. Mr. Monroe's long-winded lecture on the house of representatives had my head aching, and it was a miracle I hadn't fallen asleep again. I dropped my things off at my locker and went back to the library. This time I didn't have homework to finish, but I was hoping Archer would be tucked away in that hidden corner and I could attempt to talk to him again.

I felt very much like a stalker, creeping around trying to find Archer, figuring out his schedule so I knew where he would be. I did a quick walk-through of the library, peering through the shelves, but I caught no glimpse of Archer or his permanent frown anywhere. Maybe today he actually decided to get lunch and eat in the cafeteria like every other junior at school.

I went down to the cafeteria, slipped into the food line, and bought a salad and some french fries, then stood at the top of the steps by the senior lounge to try and scour the place for Archer. Taylor wasn't at school today—she'd texted me last night to tell me she was spending the day showing her grandparents from Milwaukee around the city—so I was a free agent for lunch.

I let out a squeak of excitement when I finally found him.

Archer was sitting alone in the back of the cafeteria at a small table, a book opened in front of him. I maneuvered my way through the tables toward Archer's and sat down in the seat across from him, popped the top on my salad container and speared some lettuce and a tomato with a fork, like this was normal and Archer and I ate lunch together every day.

The surprised look on Archer's face quickly gave way to an annoyed one as he stared at me over the top of his book. "What are you doing?" he demanded.

"Eating lunch," I said. "What does it look like?"

He actually had the audacity to wave his hands at me in a shooing gesture.

I dropped my fork into my salad and narrowed my eyes at him. "I can sit wherever I want, you know."

Archer picked up his book again and flipped it open, obviously signaling that our conversation was over.

I reached out without thinking and snatched the book from his hands. "What're you reading?" I flipped through the pages, holding the book away from him as he immediately tried to grab it back.

"*Romeo and Juliet?*" I said in surprise, looking back at him. "You're reading *Romeo and Juliet*? I didn't peg you for a Shakespeare kind of guy."

"You don't know anything about me, Hadley," Archer snapped. I was shocked to see a light blush flooding his cheeks. He was embarrassed by *Romeo and Juliet*? "And I have to annotate it for AP Lit. Give it back."

I returned my attention to the page in front of me, where Romeo and Juliet have their first kiss during the party at the Capulet's manor. Untidy handwriting was scrawled in the margin above a quote by Romeo.

> Romeo is an idiot. He's blinded by infatuation with a girl he doesn't even know. He doesn't realize that love will be his downfall. It would be better in the long run for him if he didn't even bother with Juliet. Love never ends well for anyone.

I didn't know what to think after reading that.

I wasn't a fan of the sappy love story myself, but it seemed like Archer really hated it. I wondered if he had some pessimistic, convoluted idea about love or if he really just had little patience for Shakespeare.

I gave him back the book and he shoved it into his backpack, still managing to give me a murderous glare as he did so.

"Are you normally this obnoxious, or are you just putting on a show for my benefit?" he asked.

"I'm not trying to be obnoxious," I protested. "I'm just trying to get to know you. I mean, look at what we have in common so far: we both hate Shakespeare, we both like steak fries. Imagine what else we could have in common if we just hung out."

"So compelling," Archer said sarcastically.

"But it's a place to start," I pointed out.

He examined me with a hard look in his eyes for several moments. I could practically see the cogs whirring in his brain.

Please just give us a shot, I thought.

It felt as if eons passed before he actually said something. His voice was clipped and firm as he carefully weighed his words. "All right. Fine. Only to prove we have nothing more in common. And then you'll give up whatever weird social experiment you're doing and leave me alone."

"Fine?" I repeated. I didn't process the latter part about making me give up. "Really?"

A slight smirk curled at Archer's mouth as he leaned back in his seat, crossing his arms over his chest. "Unless you don't want to anymore. Personally, I'm hoping that's the case."

"No, no, that's not it!" I said quickly. "I just . . . I'm surprised, that's all. That you actually agreed."

"Agreed is a strong word," Archer said coolly. "Meet me outside the front doors after the final bell. And hurry up. I'm not waiting around for you."

As soon as he finished speaking, the bell rang. He was on his feet in a second, swinging his backpack over his shoulder, and I immediately followed suit.

"So," I said. "I'll see you after school, then."

He gave me a slightly confusing look, his head tilted to the side, and said, "Right. Whatever."

He walked off and quickly disappeared into the throng of students filing from the cafeteria. Seemed like I had a very uncomfortable afternoon to look forward to.

"Hadley, Hadley, Hadley," I muttered, massaging my temples. "What have you gotten yourself into?"

CHAPTER 7

Cherry Danishes and Geometry

I found Archer leaning up against a lamppost outside after classes ended, his nose buried in *Romeo and Juliet* again. I couldn't keep back a sigh of relief. He hadn't blown me off. That was a good sign.

"Hi," I said nervously as I walked up to him.

He lifted his eyes from his book and gave a short nod as a greeting.

"So." I rocked back on my heels, hands clasped behind my back. "What do you want to do?"

Archer dropped the book into his backpack, swung it up on his shoulder, and gestured down the sidewalk. "I have something in mind. This way."

I almost had to sprint to keep up with Archer's considerably longer strides as we passed the buses idling at the curb outside the school. We'd made it halfway down the sidewalk before I heard a loud shout of, "Hadley! Wait up! Hey, Hadley!" behind me.

I turned back and saw one of my friends, Brie Wilson, making her way toward me. Her expression quickly slipped into a mask of shock when she saw Archer standing at my side.

"Hey, Brie," I said as she approached, shooting Archer an anxious glance.

"Hi," she said breathlessly. "Um . . . I was just wondering . . ."

The look on Archer's face was almost a mildly amused one as Brie stared up at him as if she were looking at the devil himself.

"Aren't . . . aren't you going to go over to Chelsea's tonight?" Brie asked me, biting her lip. "Since Taylor's grandparents are in town, we're going to marathon *America's Next Top Model*. Remember?"

"Er, no, sorry. I'm actually—"

"Sorry, Brie," Archer said pleasantly. "Hadley and I are hanging out tonight."

"Oh. Um. Okay." Brie gave me a quizzical eyebrow raise as she started to back away. "Right."

Text me later, she mouthed frantically before sprinting back down the sidewalk for the buses.

"I had an art class with Brie last semester," Archer said as we began to walk again. "Real *smart* girl."

Archer's voice was all but dripping with sarcasm, and I found that to be a smidge annoying. Archer didn't need to be insulting my friends when he didn't even know them. Brie really *was* smart—she just liked to pretend she wasn't because she operated under the impression that high school boys liked ditzy girls, much to the annoyance of the rest of our group who told her she was awesome the way she was.

I quickened my stride to keep pace with him as he set off down the sidewalk again. By the time we stopped walking, we had traveled a considerable distance and my feet were beginning to ache.

We were standing on the sidewalk in the shabbier part of Manhattan, outside a redbrick building that was in a rather sad state of disrepair. Above the door, swaying in the chill breeze, hung a blue-and-white sign that said "Mama Rosa's Coffeehouse . . . A Little Taste of Italy since 1898!" in peeling black letters.

The place was old, that much was obvious, but it held a certain charm I couldn't quite put my finger on.

"Wow." I looked to Archer. "What's this?"

"Family coffeehouse," he grunted before sweeping inside.

I rushed forward to catch the door, immediately enveloped in a pleasant warmth as I stepped over the threshold. Soon, the rich scents of chocolate and coffee beans assaulted my nose as I looked around.

Intricately threaded tapestries hung from the wood-paneled walls, along with paintings of what looked like different countryside landscapes. A large marble fireplace was to the left, and burning logs were in the grate, a welcome relief from the cold outside. An overstuffed red couch sat in front of it, along with matching armchairs. Off to the side, pushed up against one of the walls, was an old upright piano that looked as if it had been collecting dust for years.

The wooden floors were scuffed up, and the type that creaked whenever someone walked across. There were several round and square tables set up throughout the place with three or four chairs pushed up around each. A number of people were sitting at the tables, cups of coffee and half-eaten pastries or bowls of soup in front of them while they fiddled around on their laptops or read books or magazines.

Toward the front of the coffeehouse was a long counter with an antique register and a freshly packed pastry case. A huge blackboard tacked up to the wall contained colorful chalk displays listing the types of food and drinks offered there.

Archer didn't seem to mind that there were customers in the shop, because he shouted, "Ma! Grandma!" as he walked around the counter, toward a door in the back.

I heard a raspy voice shouting in what I thought was Italian, and then a rather short older woman came bustling out from a back room.

Her hair was a fine shade of gray, pulled back into a tight bun at the nape of her neck, and glasses perched on the edge of her slightly crooked nose. She was wearing a long gray skirt and matching cardigan, and I realized a second later that I had already seen this woman before, in a now hopefully nonexistent reality. This was Archer's grandmother, although I didn't think I ever caught her name.

"Well, it's about time you got here, boy," the old woman barked. She sounded like she smoked a pack of cigarettes a day. "I was wondering when you would show up."

"Sorry," Archer said, reaching for a cherry Danish in the pastry case. "I—"

A woman I instantly recognized as Archer's mother joined the old woman from the back room, looking almost exactly the same as when I had first met her, except that she was smiling. She was wearing a faded red sweater and a black apron covered in flour, but she looked beautiful despite the exhausted look on her face.

This was just too weird for words.

The last time I had met these women had been at Archer's funeral, yet Archer himself was standing right beside them, looking disgruntled as he ate a freaking Danish.

"Hi, sweetie," Regina Morales said to Archer. "Did you— Oh."

She stopped midsentence and stared at me with her hazel eyes wide.

"Sorry," Archer repeated. "I got held up at school."

The look he directed my way obviously said I was the reason he "got held up at school."

"Oh," Regina said again, still looking shocked. "Hi."

"Hi." I could feel my cheeks flooding with color.

"Is this your girlfriend, boy?" the old woman asked Archer bluntly, peering over the rims of her glasses to assess me with shrewd eyes.

"She's *not* my girlfriend," Archer snorted as he took a bite out of his pastry.

"Well, hello," Regina said, reaching out to shake my hand, a polite smile removing any hint of fatigue. "I'm Regina, Archer's mother."

"Hi," I said, doing my best to return her smile. "I'm Hadley."

Seeing Regina and pretending as if I had never met her when I knew for a fact that I had— How was I even supposed to act around these people?

"And I'm Victoria," the old woman added, not offering to shake my hand. "Archer's grandmother."

"Nice to meet you," I said politely.

Victoria gave a sniff, as if she found me unacceptable, and turned back to Archer. "Well, you better get to work, boy. There are dishes in the back that need washing."

"All right," Archer said, polishing off the rest of his Danish. "Just let me—"

"Oh, Archer doesn't need to work tonight, Ma," Regina

said quickly, resting her hands on Victoria's shoulders. "He probably has homework he needs to do. And it would be rude to leave Hadley by herself."

"I'd rather be washing dishes," Archer muttered.

Once his comment sunk in, I nearly smacked a hand to my forehead. Of *course*.

Archer brought me here so he could work, probably figuring I wouldn't want to hang around here only to be ignored and left by myself. It was just a ploy to get me to leave as soon as possible. And not only that, but we walked the entire way here from JFK when I knew for a fact we could've taken the train and made our travel time considerably shorter and less painful. He was just trying to make me give up, and I was fairly certain this would not be the last time.

"Idiot boy." Victoria grumbled, shaking her head, as if all the world's problems existed because Archer wasn't going to be washing the dishes. "Well, at the very least, you're going to have to look after your sister when I pick her up. I'm already late. Work fast, won't you?"

She headed off to the back room with another disapproving sniff.

"Sorry about my mother," Regina said to me, looking sheepish. "Her frontal lobe was damaged when she had a stroke a few years ago. She doesn't censor what she says. Why don't you and Archer go and start your homework, and I'll bring you both a snack and some hot cocoa?" She gave me another smile before sending a scolding look in Archer's direction that clearly said he needed to drop the attitude.

He glowered at his mother, not pleased but not bold enough to say anything in return.

"Oh," I said. "That would be . . . really nice, thank you."

It was proving difficult not to burst out laughing at the look on Archer's face now that his plans to ditch me had been thwarted. He walked back around the counter and made for a table in the back. I gave Regina a thankful smile and followed after Archer. I might as well attempt to get some homework done. I took a seat across the table from him and dragged my bag to me, pulling out my geometry notebook. Geometry was my least favorite class, and it would take me the longest to finish the work for it.

Archer was rummaging around in his backpack and came up with an AP Calculus textbook, what looked like a journal for AP Lit, *Romeo and Juliet*, *The Life of Frederick Douglas*, and a stack of notebooks.

"Holy crap," I said. "You have to do all of that? What classes are you taking?"

He dropped his stack on the table and glanced down at my work.

"Not remedial geometry, that's for sure."

"Funny," I muttered, rolling my eyes. "So I'm not good at math. Big deal."

A few minutes of awkward silence passed before Regina brought over two large mugs full of hot cocoa topped with whipped cream, a dash of cinnamon, and a sprinkle of chocolate chips. She also brought a plate of cookies, another cherry Danish, and a humongous cinnamon roll.

The hot cocoa was delicious and sent warmth shooting through me right down to my toes. I made a mental note to ask for the recipe later.

"So. Um." I leaned back in my chair, taking a bite of the cinnamon roll. "You have a little sister?"

Archer glanced up from his work, frowning. "Yeah. Rosie."

I held back a smile, remembering how adorable Rosie had been the night I'd met her, even if it had been under less-than-desirable circumstances. "How old is she?" I asked.

"Five," Archer answered briskly. He kept his head down, his pencil moving diligently. "She drives me up the wall more often than not."

That time, I did smile. "But you love her."

Archer's mouth thinned into a tight line as he looked up at me again. "You done with the psychoanalysis yet, Freud?"

I returned to my geometry work, biting my lip to keep from replying.

If the giant cinnamon roll and the hot cocoa were distracting, watching Archer work was even more so. He breezed through his homework with barely any effort. It just made me want to prove that I could do my work just as well too.

But that wasn't the case, especially because my eyes kept drifting up toward Archer as I attempted to figure out a formula while drumming my fingers against my leg. I had this irrational fear that if I took my eyes off of him, he'd disappear, and I'd wake up and realize this had all been a dream.

And the more I kept sneaking glances at him, the more I couldn't help but notice how attractive he was. He was wearing a black button-down rolled up to his elbows, and it seemed like he did enough exercise to stay fit. His hair was just starting to curl at his neck and looked soft to the touch. He had such a nice face that it seemed so wrong he was frowning and brooding all of the time. Frowning didn't suit him.

When Archer caught me looking at him and I realized I'd been staring at him for the past two minutes, I quickly ducked my head back in my work, but not before seeing him give me a look that made it seem as if he were questioning my mental sanity.

Just focus on geometry, I told myself. Because that was so much more exciting.

An hour later, night had fallen, and we'd long since polished off the plate of cookies and cinnamon rolls. It had also become clear that I was probably going to fail this semester of geometry. That, and Archer was the second coming of Albert freaking Einstein.

"I give up." I was whining pathetically. "I suck at geometry. I should just drop out of high school now and go find a cardboard box and—"

Archer grabbed my geometry notebook and skimmed over it. It took him half a second before he started laughing. Not a quiet chuckle or anything, but a full-out, shoulder-shaking, throw-your-head-back laugh. He was laughing so loudly, the few people still sitting around in the place shot us curious looks.

I was caught off guard by how rich his laughter was. I wouldn't mind listening to Archer Morales laugh again. I found myself wishing he'd do it more often.

"*This?*" Archer said with a gasp. "You're having problems with the Pythagorean theorem?"

I crossed my arms tightly, trying to ignore the burning in my cheeks. "Not all of us are mathematical geniuses."

"Yeah, but the Pythagorean theorem is totally middle school work," he told me, rather haughtily. "Even *you* of all people can do this."

"Hey! What do you mean, *me of all people?*" I demanded indignantly.

Archer ignored me, flipping to a fresh page in my notebook, beginning to scribble down numbers.

"What're you doing?" I asked.

"I'm going to show you how to do this."

I stared at him with wide eyes. I found it difficult to believe Archer was offering to help me. "Really?"

He rolled his eyes, making an annoyed sound. "I'm not doing this for your benefit. You butchering your math like this is giving me hives. Pythagoras is probably rolling in his grave right now."

I didn't particularly care for Archer's snarky remarks, but unfortunately, it looked as if he knew what he was doing, and I needed all the extra help I could get. A little extra tutoring never hurt anyone.

It took me another good fifteen minutes before I could finally say with confidence, "So I substitute A2 and B2 with seventeen and three and then solve for C2?"

Archer threw down his pencil, heaving an exasperated sigh. "Finally! She gets it!"

"Thanks very much for your help," I said sourly. "It's nice to know that you're such an altruistic tutor."

"How is it that you can't do simple geometry but you can throw out words like *altruistic?*" Archer said with a frown, pushing my homework toward me.

He had a point, I guessed, but math sucked. Anything math related made me want to curl up in a ball and cry. English was a far better subject in my opinion.

"I can't do math because math was invented by the devil," I said. "And I like to sleep with a dictionary under my pillow."

Judging by the look that came over Archer's face, he thought I was a freak. If he hadn't already, that is.

"You're weird," Archer said. "Like, *really* weird."

He was right. Hadn't I just signed a contract with Death? I *was* weird.

It was nearing seven o'clock when I began to pack up my things to head home. Mama Rosa's closed at seven, and Archer said he needed to help his mom close up shop.

"Thanks for helping me with my math and everything," I said as Archer organized his stack of completed homework. "You've got a nice place here."

"Sure thing," Archer said, though he sounded less than thrilled about it.

I figured that was the best farewell I was going to get from him, so I made for the front door after thanking Regina again for the hot cocoa and treats. That was when an idea hit me, a way to hang out with Archer without having to embarrass myself with begging him to be my friend.

"I have a proposition for you," I said, turning back to Archer when I was halfway to the door.

Archer glanced up from shoving one of his textbooks into his backpack, looking taken aback. "What kind of proposition?"

"I propose that you tutor me in geometry."

He stared at me expectantly, eyebrows raised. "*And?*"

"That's it," I said. "I'd just really appreciate it if you tutored me in geometry. My mom will kill me if I get a C in another math class."

I nearly failed algebra last year, even though I'd gotten tutoring three times a week and did copious amounts of extra credit work. I wasn't eager to repeat the experience, and this seemed like the perfect excuse to get closer to Archer. Despite the small amount of time we'd actually spent together, I knew he wasn't as standoffish and rude as he was trying to convince me he was. No big, tough guy would melt at the mention of his baby sister the way Archer did.

"And what's in it for me if I do tutor you?" Archer said, crossing his arms over his chest.

My heart did this stupid little jump in my chest. Was he actually considering it? "My charming personality," I said, attempting a witty smile. "My gorgeous good looks. All the steak fries you can eat."

It could've been a trick of the light, or maybe just my over-active imagination going into overdrive, but I swore Archer *blushed*. His cheeks were a bright pink when he quickly looked away, clearing his throat as he busied himself with his backpack. What could I have said that would make him blush?

"I'll do it for the fries."

I tried not to let out an ecstatic shout. "Fabulous!"

"Don't look too pleased," Archer muttered. "I really do have to help close up shop, though, so if you wouldn't mind . . ." He jabbed a thumb at the door, a clear invitation that I needed to show myself out.

I said good night and thanked him again for his help, to which he responded with a grunt. He obviously was done talking for the night.

I left the coffee shop then, feeling just the slightest bit smug. I took the train across town and passed the journey with the rest of the homework I'd set aside in order to trudge through geometry. I was still surprised Archer had even agreed to help me, though if he was the perfectionist I was beginning to see him as, it made sense he would want to fix something as easy as geometry seemed to be for him.

I jogged on the way home to my apartment building, wishing I'd picked a heavier jacket this morning. It was unnaturally cold for this time of the year, and I didn't like it. As I approached the apartment building, Hanson the doorman checked his watch.

"Out a bit later than usual on a weekday, aren't you?"

"I was hanging out with a friend," I said, and I couldn't keep back the small smile.

"Good, good," Hanson said with a smile of his own. "New friend?"

"Yeah," I answered. "He even helped me finish my geometry homework."

Hanson looked surprised at this news. I never kept my hatred of math a secret, so the fact that I wasn't in tears over my homework was an accomplishment of epic proportions. "Well, isn't that dandy?"

"Hanson, you have no idea."

CHAPTER 8

Sticks and Stones— 22 Days Until

Y ou're not eating lunch with us today, are you?"

I slammed my locker shut as I juggled the notebooks and textbooks in my arms, giving Taylor an apologetic look. It was Monday, and it was way too early for me to come up with a good response to that question.

She was leaning up against the locker beside mine, arms crossed over her sparkly designer shirt. The expression on her face was an unusual one. Her eyebrows were pinched together and she was more or less pouting, but at the same time she looked like she was almost bubbling with excitement.

"So you're sitting with Archer again," she said when I didn't answer her question.

I had difficulty deciding if she was annoyed that I'd bailed on her lately, or if she was having fun at my expense. "He's not a bad guy, Taylor," I said tightly. "He's actually kind of . . . nice."

Okay, using *nice* as an adjective to describe Archer was a far cry from the truth, but I'd noticed over the past few days that he had these moments where he didn't look like he wanted to slap people. I counted that as a success.

Taylor raised an eyebrow, looking disbelieving, but then she cracked a smirk and started to giggle. She kept giggling until she was breathless, making me even more confused than before.

"Is something funny?" I demanded, wondering if I should feel offended or not.

"Oh, no, no, of course not," Taylor said, waving a hand. "It's just that you must really have it bad if you think somebody like *Archer* is *nice*."

"Sorry?"

"C'mon, Hadley, I know you're not *this* stupid."

"What are you talking about?"

I had a sinking suspicion I knew exactly what Taylor was hinting at, but I sincerely hoped I was wrong.

"Just admit it," Taylor huffed out, sounding exasperated. "You *so* like Archer."

"*What*? I do not!"

I should've known from the beginning that this was where Taylor was headed. I ground my teeth together while she started babbling about how she couldn't believe I would've actually fallen for someone like Archer Morales, her sentences interspersed with laughter.

"Look, Taylor," I said as I shoved my things into my bag, straightening up. "I know I'm kind of all over the place right now, and I'm sorry, but I swear I'm not into Archer, okay? He's just a . . . a . . ."

Actually, what was Archer to me? I would've been lying to myself if I said I didn't feel something for Archer, because I did. But I didn't like him like *that*. That wasn't what this was about. It *couldn't* be about that. It wasn't even an option when the days were steadily ticking down against me. What I felt was concern. Possessiveness. A need to make sure Archer was alive. I was pretty sure Death did not intend for me to develop a crush, and therefore I wouldn't.

What did that make Archer to me, then?

"Archer's just a . . . what?" Taylor asked, looking amused.

"He's just a guy," I finished lamely, even though I knew he was so much more than that.

"You've been sure spending a lot of time with that *guy* lately," Taylor said, giggling again. "I'm not sure what you see in him, but I've been waiting for*ever* for you to actually show interest in someone, so I guess Morales will have to do for now."

"Excuse me?" I blurted, caught off guard. "Just because I'm not chasing after boys doesn't mean I—"

"Has he asked you out on a date?"

"No! We're *not*—"

"Has he kissed you yet?"

"*No!*"

Taylor heaved a sigh as she brushed her hair over her shoulder, pretending to look all hurt. "Well, when you decide you want to tell me the truth about Archer, you know where to find me."

"I *am* telling the truth!" I was at a loss to how I could steer her away from the ridiculous notion of my liking Archer. I couldn't just spill the beans and tell her why I'd suddenly attached myself to Archer's hip. "It's just that I . . ."

Taylor heaved another dramatic sigh before she wandered off, immediately cracking up again. I couldn't tell if she thought this was the funniest thing to ever happen, or if she was just trying to get a rise out of me. Probably both.

I leaned against my locker and exhaled heavily, rubbing my forehead with the heel of my palm. A part of me wanted to run after her and tell her everything that was going on, why I had no choice but to follow Archer around like a stupid, lost puppy, because it would've been a relief to share the burden with at least one person. And Taylor *was* my best friend. But even then, I didn't think she'd believe me. I couldn't afford to pass up any opportunity I got to spend with Archer, but I did miss sitting with the girls at lunch. And hanging out with Taylor after school. And even our *Top Model* marathons.

But I was down to twenty-two days now. It was bad enough not being able to pester Archer over the weekend in order to find out more about him. Two whole days, just gone. I'd debated making my way over to Mama Rosa's Coffeehouse to see if he was there that past Saturday, but I quickly decided it would have been just a little *too* stalkerish. I had to draw the line somewhere. And I suspected that if I pushed Archer too far, he'd retreat back to that corner in the library and never talk to me again.

Despite my semi-argument with Taylor, one good thing did happen that morning. As soon as I forced my way through the lunch line and got my hands on some fries and a turkey sandwich, I took off sprinting through the cafeteria to find Archer.

I had news. Big news.

I tried to stop myself from squealing once I finally reached the table in the back of the cafeteria where Archer normally sat, but to no avail.

"Archer!"

I slammed my food down onto the table and tossed myself into the seat across from him.

Archer reached out to grab a handful of my fries and popped one into his mouth, giving me a sort of amused expression. "Are you that excited to see me?"

"No, don't be stupid," I said, hoping he wouldn't notice how breathless I was. "But look."

I grabbed my geometry test out of my bag and slapped it down so he could witness the miracle for himself.

He glanced down at the test and smirked. "A B+? You're ecstatic about a B+?"

"Well, duh. I failed my last test." After getting that tutoring at Mama Rosa's and one extra session in the library earlier this week, I thought I was getting pretty good at math, if I did say so myself.

I busied myself with unwrapping my turkey sandwich and taking a bite out of it while Archer looked like he was about to start laughing again.

"Well," he said, pushing my test toward me. "Looks like you're not totally helpless. I must be a good teacher."

"Don't flatter yourself," I teased. "You just got lucky."

"Yeah, right," he snorted. "Me? Lucky? Okay."

"You're awfully pessimistic," I said. "You know that?"

Archer tossed back a couple of fries, shrugging. "Most of the time, people have reasons for their actions."

He wasn't kidding. I had my reasons for signing that contract, and I wanted desperately to believe that they were good reasons. Archer had his reasons for killing himself in the past. And hopefully I would soon be able to get him to share those reasons with me and prevent him from following through this time.

"Right," I agreed slowly. "But . . . look. Just two tutoring sessions, and I actually passed a geometry quiz. My sitting with you at lunch isn't so bad, is it?"

"Yeah, maybe for your benefit."

I kept my eyes fixed on the table as I fiddled with my sandwich wrapper. "Do I really you bother you that much?"

It wouldn't have changed a thing if Archer said I was the bane of his existence. Whether or not he realized it, our fates were entwined until further notice. I just wanted to know the answer to that question for myself.

Archer ran a hand roughly through his hair. "Hadley, just because I—"

"Well, what do we have here? Archer Morales finally got himself a girlfriend."

We both turned at the sound of the haughty voice breaking into our conversation. Standing beside our table was a big, brawny guy with carefully gelled hair and the most arrogant smirk a person could ever possibly make. This was Ty Ritter, JFK's golden boy because his dad was some big relator hotshot who owned a good chunk of the Upper East Side. I'd spoken to him before—Taylor had been known to flirt with the guys that hung out with Ty—but I couldn't imagine what he was doing, slumming it up over here. According to the rules of high school, Archer didn't occupy the same social circle as Ty. Judging by Archer's disgusted expression, he was well aware of who Ty was, and my guess was they'd never had a pleasant interaction.

I wondered if it had something to do with money. Students at JFK Prep either got in because they were smart or because their parents paid their way. I fell into the latter category, though my generally high grades in English and history classes tended to balance out the not-so-high grades I always got in all things mathematics. My English teacher, Miss Graham, who was possibly my favorite teacher, made being at this school enjoyable with her lively classes and tendency to throw candy at students who gave her good answers. I was always motivated by candy.

Even if I hadn't seen the place where his family worked, it was obvious just by the way Archer dressed that he did not come from money. The fact he wore no-brand jeans when the majority of the guys in our grade stuck with the Fifth Ave designers or ridiculously expensive vintage shops was a good indicator he was here solely based on his academic achievements. No wonder he'd snarked at me about being a rich girl. He had to work his butt off to be here, when people like me and Ty could just coast on by. I felt a little ashamed.

"Can I help you?" Archer said to Ty, sounding like he'd rather be doing anything but that.

Ty ignored Archer as he took a seat beside me, pulling my fries across the table toward him. "So we missed you at Bennett's party last weekend, Hadley."

"Partying isn't really my thing," I said, keeping my attention fixed on Archer. I wasn't sure if he was about to deck Ty in the face or storm off in a huff. He was clearly uncomfortable, perched on the edge of his seat.

"Shame," Ty said around a mouthful of fries. "We're all kind of sad we haven't seen you around lately. Taylor said it's because you've been spending all your time with Morales here."

You've got to be kidding me, I thought in disbelief. *Ty Ritter wants to talk to Archer about* me? Why did he even care? I had a sinking feeling Ty was just looking for an excuse to get under Archer's skin.

Archer leaned back in his chair, crossing his arms over his chest. "That's hardly *my* fault. Take that up with her, Ritter."

"You know, I have to hand it to you, Morales," Ty said, now looking over at Archer. "You must be something special if you can get a girl like Hadley here. She's not exactly in your league, bro."

"Oh, I'm well aware of that," Archer said dryly. "Is there any particular reason you feel the need to share this bit of information with me, or do you just get some kick out of wasting my time?"

Ty shrugged again. "Yeah, but I also want to offer you some advice too. You know, since I'm such a nice guy and everything."

I opened my mouth to tell Ty what I was going to do to him with the rest of my sandwich if he didn't shut up, but the look Archer shot me made my words die in my throat.

"And what's that?"

"Well, me and the guys have all been talking about it," Ty began slowly, "and we were thinking—you know, since your old man is in prison and everything—that you're probably going to wind up there one day too, so it'd probably be best if you left Hadley alone. You know, like *can't come within two hundred feet* alone. Pretty little thing like her couldn't possibly—"

My face felt like it had burst into flames. I didn't know what he was talking about, but this had clearly gone way too far. "Would you just leave him *alone*? Seriously! Could you be more of a jerk, Ty?"

Ty stared at me with wide eyes for a few short moments while I sat there, short of breath, flushed with color. I couldn't look at Archer. I was afraid of what his reaction would be. The last thing I needed was for a dumb idiot like Ty Ritter to throw Archer off, disrupt the progress I'd made over the past week, however minimal that progress might have been.

"Well, I really think that answers your question," Archer said, surprising both Ty and me. "Bye now."

Ty shoved back from the table and stood, slamming his hands down, leaning toward Archer. "Just think about it. Might do you some good."

I took a deep, steadying breath and looked up at Archer, bracing myself for his reaction. He was looking at me with nothing short of contempt.

"Look, Archer, I—"

"Don't ever speak for me again." His eyes were blazing as he glared at me. "You may think you just did me a favor, but you did the exact opposite. I can take care of myself. So I'll thank you for keeping your nose out of my business. The same goes for your idiot friend Ty Ritter."

He didn't give me the chance to say anything in response before he left the cafeteria. People standing nearby automatically moved to give him a wide berth and he quickly disappeared from sight.

Maybe I had jumped the gun, shouting at Ritter like that, but how could I have not when he'd said such terrible things? Yet now I was fairly certain Archer was never going to want anything to do with me ever again. And could I really blame him? Hanging out with Archer was already opening him up to more scrutiny at the hands of jerks like Ty. That wasn't helping my case any. It was his perfect excuse to stay as far away from me as possible, and I could kiss being friends good-bye.

During the rest of the day, I kept running what Ty had said during lunch over and over again in my mind. The more I thought about that conversation, the sicker I started to feel. Ritter said that Archer was going to end up in prison "like his old man." How could I have missed something as important as the fact that Archer's dad was in *jail*?

That statement alone raised more questions about this entire situation than I thought I had the capacity to handle. I wanted to believe Ty was just making it up, but there was no mistaking the look that had come over Archer's face when he'd said those words. Ty had touched a nerve with Archer, and he knew it.

But at the very least, I now knew which one of Archer's secrets I had to uncover next.

CHAPTER 9

Desperate Times Call for Desperate Measures— 21 Days Until

I had begun to develop a morning routine since I'd signed the contract with Death. I would ride the bus with Taylor in the morning, we'd part ways at our lockers, and I would spend the first half of the day chatting with Brie in the hallways between classes. I'd do my best to pay attention in classes like American Government and Chemistry, where my lab partner, Chelsea, was much more fun to talk to than memorizing the periodic table of elements. Archer and I didn't have any classes together, seeing as junior year was when classes were divided based on which students were going the Advanced Placement route—which Archer was clearly intelligent enough for and had decided to take advantage of.

When it was time for lunch, I would buy a sandwich or a salad and some fries from the food line and sit with Archer at the table in the back of the cafeteria. Lunch was the only opportunity we actually had to spend time together during the day. I'd decided that today I would bring up geometry tutoring again and more or less pester Archer into setting up a schedule for him to teach me shape formulas, which would also serve to get to know him better. I may have wormed my way into his life, but I had no idea if I'd made a dent in his decision to end that life.

When Archer wasn't at our usual table toward the back of the cafeteria on Tuesday, I was caught off guard. I did a quick scan of the place, leaning up on my tiptoes, looking for any sign of Archer, and it quickly became apparent that he wasn't anywhere in sight. Our junior class had less than two hundred students. If Archer was at lunch, I I would've seen him already.

I didn't want to admit it, but I was afraid. It was unrealistic to expect that I could keep tabs on Archer *all* of the time, but my stress level noticeably shot through the roof when I didn't know where he was. Almost a week had gone by since I'd been sent back in time, but I'd already grown accustomed to being around Archer. I savored each moment I was with him, and I'd begun to notice this hollow feeling in the pit of my stomach that would immediately take hold when we parted ways.

My first thought was to go to the library to look for him, maybe take up post at his locker, but I had the sense that would only annoy him. And then I remembered what had occurred during lunch yesterday with stupid Ty Ritter. I held in a groan, squeezing my sandwich between my fingers. After *that*, it made sense Archer would avoid the cafeteria. And me.

"Archer's fine," I muttered to myself as I changed direction and made for the table Taylor, Brie, and Chelsea normally sat at during lunch with other girls in our class. "Of course he's fine."

"Uh-oh," Taylor said when I flopped down into the seat across the table from her. "Trouble in paradise?"

"Nope, just wanted to spend some time with you," I said confidently, trying to convince myself just as much as Taylor. "Archer is busy anyway. He's in all AP classes, so he always has a lot of homework."

The words didn't ring true, even though I'm sure Archer *did* have a lot of homework. The girls didn't seem convinced by it either.

"You have to tell me something, girlfriend, because I just don't get it," Chelsea cut in, leaning toward me. "What do you see in that boy? He's kind of intense."

I swallowed hard as I unwrapped my squished sandwich with trembling hands. *I see a* lot, I wanted to say. More than anyone else did in this place, at least. "He's been tutoring me in geometry," I half lied, and my insides immediately twisted with guilt.

I didn't like to bend the truth, and I definitely didn't like doing so to my friends, but what else could I do being put on the spot like that?

"Uh huh," Taylor said, clearly unconvinced. "Sure."

"Seriously!" I shoved my hand into my bag and rummaged around until I came up with my geometry test from the other day, and then I shoved it across the table toward them. "Look!"

Brie let out a whistle as she looked over my test. "Not bad, but let's see you do this *without* a calculator."

"That's impossible," I said, snatching my test back. "Mrs. Lowell's class is hard enough as it is."

"Geometry isn't *that* bad," Brie disagreed. "I had Mrs. Lowell freshman year, and her class was a breeze."

"Careful," Chelsea said to Brie. "Jensen Edwards is sitting at the table next to us. He might overhear that you're actually a mathematical genius."

I began to relax as conversation moved away from Archer, though I still wasn't able to completely stop worrying about him. Talking with the girls, chatting away like we normally did every day, was a nice distraction, but it wasn't perfect. I could momentarily forget what was bothering me, but the second I was left alone with my thoughts, it would all come rushing back. Relaxing with my friends was something only the pre-contract Hadley could afford to do.

After the final bell, I spent a few moments standing around by Archer's locker, peering through the crowd to try to catch any sight of him. Nothing. When the hallway had almost completely cleared of students, I knew it was pointless to stay there any longer. I gave up with a frustrated sigh and stomped my way down the stairs.

I had to take the train home because I'd missed the bus while waiting around for Archer. I pulled out my cell phone as I walked into the apartment an hour later and texted Chelsea, Taylor, and Brie. If I stayed shut up in my apartment, trying to do my homework, I'd be consumed by my own thoughts and drive myself crazy.

NETFLIX NIGHT AT MY PLACE? CHINESE
TAKEOUT ON ME.

I received enthusiastic responses in just a few minutes, and I was happy to dump my bag on a chair in the dining room and totally forget about my homework, and the hurdles I'd only just begun to face. One night off couldn't hurt, could it? I needed to feel normal again, at least for a little while.

But the next day, Archer was absent again. When I didn't see him at his locker, I had difficulty breathing for a few tense moments. I leaned up against the wall and forced myself to take deep, calming breaths as I tugged on the strands of ghost beads I'd religiously kept on my wrist for the past week. The beads now hid the number 20. I only had twenty days left. Only twenty days, and I still felt like I was wandering around in a daze, unsure of what I was doing, constantly worrying that I wouldn't be able to save Archer. I needed to take action. I needed a plan.

Just because Archer hadn't been at school didn't mean anything. Maybe he was sick. Everybody missed a day now and then. It wasn't cause for a panic attack. Yet my automatic response was to assume that the worst had happened and that Archer . . .

Stop it, Hadley! I snapped at myself. *You're being ridiculous!*

Ridiculous or not, though, I wasn't going to waste any more time. After the final bell, I walked outside, quickly pulling my cell phone out of my pocket to look up the address to Mama Rosa's Coffeehouse. If Archer wasn't at school, then it stood to reason that the next best place to check was his family's coffeehouse.

A light dusting of snow swept through the streets as I jogged my way up from the subway and walked the two blocks over to the coffeehouse. When I was finally standing in front of the red door of Mama Rosa's, I had done my best to convince myself that it didn't matter what Archer would think about my showing up announced—I had to do it anyway.

I gripped the doorknob and wrenched the door open, stepping inside before I lost courage and turned to go home.

There was a fire burning in the grate, just like last time, and a few people were lounging about at tables with coffee and magazines. There was a hidden radio somewhere set to a classic station, music filtering quietly throughout the place, but for the most part, it was empty.

I approached the front counter, wondering if Archer was crouched down behind the pastry case or somewhere in the back, only to come face-to-face with Regina as she walked out of the kitchen.

"Oh!" A smile crossed her face. "Hadley!"

I was pleasantly surprised to find that she remembered who I was and that she seemed genuinely glad to see me. "Hi," I said, returning her smile. "Nice to see you again."

I really did mean it. If Regina was smiling and all perky, that had to mean nothing terrible had happened to Archer. We made a few minutes of small talk, discussing the sour weather and Thanksgiving, which was just next week.

"Are you looking for Archer?" Regina asked as she wiped up a spill on the counter.

"Um, yes." I tried not to flush in embarrassment.

"Well, I'm sorry to say that he's not in," Regina said, looking apologetic. "He's out running errands with my mother right now."

Sweet relief coursed through me. Archer was *okay*. Thank God there was that.

"Oh." I still couldn't keep back the defeated sigh that seemed to be becoming the norm for me. That walk in the snow had been for nothing, then, but at least I knew Archer was all right. "Well. Okay. Thanks anyway. I should probably—"

"Wait a moment, Hadley!"

I turned back to Regina, halfway to the door already. "Yeah?"

"You could always stay for a cup of coffee, you know," she said. "I'm sure Archer will be back soon, and besides, it looks like the snow is picking up outside."

I looked out the window, and sure enough, snow was now falling with a considerable amount of force. A hot cup of coffee sounded much better than stepping into the flurry. "You know what? That would be lovely, thank you."

Regina's answering smile lit up her eyes. "Great! Have a seat. I'll whip up a special blend."

I took a seat at a square table by the counter, and Regina joined me a few moments later with two steaming mugs of coffee. I said my thanks and brought the mug up close to my face, inhaling the rich scent of what I thought was cinnamon.

"This is delicious!" I exclaimed when I took a sip. "It tastes like a snickerdoodle!"

Regina laughed, sipping at her own mug of coffee. "Thank you. Our coffee is the only reason this place stays in business. Well, that and we own and live in the apartment upstairs."

Regina then told me how she and her two sisters and brother had grown up in the building, and how the Incitti family had been in the coffee business ever since her great-grandmother, Rosalia Incitti, had emigrated from Sicily to the United States in 1895. Now she and Archer, her daughter, Rosie, and her mother, Victoria, still lived in the apartment above the coffeehouse.

"Well, it's a lovely place," I said, sipping at my coffee as I glanced around. "It's very . . . charming."

"Thank you," Regina said. Then she paused. "So . . . do you have a crush on my son?"

I spat out a mouthful of coffee and stared at Regina with a look of pure horror on my face. She did *not* just ask me that.

"Um, no," I spluttered out. "I don't have a crush on Archer. I don't."

Regina raised her eyebrows, clearly skeptical.

"Well, I mean, he's a nice guy, and, um, certainly good looking, but . . ." I slunk down in my seat, hiding my face in my coffee mug. This was a lost cause. "No, I don't."

"Oh, I see," Regina said as she began to grin. There was this knowing look in her eyes that made it seem as if she was totally aware of the conflicted thoughts currently racing through my mind. But I really wasn't interested in Archer. Not like *that*, at least.

"Sorry for asking, but I was just wondering, of course. Archer's not one to normally bring home friends, let alone a girl who's a friend, so you can imagine my curiosity."

"I have noticed he's a little antisocial," I murmured into my coffee mug.

Regina nodded. "Archer's always been the quiet type."

"Why is that?"

She stared at me in surprise for a moment, letting what I'd blurted out sink in. I regretted my abrupt question almost immediately, but then she let out a quick breath, clutching her coffee mug tightly.

"There are things in Archer's life that he shouldn't have had to deal with, as young as he is. Things nobody should have to deal with. He's the man of the house, of course, and thinks it's his duty to look after me and his grandmother and his little sister more than himself. The Lord knows it hasn't been easy on him. I've always said he seems more middle-aged than seventeen."

So there actually was some truth to Ty's words. Archer's father wasn't in the picture, not if Regina had called Archer the man of the house. The question that still remained was, where was Archer's father? Prison? Was he just a deadbeat who had skipped out years ago?

"Oh," I said stupidly. "I'm . . . so sorry. I shouldn't have asked, I—"

"No, it's fine," Regina said. "I'm glad you did. You should know Archer isn't as rough around the edges as he seems. He's actually a real sweetheart."

Archer's sweetness had to exist very far beneath his rough exterior, if at all, but I doubted anyone knew him better than his own mother.

"At any rate, I'm glad you're spending time with him," Regina told me. "You're always welcome here."

"Thank you," I said.

It was surprising to realize just how much I meant that. The Morales family were almost total strangers to me, but I knew Regina was telling me the truth.

I ended up staying, talking with Regina much longer than I expected. The clock above the mantel had just chimed the hour—five o'clock—when Regina looked to me with a curious expression that had me a little worried about what she was going to say.

"The after-work rush is about to start, and since Archer and my ma aren't back yet, would you mind giving me a hand?"

I felt my jaw drop. "B-But I've never even had a job before, and I've never—"

"Honestly, there's not much to ringing up orders and delivering soup and sandwiches to tables," Regina assured me. "Really, you'd be helping me out a lot."

"Um . . . okay?" I said, noticing the tremble in my voice. "Sure."

"Great!" Regina stood and gestured for me to follow her back to the kitchen. "Let's get you an apron."

I let Regina pull me behind the front counter and into the kitchen, wondering what on earth I had just agreed to do. Five minutes later I was armed with a clean black apron, standing behind the register, watching the front door, just waiting for a whole slew of people to come rushing inside to throw orders at me left and right.

"Don't look so nervous, Hadley," Regina told me with a smile as she placed wrapped cold cut sandwiches on the bottom shelf in the pastry case. "I promise; our regulars are as kind as can be."

Before long, the bells tied to the front door gave a jingle and a couple with six screaming children came strolling inside. I told myself I could do this. That Regina was right and there really was nothing to ringing up orders. I forced on the brightest smile I could manage.

And by the time closing at seven o'clock rolled around, I fully understood just how right Regina had been when she'd called it the *rush*. Mama Rosa's got packed as soon as five thirty rolled around.

Regina took care of the drink orders with a swift sort of efficiency I found a little frightening. She whipped up mochas and lattes and espressos in quick succession, and didn't even look remotely frazzled. She was all grins as she handed out drinks and pastries, chatting with the customers as if they were old friends.

It took me a few tries to figure out how to work the ancient register, and once I got the hang of it, I fell into an easy routine of taking orders, as well as helping Regina carry drinks and bowls of soup or sandwiches. The task wasn't as difficult as I had been expecting, and after I had finally calmed down a bit, it was almost sort of fun.

Most of the people that came through the front door must have been regulars, as I was asked more than once when I'd started working here.

"She's a friend of the family," Regina had answered once, smiling as she handed the old woman her mocha in a to-go cup.

I felt a surge of warmth at her words, and smiled in spite of myself. Even if this was only temporary, it was still nice to feel as if I was a part of something.

The front door burst open with a tinkle of bells and a gust of cold air as I was wiping down the counter and Regina was removing the unsold pastries from the pastry case. I whipped my head up and squeaked in shock as Archer came striding inside, closely followed by Victoria, who was balancing a little girl with dark curls on her hip.

Archer came to a sudden stop in the middle of the coffee-house and stared at me with wide eyes. "Jamison? What're you doing here?"

"Oh, I was just—"

"Hadley was just giving me a hand during the dinner rush," Regina told Archer, giving him a look that said *Don't you dare start anything*.

"Hadley. How nice," Victoria said as she shoved past Archer

with the little girl, marching around the counter to Regina. "Sorry we're late. One of the trains broke down."

"Mom!" the little girl squealed. "I drew you a picture at school today!"

Regina beamed as she took the little girl into her arms and kissed her forehead, hugging her tightly. "Rosie, this is Hadley," she said, introducing us.

Rosie gave me a big smile and waved, her nose crinkling cutely. "Hi," she said shyly.

Rosie seemed just the same as she had the night of Archer's funeral, all sweet and bubbly despite any circumstance.

"Are you friends with Archer?" Rosie asked me, reminding me again of that night. "Archer's my big brother."

I shot a furtive glance toward Archer, who was going around flipping chairs upside down and placing them on the tables.

"Er . . . sort of," I said to Rosie.

Rosie squirmed in Regina's arms as a signal to be set on her feet, and then she came over to yank on my pant leg, wanting me to bend down to her level. "I gotta tell you something."

"Sure," I said, grinning as she looked up at me with those big blue eyes of her. "What is it?"

She leaned up on her tiptoes to whisper in my ear, "Archer is a big, fat meanie."

I had to bite my lip to keep from letting a giggle escape. "I'm sure he is."

"Rosalia, what nonsense are you saying now?"

Rosie stopped talking midsentence as Archer leaned over the counter, giving his little sister a stern glare.

"Nothing!" she chirped with a bright smile.

Archer rolled his eyes before he launched himself over the

counter, jostling me to the side as he scooped Rosie up into his arms and started tickling her. I watched in astonishment as Rosie giggled in delight, struggling to get out of Archer's arms. She wasn't having much luck, but I didn't think she minded.

It was a heartwarming scene, Archer playing with his little sister. But it was also a little strange. Archer put up such a hard, strong front at school that it seemed almost . . . unnatural for him to not be on guard like this.

"All right, all right!" Regina said loudly over Rosie's squealing. "I think that's enough, you two."

Archer set Rosie on her feet and turned to me as Regina struck up a conversation with Victoria in Italian.

"What are you really doing here, Hadley?" he asked quietly, turning to me. "And I know you didn't come here just to help my mom out."

He wasn't pleased that I was there, that much I could tell. "Look." I took a deep breath. "I came here so I could—"

"Listen, Hadley," Regina said, coming over to us. "Would you like to join us for dinner? As a thank you for helping me this evening."

First I worked a shift at their coffeehouse, and now I was being invited to stay for dinner?

"Oh, Hadley can't stay for dinner, Ma," Archer said quickly, looking incredulous. "She has to—"

I wanted to laugh, because there was actually nothing I needed to do, apart from getting some time with Archer. I'd finished my homework in sixth-period study hall, and my parents would probably be eating in their offices at work as usual.

Besides, now I was even more determined to stay despite

Archer trying to shove me out the door. "I'd love to stay for dinner, Regina," I said, smiling at her. "Thank you."

"Great!" Victoria barked. "Now that we've settled that, let's actually go upstairs and make dinner, shall we?"

I followed after Archer as he slouched his way into the kitchen, not wanting to see the look on his face.

10

Dinner in the Apartment Upstairs— 20 Days Until

The apartment above Mama Rosa's Coffeehouse was nothing like I would have expected. It was small and cramped, the living room the size of a postage stamp and containing an old couch, a coffee table, and a TV set that had to have been purchased in the 1970s. There was a long table with a pretty lace cloth in the dining room, the windows behind it covered with heavy drapes.

The kitchen, positioned off to the side of the dining room, was full of appliances definitely not from this century, though they did have marble countertops and an island counter in the middle. Beyond the kitchen and the dining room was a long staircase that led up to the second floor.

It was hardly anything like what I was used to living in, yet it had a sense of home that I had never felt in my parents' five-star digs. You could tell that the people who lived here were family, and that memories lived inside the walls.

I loved it.

"Wow," I said, still taking in the sight. "This is nice."

I heard a snort behind me. "Yeah, whatever. Would you kindly get out of the way so I can start dinner?" Archer shoved past me into the apartment, heading for the kitchen.

"Come on, Hadley, let's watch *Dragon Tales!*" Rosie chirped, grabbing my hand and pulling me into the living room.

I took a seat on the edge of the couch while Rosie snatched the remote and started flipping through the channels on the TV. Regina and Victoria were still closing up shop downstairs, so Archer, Rosie, and I were the only ones in the apartment.

I wanted the chance to talk to Archer about Monday. What had been said during lunch the other day with Ty Ritter was still following me around, like an itch I couldn't scratch. I doubted I would be able to rest easy until I had at least attempted to make amends with Archer. I needed to figure out why I'd upset him and apologize for it.

While Rosie was riveted by a particularly colorful commercial, I got to my feet and walked to the kitchen, taking a seat on one of the stools at the island counter. Archer looked up from slicing tomatoes on a chopping board, gave me the once over, and returned to his task.

I awkwardly cleared my throat, folding my hands together on the counter. "So. Um. Do you need any help with dinner?"

I couldn't see his face, but I was fairly certain he was laughing silently from the way his shoulders were shaking. What was so funny about my offering to help him with dinner?

"Don't bother," he said. "I'm just reheating leftovers and making a salad."

"Oh . . . all right."

I didn't know how to start this whole apologizing thing. I knew he wasn't going to be thrilled that I was bringing up the subject.

"So, um." I started drumming my fingers on the countertop, frowning. I had to stop saying *um*. "Did you have a nice day?"

"The best day ever," Archer said sarcastically.

"That's . . . good," I said awkwardly. "But look. I really just wanted to—"

"Hey, Hadley!" Rosie called from the living room. "Come watch with me!"

Archer nodded his head toward his little sister. "Keep her company, would you? She'll start bouncing off the walls if she doesn't get enough attention."

"Sure," I said. "Okay."

There went nothing. I slid off the stool and headed back to the living room, wondering if Archer had known what I'd been trying to say, or if he really did just want me to spend time with his sister.

Rosie chatted away as a *SpongeBob SquarePants* rerun played on the TV, telling me about her day at preschool, which was full of many more perils than I remembered, like missing colored pencils and the little play kitchen being so popular that only the kids Rosie called "the mean girls" got to play with it.

"Enjoy preschool while you can," I told her. "High school's no fun. I think Archer would say the same thing too."

"I like staying with Mommy and Archer," Rosie said, pulling a dramatic pout. "I like being at home."

"Yeah, I know," I said. I could relate. It had taken months after I first started kindergarten to stop being so homesick. "You have a very nice home too."

Rosie giggled. "I know. It's comfy. Plus, I get see my daddy here." She rolled off my lap and scrambled across the couch to the table beside it, snatching up a picture frame. "Have you seen a picture of my daddy?"

"No, I—"

Rosie shoved the photo under my nose. "Look! Aren't they pretty?"

I took the photo and examined it, obviously taken at a wedding—Regina's wedding.

Regina looked beautiful, dressed in a gorgeous lace dress, her hair done up in a waterfall of curls. The man who had his arms wrapped around her was tall and very handsome, his eyes a bright blue, his wavy hair dark, and a wide smile was on his face. The way the man and Regina were staring at each other . . . you could tell that they were head over heels in love. You couldn't mistake the looks in their eyes for anything but.

"This is your dad?" I asked Rosie, pointing to the photo.

Rosie beamed up at me. "Sure is!"

"I've never met him before," I said.

She blew out a sigh—this type of sad sigh I didn't think was possible for a five-year-old to make—and took the photo back, running her fingers over her parents' faces. "I never got to meet Daddy, either. Mommy says he went to heaven before she had me."

I felt a little sick to my stomach hearing those words. Rosie and Archer's dad, Regina's husband, was dead? I may not have been all that close with my own father, but I couldn't imagine what it would be like to not have him there anymore.

Rosie was five. If what she said was true, that meant Archer's father had only died, at the very least, a little less than six years ago. The thought that was why Archer had ended his life the first time around crossed my mind. Being depressed would naturally be the side effect of something like losing your dad. Depressed enough to commit suicide, though? I had no idea.

What about what Ty said? I thought. *He said Archer's old man was in prison.*

I was obviously missing something here. Either Ty was lying—which was a definite possibility—or Rosie was wrong. Maybe her dad wasn't dead but in prison, and Regina didn't know how to tell her. That couldn't be an easy conversation to have with a little girl.

I took a deep breath while rubbing my forehead with the heel of my palm, and made a mental note to add this little detail to my growing list of mysteries.

Regina and Victoria walked in about fifteen minutes later, while Rosie and I were watching another episode of *SpongeBob*.

"Dinner ready yet, boy?" Victoria asked as she whisked into the kitchen.

"Nearly," Archer answered.

"Rosie, come help me set the table," Regina called to her daughter.

Leftovers or not, dinner ended up being a lovely dish of fettuccine with a spicy marinara sauce, some fruit on the side, and a salad with vinaigrette. And I quickly learned that dinner with the Morales family was not a quiet affair.

Victoria was the loudest, speaking with so much enthusiasm that she might as well have been giving some dramatic monologue. She had this tendency to slap her hand down on the table when she was making a point, which, incidentally, was rather frequent.

She traded stories with Regina about the fiascos of running

a coffeehouse, while Rosie interjected now and then, sharing her opinions about almost everything. I found myself laughing during that dinner more than I had in the past few weeks. I couldn't remember the last time I actually had a sit-down dinner like this. I liked it. It was easy to forget your troubles when you were surrounded by people who never stopped laughing.

Not surprisingly, the only person who didn't seem to be enjoying himself was Archer. He was silent throughout the whole meal, eating his pasta with his head down, his hand clenched into a fist on the table beside his plate. I wasn't sure if this was normal behavior for him, but Regina and Victoria made no comment about it.

Rosie's head began to droop low over her plate shortly after Regina brought out cups of pudding for dessert, and soon she was yawning after every other word. I was feeling tired myself, but still antsy, knowing I needed to find a chance to get Archer alone to talk to him.

"Bed!" Victoria declared, slapping a hand down on the table when Rosie tried to take a bite of pudding, missed, and smeared the chocolate on her face.

Archer quickly stood, probably eager to make an escape. He wiped Rosie's face off with a napkin, then scooped her up into his arms and made for the stairs. Rosie wrapped her arms around his neck, laid her head on his shoulder, and was asleep before he even made it to the first step.

Something about the sight made my heart ache in a way I didn't understand. How could Archer have ever felt like he needed to end his life? Didn't he see how heavily his family relied on him? How much they loved him? How could he have wanted to leave something like that behind?

Victoria got to her feet and followed after her grandson as Regina started to pile up the dirty plates in her arms.

"Here, let me help," I said, standing.

"Oh, Hadley, that's okay, you—"

"Really, it's okay. I want to help."

Regina gave me a grateful look and made for the kitchen with the dishes. I gathered up the rest of the dinner dishes and pudding cups and set them on the counter as Regina filled the sink with hot, soapy water—no dishwasher.

"I'll wash, you dry," she said, tossing me a dishtowel.

"Sounds good," I said.

We fell into a comfortable silence as Regina scrubbed the dishes clean and I rinsed and dried them off. And even though we were just doing the dinner dishes, it was sort of nice to realize that there were moments silence was an okay thing. Sometimes not saying anything could say just as much as words did.

"You know, I really appreciate your help tonight, Hadley," Regina told me as she handed me the last of the dinner plates to dry. "You did great."

"It was no problem," I said. "It was sort of fun."

Regina laughed, pulling the stopper in the sink, letting the water drain. "Just wait until it starts to get *really* cold. Then it's not so much fun. We go through so much hot cocoa mix, it's not even funny."

"I don't doubt that," I agreed.

"You know . . ." Regina set the stack of plates in the cupboard and leaned up against the counter. "I'm sure we could find you a waitressing job downstairs. We could always use the extra help. If you wanted, of course."

What?

"You . . . I mean, you're offering me a job?"

"If you want," Regina said again with what seemed to be hopeful eyes.

I tried to run through every scenario of what could happen if I accepted Regina's offer. The possibilities were endless. Archer wouldn't be too happy, but his displeasure was just something I would have to deal with. This was too good of a chance to pass up.

"Sure," I finally said, forcing a smile, realizing I'd inadvertently been tugging on the ghost beads that hid the numbers tattooed on my wrist the entire time I'd had that internal debate with myself. "That would be really nice."

"Fantastic." Regina beamed at me. "I'll just have Archer—"

"You'll just have Archer what, exactly?"

We both turned and saw Archer standing at the island, watching the two of us with a wary expression.

I looked to Regina for help, unsure of what to say. "Um . . ."

"Why, Hadley has just agreed to start working part time for us down in the coffeehouse," she said, looking pleasantly at him.

The expression on Archer's face at hearing this was akin to having been clubbed on the back of the head. "You're joking."

"Afraid not, sweetheart," Regina said. "We could use the extra help, what with the holidays coming up and everything."

"Then ask Carlo or Lauren for help," Archer snapped. "You don't need to hire Hadley. It's not like she needs the money."

I swallowed uncomfortably. He wasn't wrong. There was probably someone out there who needed the job more than I did.

"Unfortunately for you, Archer, that's not your decision to

make. I run this shop, not you," Regina said in businesslike voice I hadn't heard her use before. She added something in Italian that made Archer's expression go from incredulous to stoic in half a second.

"Fine," he said stiffly. "Fine. Whatever you like, Ma."

"Good," Regina said, seemingly satisfied, before turning back to me. "Thanks again, Hadley, for your help."

I was shocked when she reached out to hug me. I couldn't remember the last time I had been hugged like this—by someone who actually meant it, and not just some fleeting, one-armed hug from my parents, or in the hallways at school from a friend.

"Of course," I said, finally remembering that I was supposed to hug her back.

"Give Archer your number, and I'll have him call you and let you know when we can get you in for your training."

"Sounds great, Regina."

"Come on, Hadley." Archer crooked his finger at me and gestured toward the front door. "I'll help you catch a cab home."

I bit my lip, unsure of how to react at hearing this. Archer was actually offering to do something nice for me. What had Regina said to him? "Or I don't have to help you find a cab," he said, giving me an exasperated look. "Your choice, really."

"No, no, that's—um. Great," I said awkwardly. "Thanks."

I said good-bye to Regina again and grabbed my coat and bag off the couch, then followed Archer to the door. Neither of us spoke as she shut the front door behind us and set off down the four flights of stairs to the back of the coffeehouse.

The moment Archer reached the bottom of the stairs, he rounded on me with the furious reaction I'd been waiting for.

"Archer—" I began, but his voice quickly overpowered mine.

"Just what were you thinking, coming here and spending the afternoon with my mother? That's really freaking creepy, and I distinctly remember saying that we would hang out one time and maybe sit together at lunch, and I don't think that exactly includes coming back when I'm not here to—"

"ARCHER, WILL YOU JUST SHUT UP A MINUTE AND LET ME EXPLAIN?"

Archer snapped his mouth shut, his eyes hardening as he glared at me.

I was definitely walking on thin ice here. From his perspective, I could see where I looked like some crazy wannabe girlfriend, stalking him to get his attention. It was so far from the truth it was laughable, but I couldn't tell him the reasoning behind my actions. I needed to settle for somewhere in between.

"Look." I took step down on the staircase, closing the distance between us. "I came to apologize. I didn't plan on staying for so long, helping out your mom. It just happened. And anyway, your mom is a nice person, and she's easy to talk to."

"You came to apologize?" Archer looked momentarily confused. "Apologize for what?"

Wasn't it obvious? "For . . . what I said at lunch the other day," I forced out. "You were right; I shouldn't have said anything to Ty. You're a big boy. You can take care of yourself."

Archer was quiet for a moment. "You know what?" He let out a harsh breath, squeezing his eyes shut, pinching the bridge of his nose with two fingers. "Just forget it, okay? Ritter is a jerk. He makes everyone do stupid things."

I almost snorted. He had a point there. "Then just . . . don't listen to him, Archer," I said without thinking. "He talks a load of BS, and you don't want to damage your ears."

Archer actually cracked a smirk at that. "I know."

I felt a flood of relief rush through me when he smiled. "Right," I said, taking a deep breath. "So about the job . . ."

The smile vanished and his usual annoyed expression took over his face again. "Yeah, about that," he said sarcastically. "You're that desperate to spend time with me you had to beg my mother for a job?"

"No," I snapped, slightly offended. "For your information, your mother was the one who offered me the job. I'm not desperate to spend time with you at all."

Archer rolled his eyes, clicking his tongue, and I suspected he saw right through my lie. "Right."

I shrugged off his comment and instead asked the question that had been bothering me for two days. "Why didn't you come to school yesterday and today?"

Archer, in the process of opening the back door, turned to stare at me with this crooked grin that made my stomach do an uncomfortable flip-flop. "I was at school. I was just avoiding you."

I felt my cheeks fill with color in embarrassment. It was bad enough Archer was avoiding me, and it was even worse that he knew I'd been looking for him. It made me feel so *creepy*.

"Come on," Archer said, jabbing a thumb over his shoulder. "Let's get you a cab."

I headed after him, hoping my new job would give me a chance to get to know the *real* Archer. I had to show him that I wasn't some crazy girl following him around all the time but someone genuinely interested in getting to know him, because I wasn't going anywhere for the next twenty days.

CHAPTER 11

Accidental Revelations— 19 Days Until

S on of a— *Hadley*! You burnt my hand!"

"I'm sorry, I'm sorry!" I wailed as Archer sprinted for the kitchen to run his very red hand under a stream of cold water. "I told you, you shouldn't have made me do anything with making coffee, I—"

"You weren't supposed to be making anything—you were supposed to just empty out the espresso grounds," Archer snapped. "How did you manage to spray hot water everywhere?"

"I don't know!"

My first official shift at Mama Rosa's was not going well. Yesterday was starting to seem like beginner's luck.

I'd accidentally dumped half a bag of their imported Colombian coffee beans in the sink, nearly spilled a bowl of soup on some poor man's lap, messed up on more than one order, and I'd just burned Archer's hand. I'd been so nervous the entire time, what with Archer hovering around me as he barked out orders, telling me how to do this and that. It was a miracle I hadn't burned down the whole building. This afternoon was completely different than working with Regina the other night, and not nearly half as enjoyable.

I had high hopes for this job at Mama Rosa's. Getting to spend extra time with Archer outside school, with little interruption, had seemed like a blessing when Regina offered. But really, the only thing I discovered about Archer was that he had a future career as a drill sergeant. I'd never seen someone boss people around without any hesitation and with such ease.

I had to hand it to Archer, though. I'd always assumed any work environment was a stressful one, but he kept business running smoothly and with little difficulty—save for the difficulty that was me, that is.

"Well, you'll definitely be sticking to waitressing, that's for sure." Archer twisted off the faucet and gingerly dried his hands off with a towel before turning back to me with a frown. "I'm not so sure you're cut out to be a barista."

"Yeah, I've been wondering that myself," I said, rubbing the back of my neck. "Third time's the charm, though."

"Sure," Archer said sarcastically. "Look, go clear off the tables and wipe them down. I'll finish up back here."

"Okay."

I grabbed a large plastic tub from under the counter and got to work stacking dirty mugs, bowls, plates, and cutlery into the bin. After I finished with that, I grabbed a wet cloth and wiped down the tables, then flipped the chairs upside down and stacked them on the tabletops.

I carried the now-full bin into the kitchen, ready to hand it off to Archer and help Regina, but Archer wasn't in the kitchen. Deciding not to annoy him more than I already had, I rinsed off the dirty dishes and stacked them in the dishwasher. At least I could handle the cleaning aspect of the job with no trouble.

When I finished, I left the kitchen and joined Regina up front, where she was counting the day's earnings in the till.

"I think that's about it for today," she told me. "You can go ahead and go home. We'll let you know when you're scheduled to work again."

"Thanks," I said awkwardly. "Um. About today . . . I'm sorry, I didn't mean to mess up so much—"

Regina held up a hand to cut me off, smiling. "Don't even worry about it, sweetheart. It's your first day on the job, and sometimes first days don't go smoothly."

To say things hadn't gone smoothly was putting it lightly. Today had been horrendous.

"And about Archer?" Regina took a step closer, lowering her voice. "Listen, it's just going to take time for him to get used to working with other people. It's been him, my mom, Rosie, and me for the longest time. He doesn't do well with change."

That I could understand better than anything else about Archer. Change was difficult. Sometimes change wasn't always for the better. I hoped that my being hired wasn't one of those cases.

"Right," I said. "Well, I think I'll head out now, then."

Regina nodded and squeezed my forearm. "Of course. I'll see you later."

I said my good-bye and walked through the kitchen, to the back room where the stairs led up to the apartment. I pulled my jacket off one of the hooks and slipped into it, pulled on my knit hat, and slung my bag over my shoulder.

I opened the back door and stepped outside into the cold night air, only to let out a shriek of surprise when I nearly tripped over Archer sitting on the curb right beside the door.

"You scared me!" I gasped, clutching at my chest.

"You scare easily, then."

Archer looked . . . different underneath the yellow glow of the porch light. His shoulders were slumped over as he leaned back against the brick wall. There were dark circles underneath his eyes, as if he hadn't been getting a good night's sleep for a while now. He didn't really look seventeen. He looked much, much older than that.

I wasn't sure how I hadn't noticed it before. So far, all I'd seen from Archer was his stay-away demeanor. But catching him with his guard down like this made me realize that there was more behind Archer than a prickly attitude.

I blew out a sigh, suddenly feeling old myself, and took a seat on the curb beside him. "I'm just tired, sorry."

"Yeah, ruining drinks and burning people's hands can be exhausting," Archer said sardonically.

I had no comeback to this, seeing as that was exactly what I'd done.

We sat in silence, listening to the sounds of noisy traffic on the next street over. Archer's mind was obviously somewhere else, and so was mine. I was thinking about what Rosie told me the other night, about their dad being dead. I'd been trying to find a way to bring it up with Archer, but now didn't seem like the right moment.

I decided to keep silent.

"You can go home, you know," Archer said after a while.

I shook my head. This was one of the few chances I had

to talk to him away from work and school and everything else. "I'm good," I told him. "Why don't we just talk or something?"

"Talk about what?"

"You," I answered honestly.

"And why would you want to talk about me?" Archer asked, and I couldn't tell from his tone whether I'd made him angry or not.

"Well, I'm really just . . ." I bit my lip, hesitant to continue. "Trying to understand you."

Archer's eyes widened in surprise, and for a moment he looked as if he didn't know what to say. I had the thought that this was the first time someone ever said that to him.

"Rosie told me your dad died."

I immediately clapped a hand over my mouth, squeezing my eyes shut. What had I just said? The words had just fallen out of my mouth without preamble. I forced myself to open my eyes, anxious to witness Archer's reaction.

He was now on his feet, his back turned to me. One hand was on his hip, the other hand fisted in his hair; and when he finally did turn around to face me, his shoulders sagged and his hand dropped from his hair to cover his eyes as he let out a long, slow breath.

"Rosie and I don't have the same father." He moved his hand, looking defeated. "But she's right. He is dead."

Did that mean Ty had been right in saying that Archer's real father was in prison? My mind flew into overdrive, thinking of all the thousands of possibilities that could be the answers to the new questions cropping up because of what I'd just heard.

"I'm so sorry," I managed to say in a faltering voice. "That's terrible."

Archer gave a harsh, bitter laugh. "You don't know the half of it."

He sat down on the curb again, leaning his head back against the brick wall of the building. After a hesitant moment, I moved over to sit beside him, making sure to put a few inches of space between us.

"You don't have to say anything to me," I said, even though my mind was screaming, *Liar, liar, you want to know everything!*

"I know I don't," Archer said, giving me a sideways look. "I never do anything I don't want."

I didn't doubt that.

"But . . ."

A small surge of hope ran through me as Archer kicked at a pile of pebbles on the ground with his shoe, scowling. He shrugged. "I'm not as crazy as I might seem."

I bit the inside of my cheek to keep from laughing. I'd made a deal with Death to go back in time to stop Archer from ending his life, which so far had consisted of following him around and all but pining for his attention, and he thought he was the crazy one? The thought was ludicrous.

"Archer, you're not crazy," I told him confidently. "Trust me."

"What would you know about crazy?" Archer said, and he suddenly sounded bitter. "From where I'm sitting, it looks like you have the perfect life."

I was laughing before he even finished his sentence. "I do *not* have the perfect life, Archer. You know my parents make lots of money, but what good does that do when they're so busy all of the time? Most days, it feels like I spend more time with the doorman at my apartment than with my parents."

"You have a doorman?"

"Yeah, and you have your mom, Rosie, and your grandmother."

Archer didn't have an answer to that, and I was surprised at myself for admitting something so personal. So far, it had been all about Archer, and I had been positive that was the way it needed to stay. I had more or less put myself on the back-burner, but maybe opening myself up to Archer, sharing things about my life, would show him he could do the same with me. Friendships were all about give and take, weren't they?

"And I know I'm going to need *a lot* more training, but I think this job will do me some good," I continued, smiling as I glanced over at him. "Get me off my high horse or whatever it is you think about me. A fresh new face around the coffee shop can't hurt, can it?"

"Well, my mother likes you," Archer said after a moment, "but the real test is getting my *grandmother* to like you."

I tried and failed to hold back a shudder. "Yeah, that might be a *bit* more difficult, but I think I'm up to the challenge."

I had a lot more challenging things to tackle for the foreseeable future. Winning over Archer's grandmother seemed like a piece of cake in comparison.

12

High School Clichés— 18 Days Until

A rcher was not at his usual table that next day during lunch.

I stood there, holding my ham and cheese sandwich and fries tightly in my grasp, trying not to take notice of the sinking feeling in my stomach. Where *was* he? Surely he wasn't avoiding me again?

After the discussion we'd had last night after my disastrous first shift at Mama Rosa's, I'd thought things were going to return normal between us. Well, things had never exactly been normal between us—and they probably never would be—but at least I was under the impression we would no longer be at each other's throats like we had been so far.

My chest tightened as I set my food on the table and looked around, hoping to catch at least some small sign of Archer here or there.

I unwrapped my sandwich and took a bite, ignoring the few stares that came with sitting alone during lunch in high school. Archer would be here soon; I had no reason to worry. I knew he was here because I'd seen him at his locker earlier in the morning, so he was probably just running late.

"Hey there, pretty lady. What's the matter? Did your boyfriend ditch you already?"

I looked up, and much to my dismay saw Ty Ritter standing at the front of the table, flanked by two of his companions—Hayden Keller, another football player, and Aimee Turner. I'd hung out with Aimee before and she wasn't so bad, but I didn't like seeing her with Ty. She could definitely do better.

"What?" I swallowed the hard lump in my throat. "I'm not sure I—"

"Where's Archer?" Aimee plunked down into the seat across the table from me, resting her chin in her hands, giving me an indulgent smile. "You guys are such a cute couple."

"We're not dating," I said. "I think you—"

"Ty told us about everything the other day," Hayden said as he took a seat beside me, ruffling his hair in that stupid jock-ish way. "Said you two were looking at each other with gaga eyes the entire time."

"Excuse me?"

"It's true," Ty said with a shrug, now sitting on the other side of me and sliding my fries toward him again. "No offense, Hadley, but it was a little gross."

"Oh, come on, Ty," Aimee said. "They're obviously in love. Gaga eyes are required. Don't worry," she added, giving me a wink. "I think it's adorable."

I was positive my face had never been as red as it was at that moment.

"Look," I said sharply. "Archer and I are not together. We're just friends. I don't know where you're getting your information, but it's not true."

"Oh, honey." Aimee was staring at me with obvious pity. "You don't need to lie about it. It's okay."

"I'm not—"

"But since we're your friends, Hadley, we all agreed it would be best to warn you," Hayden said, nudging me with his shoulder. "You know, for your own personal safety and everything."

"Exactly," Ty said, nodding. "We have your best interests at heart."

"And we don't want to see you get hurt," Aimee added. "Of course we don't."

"Gee, thanks," I said sarcastically. "I feel all warm and fuzzy inside now. Your worries are unnecessary, though. You don't need to warn me about Archer."

"I wouldn't be so sure about that," Ty said, exchanging dark looks with Hayden and Aimee. "Morales has problems, babe."

"Is that so?" I said dryly.

"You do know his dad killed somebody, right?"

Ritter's words from the other day came rushing back. He said that Archer would end up in prison like his old man. That was what Archer's biological father had done to end up in prison? He *killed* someone?

The noisy chattering of the people around us seemed to fade away as I took a few deep breaths, digging my fingernails into my jeans as I gripped my thighs.

"I don't believe you," I finally said. I might as well have just run a mile with how breathless I sounded. "You're lying."

"Oh, Hadley," Aimee said, shaking her head. "How could you have not known?"

"Yeah. I mean, it was all over the papers and the news," Ty said energetically. "Morales's old man broke into their apartment one night and stabbed his stepdad twenty-seven times. Talk about overkill, right?"

Hayden and Ty shared identical smirks, and it made my stomach turn.

"Overkill," Hayden repeated, still giggling. "Good one, Ty."

"That isn't true," I said, gritting my teeth. "You're lying. This isn't funny."

"We're not lying, Hadley," Aimee said. "Look it up on the Internet. Google never lies."

"He's bad business, babe," Ty said with a nod. "So be careful."

"You know, I don't think I've ever heard that version of the story before. I appreciate your creativity, really, but I'm not so sure that's quite how it actually happened."

I looked around in horror at the sound of that voice, and my heart nearly gave out as I locked eyes with Archer. He was leaning up against the wall a few feet from the table, arms crossed, watching us with a fascinated expression.

"Morales!" Ty smiled brightly and gave a wave. "Nice of you to finally show up, man."

"Oh, were you waiting for me? Sorry to disappoint." Archer moved away from the wall and approached the table. I inadvertently drew back in my chair as he came closer, on edge because of the look of barely contained fury now on his face.

"Well, go on, then," he said, clapping Hayden on the shoulder, giving him a friendly shake. "Don't let me stop you from finishing the story. You were just getting to the good bits. Or would you rather I set the record straight and tell you what really happened that night?"

Aimee, Hayden, and Ty said nothing, exchanging looks with one another. I got the impression they weren't sure what to do now that Archer had unexpectedly shown up.

"Archer." I reached out and grabbed his hand without thinking, holding on tightly. "You really shouldn't . . ."

"It's all right, Hadley," Archer said, not looking at me. "If they want to know, I'll tell them. I don't have a problem with it." He slipped his hand out from mine and grabbed an empty chair, swung it around and sat down, propping his elbows up on the table.

"So. What do you guys want to talk about first? How nice it was to see my mom with a guy who actually treated her right, or how happy she was until my abusive father found out? What it was like finding my murdered stepfather in the middle of our kitchen floor? Testifying at the trial?"

An eerie silence followed Archer's words, and I felt my insides beginning to chip away. Suddenly it seemed like I knew *exactly* why Archer had ended his life. How would he have been able to leave that all behind, especially when jerks like Ty took enjoyment in reminding him?

Archer stared at Aimee and Hayden and Ty in turn, waiting for them to say something. They gave him wide stares instead. "Well?" Archer pressed. "I can assure you it's not a boring story. You're not giving it the credit it deserves."

Aimee shoved back from the table and stood, looking expectantly at Hayden and Ty. "Well, we should leave the happy couple alone now, you guys."

"But we were just—" Hayden started to say, but Aimee was quick to cut him off.

"Seriously," she said, glaring at the two boys. "It's time to go."

Aimee practically had both of the boys by the neck as she led them away from the table, but not before she glanced back at me and mouthed *sorry*.

I looked to Archer, a feeling of total helplessness washing through me. What was I supposed to say to him?

"Archer . . ." My voice was pathetically small when I managed to speak. "I don't . . ."

"Get up."

"Excuse me?"

Archer quickly rose to his feet, snatched his backpack off the ground, swung it over his shoulder. "Get *up*," he repeated forcefully.

I scrambled my way to my feet without hesitation. "What's going on?"

He gripped my forearm tightly and pulled me from the lunchroom, down the hallway. It took me a moment to realize we were heading for the library.

"Archer, what are you doing?" I demanded, trying to pull my arm from his grasp. "The bell is going to ring in a few minutes. We're going to get caught."

"So what?" Archer said, moving with purposeful strides. "Like that even matters."

"I'm sorry, but skipping class does matter, no matter how you feel about our fellow classmates."

Despite my attempts to get some kind of response from him, Archer remained silent until we reached the library. He pulled me through the rows of bookcases, toward the back of the library, to that little corner with the chair I'd found him sitting in the other week.

"Look. If I had it my way, you never would have found out about my family's deep, dark secret," Archer told me, speaking quickly. "I'm sure you can understand why that's not something I usually broadcast. But if you think I'm just going to let you walk away under the assumption that what they told you is actually the truth, you're insane."

I couldn't properly formulate any thoughts that would come out as something remotely intelligent. What was I supposed to say? Thank you?

"Okay," was all I could manage.

Archer gave a short nod. "Okay." He pointed to the armchair tucked away in the corner. "Sit."

CHAPTER 13

Truth Will Out

I scuttled over and sat down. It was impossible not to fidget while Archer just stood there, biting his lip, eyes narrowed at the ground.

"This . . . the whole story," he began slowly, "it's not . . . it isn't like what they were saying. It didn't start that way."

"I didn't think it did," I said softly.

He blew out a sigh. "I guess . . . Well, I guess everything started before I was even born. Back when my mom met my biological dad, Jim St. Pierre, in high school. They started dating their junior year, and then my mom ended up getting pregnant with me a few months later. And, naturally, my grandparents—being strict Catholics—really wanted them to get married. I guess things were okay after I was born, I'm not really sure. My mom doesn't really like to talk about it, and I can't say I blame her."

As Archer spoke, I watched his hands curl into fists at his sides, and there was that tick jumping in his cheek again.

"But I'm sure you've already figured out by now that St. Pierre wasn't the best of people. After a while, he started to get really screwed up with drugs and alcohol. I guess his relationship with his parents wasn't so great, and having a kid at eighteen didn't really do him any good. There's no excuse for it either way. My mom, though, she loved him, you know? Despite everything he did, how much he treated her like crap. But then he started knocking her around. And the one time he laid a hand on me, she finally snapped."

He was pacing now, raking his fingers through his hair, and it was distracting, listening to him speak and watching his frantic movements at the same time.

"She called the police, filed for a divorce, the whole nine yards. We moved in with my grandparents. Even though there was a restraining order taken out against him, my dad didn't pay much attention to it. He'd come around at all hours of the night and day, banging on the doors, shouting about how my mom wasn't going to take me away from him. It took a while, but he finally just stopped, and we figured that was the end of it. And then my mom met Chris."

Chris must have been Rosie's father, Regina's late husband.

"Chris was definitely a good change from my biological dad," Archer said. The look on his face was much different now. Softer. "He came into the coffeehouse one day, and it sounds stupid to say, but I think it was love at first sight for them. I swear I've never seen my mom as happy as she was when she was with Chris, and they got married pretty soon after. He was one of the good guys. Ex-Army. Helped me with my homework, taught me how to do math, how to play baseball, helped out with the business whenever he could, did all these things with the rest of the family, and . . ."

"He was your dad."

It was obvious by the way Archer spoke about him, and by his expression, that Chris was the man he considered to be his real father. Blood had nothing to do with it.

Archer stopped pacing long enough to look over to me. "Yeah. He was." He was silent for a few moments.

"And then . . . Rosie?" I pressed when the silence stretched on.

"Rosie." Archer let out a small laugh. "Rosie was an unexpected surprise. I love her, don't get me wrong, but she's definitely a handful." Just as quickly as that smile had appeared at the mention of Rosie, it was gone. "But before Rosie was born . . . Well, that's when it all happened. Of course you can imagine that St. Pierre was not at all happy that my mom married another man and was having a kid with him. I don't know how he found out about it, but he knew."

Judging from what I'd heard about Jim St. Pierre so far, I could definitely imagine he wouldn't be happy Regina found another man.

"So, one night . . . One night, St. Pierre broke into our apartment. And Chris went downstairs to . . . to see what was going on and . . . and then the next thing I knew, I heard all this yelling and shouting, lots of stuff breaking, and I ran into the kitchen, and he was . . ."

The heart-wrenching thing was that I knew what Archer was trying to say even if he couldn't find the words. Because I had already known from the beginning that this story did not have a happy ending.

"Archer, you . . . you don't have to finish. I . . ." I couldn't even find any words to say myself.

Archer leaned against the wall beside the armchair, letting out a small, frustrated groan as he rubbed his forehead with the heel of his palm.

My fingers twitched with the urge to reach out and comfort him somehow, but I held back. "Archer, I'm . . . I'm so . . ."

"Do *not* say you're sorry," Archer snapped, his eyes bright as he glared at me. "And don't you dare pity me. I hate that look people get when they hear about what happened and they want to try and make everything all better for me."

I'd wanted from the beginning to make everything better for him, but I could only do so much. I was thinking then that Archer was going to have to realize that he was the only person who could make everything better for himself.

"I don't pity you," I said honestly. And I really didn't. I *hurt* for him. "I just . . . I want to help you."

"I don't want help," Archer ground out between clenched teeth. "I don't *need* your help."

That was a lie. I knew he needed help. And if he didn't get it from me, that was fine. I just wanted him to get it through his thick skull that he wasn't alone in this.

"Look, go ahead and hate it all you want, but I'm not going anywhere anytime soon. You don't see me running and screaming just because you told me what happened to your family, do you?" I said. "So can we just stop picking on each other? Maybe actually give being friends an honest chance?"

"Friends," Archer repeated, sounding skeptical. "I don't even know what being a friend means."

"You know what? I don't think I do, either," I agreed, thinking of how much of a crappy friend I'd been to Taylor and everyone else lately, blowing them off with some halfhearted excuse about geometry tutoring with Archer. "I'd be happy to find out, though."

Silence fell again. I didn't know what to say to Archer. I

was sure I was pressing my luck, hoping he would share anything more with me. This was the most I'd ever heard him talk before, and even though he'd done it unwillingly, I was honored he felt the need to tell me what had happened.

"Archer, this . . . What you said to me, it stays between us, you know," I said, wanting to take his hand in mine again to reassure him. "Thank you. For telling me."

He rolled his eyes, but the corners of his mouth twitched, like he was fighting back a smile. "Yeah, whatever. Sure."

And there was snarky Archer again. Good to see he hadn't completely disappeared.

The bell rang overhead, cutting through the tense atmosphere wavering between us. It was a shock to realize we'd already missed all of fifth period.

"We should probably get out of here," Archer said, glancing at the nearby clock.

"Right," I agreed, getting to my feet. "Don't want to miss study hall."

"Of course not," Archer muttered as he swung his backpack up on his shoulder. "God forbid you miss *one more* class. It's all because I'm such a terrible influence on you, right?"

"Oh, *please*," I said, fighting back a snort of laughter. "*You*? A bad influence on *me*? If that's the case, then shouldn't I be a good influence on you?"

Archer stopped to ponder what I'd said, his lips twisting into a frown. "Maybe," he said after a moment. "At any rate, my mother would agree with you, but . . . we'll see."

"Right," I said, having difficulty holding back my smile. "We'll see."

It'd taken eight days, but I was finally making progress.

CHAPTER 14

Cautionary Words— 15 Days Until

It felt as if we'd reached a stalemate. I had actually begun to feel hopeful that I'd made headway with Archer, that we were slowly but surely inching our way toward friendship. I'd learned things about him I was pretty sure he never acknowledged unless absolutely necessary, things he said he felt like he *needed* to explain to me. I was positive that counted for something. But three days had passed, and the only semi-exciting things that happened were two frustratingly short tutoring sessions during rather slow shifts at Mama Rosa's. Archer had been decidedly tight-lipped, like maybe he wished he could take back everything he'd told me.

I couldn't help but think that I was going about this all wrong. What if being his friend wasn't enough? There was so much more about him underneath the surface that I couldn't possibly uncover it all in only fifteen days. I could tell talking about what had happened to his stepfather had taken a lot out of him. What was going to happen if I kept digging the way I was?

The church Archer's funeral had been at was empty when I stepped inside. The only source of illumination came from the rows and rows of flickering candles lined up neatly beneath the windows and beside the main entrance, along with the occasional flash of lightning. The overall effect was rather creepy. I made the sign of the cross just to be safe.

Saving Archer meant more to me now than ever before, especially after getting to know him and his family. But now there was a small seed of doubt always settled at the back of my mind, the possibility I would ultimately fail, and it was steadily growing. I only had fifteen days left. The constant burning of the numbers on my wrist made that impossible to forget, and I couldn't help but shudder every time I looked down at the ghost beads on my wrist. I wasn't convinced they were keeping *all* the bad things away.

I took a few steps forward and sunk into a pew, tightly holding my hands together in my lap. "Um. Hello?" I sucked in a deep breath of air, trying to slow my erratically pounding heart. "Look, I figured I would come here since this is where it all started, and I . . ." Coming to this church seemed like a better alternative than going to the Starbucks where I signed the contract. I wasn't going to get any answers from a coffee shop.

"Okay, the thing is, I have no idea what it is I'm supposed to be doing here. Archer is . . . Well, Archer's not the easiest person to be around, you know? I don't have any idea how I'm supposed to help him. I've honestly never felt so stupid. The only thing I really know is that I like being with him, even if he is the most frustrating person I've ever met. I like being with him, and his mom and his little sister and even his grumpy old grandma, and it's just like . . . when I'm with them, I almost forget what it is I'm supposed to be doing. Is this even making any sense? It probably isn't, is it?"

I stopped talking. What *was* I supposed to do next? I'd come to the church for some kind of guidance, but I still felt lost. There were these few times in the morning when I would first open my eyes, and just for a few seconds it was easy to believe that I hadn't signed that contract with Death, and that my life was totally and completely normal. And then I would catch sight of the numbers or the beads on my wrist, and that illusion would be shattered. I exhaled and got to my feet, pulling my coat more tightly around me.

"You weren't looking for me, were you?"

I spun around on my heel and felt shock run through me as I locked eyes with Death. He was leaning up against a marble pillar beside a shelf of hymnals and a row of candles, an unsettling smirk curling at his mouth. The candles cast part of his face into shadow, giving him this sort of inhuman appearance.

"Um," I said, at a loss for what to say. "Were you listening this whole time?"

He definitely heard something if he had shown up out of the blue while I was talking. I didn't like the idea of him spying on me like that.

"Of course," Death said with a nod.

"So . . . can you help me?" I asked, realizing he was probably the last person who would.

"No, Hadley. I can't."

Despite myself, I felt crushed. I needed to know I was doing the right thing, that I was on the right track. There was too much at stake to mess up.

"I don't understand," I finally said, sounding winded. "Why? Why me? Why would you pick me of all people to do something like this?"

Death shrugged a shoulder again, his face a blank slate. "We all have reasons for our actions."

"That's not good enough! I'm in the dark here, Death, and I have no idea how I'm supposed to do this! You didn't exactly explain my job description all that well when you had me sign that contract, you know! Why would you make me sign it if you knew I couldn't do it?"

My voice bounced off the walls, ringing through the church with a hollow echo.

I was out of breath and clammy all over, but I felt a sense of relief at having blurted that out. Death pulled away from the wall and came closer, like a predator moving in for the kill. I quickly stepped back, clutching at the pew behind me.

"Let's get something straight, Hadley Jamison." He kept moving closer until he was gripping the pew on either side of me, bending down so we were level with one another. "I didn't make you do anything. You signed that contract of your own volition. And I may not be able to read people's thoughts, but don't doubt for one second that I know what's going through your mind right now."

My eyes were beginning to cross from trying to stay focused on Death. That same feeling I had the first time I'd seen him, of ice spreading through my veins, returned, only ten times more intense.

"You're scared. I know you are. I've been at this job a lot longer than you could ever possibly imagine. I've seen it all, Hadley. Nothing you can say would ever surprise me."

I was not comforted by Death's words.

"You . . . Well, you could have at least told me Archer's stepfather was murdered," I managed to force out.

"Just a piece of the puzzle," Death said, leaning away from me.

"Archer's not a puzzle. I don't exactly understand half the things he does, but . . . he's a human being."

"Then you're already halfway there, aren't you?"

"Halfway there? Death, I . . ." My voice broke, and it was all I could do to keep from sobbing. "What am I supposed to do?"

It was such a fleeting look that I couldn't be sure, but for just a second Death looked sympathetic. "Hadley, I'm not the one with all the answers."

With those final words of advice, Death just . . . disappeared. I made it a few steps before my legs gave out and I landed awkwardly in the pew. The tears I had managed to keep back for days finally escaped, and it was as if floodgates had been opened.

I sat there and cried, thankful no one else was around to witness my pathetic display.

"Excuse me. Excuse me, miss. Are you all right?"

I whipped my head up and saw one of the church's priests standing in front of me, a concerned expression on his weathered face. I recognized him almost at once as the priest who had performed Archer's funeral service.

"Oh, no, I'm fine," I said quickly, rubbing at my cheeks. "I'm so sorry, I didn't mean to . . ."

"It's quite all right," the priest said with a kind, small smile. "People often come here during the day for the quiet, and to pray."

I bit my lip to keep from laughing. I wasn't so sure the conversation I had with Death could be considered prayer.

"Right," I said uncomfortably, getting to my feet. "I should just . . ."

I couldn't force out any other words, so I settled for gesturing to the exit behind me.

"Are you sure you're all right?" the priest asked, his brow furrowed. "You came here for a reason, didn't you?"

"Well, it's . . ." I sighed heavily, dropping back down into the pew, suddenly feeling defeated. "No, Father. I guess I'm not all right."

The priest let out a sigh almost identical to my own and took a seat beside me in the pew. "Do you want to talk about it?"

I stared over at him with a frown. "Why would you want to listen to me talk about my problems?"

The priest chuckled, giving me a bemused look. "It's what I do."

"Right. Of course," I said. "Sorry. I . . . haven't been to church in a while."

The priest shrugged. "There's no time like the present."

"Well, sure, I guess, but . . ." My fingers started twisting and pulling at a loose thread on my coat sleeve. "Well, I'm sort of stuck with something."

"And what are you stuck with?" the priest asked.

I told him the truth. Well, as much of the truth as I was capable of telling. "I'm sort of supposed to be helping this person," I said carefully. "But the problem is, he doesn't want my help."

"Supposed to be helping someone?" the priest repeated in confusion. "What do you mean?"

I sucked in a deep breath through my nose, debating the right way to answer the question. "This person is in trouble. Like, big trouble. And if I don't find a way to get him to listen to me, he's going to . . . He's going to do something bad. Really bad."

The priest gave a nod, crossing his arms over his chest. "He must be a troubled man, then."

"Father, you don't know the half of it," I said. "I know he's hurting. But he won't let anyone help him."

The priest nodded again, his thoughtful frown back in place. "Why do you want to help him?"

"Because I have to," I said immediately.

"But why?" he pressed. "Helping others is always the right thing to do, but nobody can force you to do it if you don't want to."

I had no other answer to that question. "Because . . . because . . ." I swallowed hard, trying to get a grip on my erratic emotions. Archer was my friend. I cared about him. I cared about Archer and his family, so much so that it felt as if I had known them for a lot longer than just twelve days. "I care about him," I told the priest. "I don't want anything to happen to him. I need him to be okay."

"So, he's important to you," the priest said aloud for confirmation. "Sounds to me like that's exactly the right reason for helping someone."

"Okay, yeah, but what if . . . What if you don't have everything you need to help that someone?"

"Then you show him love."

I stared at the priest in utter confusion. I was hardly able to believe he had just said that. Show him *love*? He stared back expectantly, and I realized he was absolutely serious.

"God loves us all equally, as his children, doesn't he?" the priest asked me. "He wants to help us, and for us to help one another."

"Sure," I said, wondering where he was going with this.

"Then all you have to do is pass that love on," the priest said, shrugging again, like it was all just that simple. "Sometimes it's all you can offer."

"But what is love?" I demanded exasperatedly. "How on earth am I supposed to know what love is if I can't even pass a stupid high school geometry class? I'm only sixteen!"

The priest laughed. "I believe you, but I think you're not giving yourself enough credit. Love has a different definition for every person. Just look for it underneath everything, and you'll find it."

I pondered his words for a second. "Father, I hate to say this to a holy man, but that makes absolutely no sense."

"Life doesn't always make sense," the priest said. "But I think . . ." He made a thoughtful humming noise, then grabbed a Bible from the stack at the end of the pew and flipped it open, thumbing through the pages until he found what he was look-ing for. "I think this might clear things up a bit more."

He pointed a finger to a passage in the gospel of John. I read it aloud. "There is no greater love than to lay down one's life for one's friend."

I looked up at the priest, unsure of what to say.

"Just think about it," the priest repeated, reaching over to pat my hand.

He got to his feet, and I quickly followed suit.

"Thank you, Father," I told him honestly.

"I'll pray for you," he said, giving me a kind smile.

And for some reason, that thought was comforting to me. "Thank you," I said again.

He began to make his way up the main aisle.

"Wait! Father!"

The priest turned back around. "Yes?"

"If you knew you had to do the right thing, but that something bad might happen to you because of it, would you do it anyway?"

"The right thing is always the right thing."

The priest gave me another smile and then continued on his way, whistling a quiet tune under his breath. Before leaving the church, I dropped a few dollars into a donation box, lit a candle, and said a silent prayer.

Bottled-Up Emotions— 14 Days Until

When I woke up the next morning, I spent a good half hour staring up at the ceiling, lost in my own thoughts. I couldn't force the conversations that I'd had with Death and the priest out of my head. Their words were buzzing around in my mind, annoying and frustrating and completely confusing.

When my alarm finally went off at eight, I rolled out of bed and padded my way to the kitchen, ready to eat as large a breakfast as I could make.

I stopped short when I reached the dining room. "Mom? Dad?"

My dad looked up from the newspaper spread open in front of him and gave a smile. "Morning, Hadley."

My mom was too fixated on whatever was on her iPad, and the yogurt cup in her hand, to pay me much attention. She barely managed a brisk wave in my direction.

"What are you doing here?" I asked, very confused. "You guys are normally gone by now."

"I know," my dad said as he took a swallow of orange juice.

"Your mother and I are leaving on a business trip in a few hours."

That made even less sense than them actually being at home instead of their offices at this hour. "What? Why?" I said. Dad was a defense attorney, and Mom was a CFO at a Fortune 500 company. Their business paths didn't cross often.

"Your father's firm is representing us in a breach-of-contract suit," my mom said, turning off her iPad. "Our flight leaves for Miami in a few hours."

I had to stop myself from slapping a hand to my forehead. I felt like an idiot for forgetting that I'd spent Thanksgiving alone the first time around—well, apart from sharing some runny pumpkin pie with my ancient neighbor, Mrs. Ellis— because Taylor had gone out of town for the week to see her grandparents in Wisconsin. I'd been preoccupied with more important things to remember. And after spending the past week with Archer's family, the thought made me feel depressed. Who wanted to spend a holiday alone, especially one that represented coming together as a family like Thanksgiving?

I opened the freezer and grabbed a package of waffles, pulled two out, and popped them in the toaster beside the sink.

"Hadley . . ." I glanced back toward the dining table as my dad spoke, looking rather sheepish as he adjusted his red tie. "This means we won't be here for Thanksgiving. Will you be all right?"

"Of course I'll be fine," I said shortly. "This isn't the first time I'll be left alone."

My mom looked over at me with raised eyebrows.

"Well, we figured one of your friends invited you over for Thanksgiving dinner," my dad said awkwardly.

"No," I said flatly, banging the fridge door shut as I poured myself a glass of milk to go with my waffles. "I'll just order out or something. And besides, I have to work this week anyway, so I won't be here alone too much."

"Excuse me?" my mother said. "You have to work?"

My parents didn't know I'd gotten a job. I'd barely seen them in the past few days, and I'd been so preoccupied that I hadn't even thought about telling them. The opportunity had suddenly presented itself, though.

"Yeah," I said, turning around to face them. I couldn't tell if I was proud or defensive, or somewhere in between. "I have to work."

"Why would you get a job?" my mom demanded. "It's completely unnecessary. You should be focusing on your studies."

"Hang on a second, Michaela," my dad said. "Lots of kids in high school have jobs."

"Well, yes, but our child doesn't need a job, Kenneth," my mom retorted, shooting my dad a look. "Getting a job simply puts her grades in jeopardy, and her grades are bad enough as it is."

"Hey! My grades aren't that bad, and—"

"Do you really think that's fair?" my dad asked. "If Hadley wants a job, I think it's her decision, not ours."

"You're missing the point," my mom snapped. "Hadley, you have more than enough money in your bank account to do whatever you want. I don't see why you—"

"You know what, Mom? Getting a job is better than being shut up in this stupid apartment by myself all the time!"

My parents looked as if I had just struck them across the face. I was sure I looked the same way too. I'd never talked back to either of them in my entire life. They weren't usually around enough for me to do so.

But now that those words had finally left my mouth after years of being on the tip of my tongue, the rest decided to follow suit, and I went with it. After spending a couple of days with a *real* family, I realized how much I had been missing.

"Do either of you even realize how often you're gone? You're away so frequently, it's like I'm the only one living here! And during those rare moments where you decide to check and see if I'm still alive, it's as if I'm talking to total strangers! I'm your daughter, not one of your business partners!"

I snatched my waffles from the toaster and my glass of milk and then stomped from the kitchen back to my room, not giving myself time to read the expressions on their faces. They didn't come after me. That in itself said more than enough.

I didn't come out of my room until I had to leave for my shift at Mama Rosa's. My parents were already long gone, off on their business trip in Miami without saying good-bye. I tried to tell myself that their absence didn't matter, that I had more important things to worry about, but doing so was pointless. It did matter, and it hurt.

I took the train across town and walked the few blocks over to Mama Rosa's, still in a tremendously foul mood. I already knew it was going to be impossible to put the conversation I'd had with my parents out of my mind and fake a happy face.

I stepped inside the coffeehouse, immediately enveloped in the cozy warmth the fire in the grate was giving off. I made my way behind the counter and to the kitchen, where I was met with pure and utter chaos. Regina was at one of the sinks, furiously scrubbing what looked like burnt cinnamon rolls off a cookie sheet as Victoria was unloading glass plates from the dishwasher, stacking them on the counter with a speed I didn't know someone her age was even capable of, all while she was shouting at Regina in Italian.

And then there was Rosie, who was sitting in the middle of the floor, playing with a bunch of pots and pans that she was repeatedly hitting with a wooden spoon, while also singing at the top of her lungs. The cramped space was stiflingly hot, and with the racket everyone was making, I wanted to turn around and walk right out.

"Hello?" I said, cautiously edging my way into the kitchen.

Regina whipped around and let out a huge sigh of relief when she saw me. "Hadley, thank God. Would you get Rosie out of here? I can barely think straight with all of this noise."

"Um, sure," I said. "Do you want me to—"

"Archer is doing some accounting upstairs," Victoria said briskly. "Tell him he needs to take his little sister out for the afternoon."

"And by all means, join him," Regina added. "Take the day off. This is your Thanksgiving break, after all."

"But this is only my third shift, I really should—"

"Honey, trust me." Regina gave me an imploring look. "Watching Rosie for an afternoon is work enough."

"Go on, then," Victoria said, giving me a dismissive wave. "Take the girl and go."

I would have kept protesting, but I didn't dare refuse any order from Victoria. The woman looked like she could kill someone simply by raising an eyebrow at them.

I crouched down beside Rosie on the floor; she was still banging away with the wooden spoon to her heart's content.

"Um, Rosie?"

Rosie stopped banging on one of the pots and looked up at me with a frown. It was almost impossible not to melt at her big, blue eyes.

"I'm singing," she told me earnestly.

"You are," I said. "You sing beautifully."

"I know," Rosie said.

"So. What say you and I go upstairs and see if we can convince Archer to take us out for some brownies and hot chocolate?"

Rosie's face lit up like the Fourth of July. "Okay! Come on! Let's go!"

She dropped the spoon and jumped to her feet, grabbing at my hand, pulling me toward the stairs that lead up to the apartment. Rosie knocked open the front door when she reached the apartment and burst inside, shouting, "Archer! It's brownie time!"

Archer was sitting at the dining table, fingers tapping away on an adding machine while he scribbled something down on a piece of paper. He looked up as I entered, and scowled as I shut the door.

"What are you talking about, Rosie?" he said as Rosie climbed into the chair across the table from him, now singing about brownies.

"Hadley said you're going to take us out for hot chocolate and brownies!"

"Excuse me?" Archer gave me an incredulous look. "When did this happen?"

"Just go along with it," I said, low enough so Rosie couldn't hear me. "It doesn't have to be brownies. Your mom and grandma just want us to take Rosie out."

"Why?" he said. "I don't—"

"Archer, I said it's *brownie time*," Rosie said loudly before snatching at the pile of papers beside him and throwing them into the air.

Archer stared at Rosie in astonishment for a moment, and then released a heavy breath, dropping his pencil. "Go get your jacket, Rosalia."

Rosie let out an excited squeal and leapt off the chair, making a mad dash for the stairs.

"Is she normally like this?" I asked curiously.

"When sugar is involved? Usually." Archer stood and made for the living room, grabbing his jacket off the back of the couch and slipping into it. "But this is an excuse to take a break from crunching numbers, so I'm not complaining."

"So, uh . . . how's business?" I said, nodding toward the mess on the table.

Archer shrugged, not meeting my gaze. "Business is as good as it can be."

I wasn't sure what that was supposed to mean, but I decided not to pester him on the subject.

Rosie came skipping back down the stairs a moment later, bundled up in her jacket, hat, and scarf. "Come on, let's go."

Archer and I followed Rosie down the stairs to the back door of the coffeehouse, said a quick good-bye to Regina and Victoria, and then we stepped out into the November chill. We made our way through the alley and out onto the sidewalk, heading off down the block.

"There's a bakery a few blocks over," Archer said as we walked. "We can see if they have brownies. Not that Rosie needs the sugar or anything."

I grinned in spite of how miserable I still felt from the words I'd shared with my parents earlier that morning, but said nothing. There was too much going on in my head to keep up a conversation.

We had been walking in silence for a few minutes before Archer spoke again. "So."

I glanced up at him with raised eyebrows. "So."

"Are you going to tell me what's bothering you?"

He was watching me with a guarded expression, his eyes narrowed. While I couldn't rightly say there was concern in his eyes, he did look interested.

"I'm not . . . Nothing is bothering me," I said uneasily. "I'm fine."

"You're a dreadful liar," he said flatly. "And I'm not an idiot. Something is eating at you."

"Well, I guess . . . it's just . . ." I let out a small moan, resigning myself to defeat. "It's my parents."

"Your parents." Archer nodded. "Okay. What about your parents?"

"They . . . went on a business trip," I began carefully. "To Miami. And it wouldn't be the first time they've run off for weeks at a time, so it's not a big deal. I'm used to it. But today I kind of lost it, and yelled at them for being crappy parents because my mother pitched this fit about me having a job, making all these presumptions that I have this perfect life with all this money, that I don't have to lift a finger. And she doesn't know me. Neither of them do."

My throat felt tight when I finished speaking.

"Good."

I stared up at Archer in confusion. "What?"

"Good," he repeated. "I'm glad you told them they were crappy parents. That's nothing on you, you know. You've got people in your life that care about you. Sometimes parents just don't show it as much as they should."

This was true. Taylor, Brie, and Chelsea cared about me. I'd even go as far to say that Regina cared about me too.

I was touched by what Archer said. He was a bit brisk about it, but the intent was still there. "Are you trying to make me feel better, Archer Morales?" I asked slyly.

Archer opened his mouth to respond, but was cut off by Rosie's loud shout of, "Will you please hurry up? I really want brownies!"

After making a quick stop at the bakery Archer mentioned, and getting Rosie only one brownie instead of the seven she demanded, we were now walking down one of the many paths in Central Park. I figured it would be a good idea to let Rosie blow off some steam before we circled back to Mama Rosa's. Regina and Victoria would probably be glad if Rosie was tired enough to go down for a nap when we returned.

"I have an idea," I said to Archer as we strolled along.

"Well, there's a novelty."

"Don't be rude."

"Fine, fine." He looked down at me in question as he hooked a finger into the back of Rosie's coat to keep her from getting too far ahead of us. "What's your idea?"

"I want to take us somewhere."

Archer looked as if he didn't like the sound of that. "Where? Not to get more junk food, is it?"

"No," I assured him. "Just follow me."

He followed suit as I turned back down the path, heading off in a different direction, and when I glanced back I saw he was steering Rosie with his hands on her shoulders. It took a few minutes to get to my intended destination, and we were almost there when Archer figured out where I wanted to go.

"Oh, no. No. We are not—"

"The zoo!" Rosie squealed loudly.

"The zoo?" Archer hissed at me. "Why do you want to go to the zoo?"

"The zoo is fun!" I protested. "Central Park Zoo is classic! Look how excited Rosie is!"

"She gets that excited about macaroni and cheese for dinner."

"Fine. We're doing this for me, then," I said, ushering the two of them toward the entrance. "The zoo reminds me of happier times with my family. Unless you'd rather go back to accounting?"

That seemed to change his mind pretty quickly. I bought three tickets, and Archer and I ended up chasing after Rosie as she dashed through the front gates ahead of us.

"Where do we go first?" she asked us excitedly when we finally caught up to her.

"You pick," I told her. "Archer and I will follow you."

Rosie looked as if Christmas had come early, and immediately said, "Penguins!"

Archer groaned. "Penguins? Really, Rosie? Penguins are loud, and they smell like—"

"Penguins it is," I said loudly over Archer, shooting him a disapproving look. "Let's go, then."

Rosie squealed happily and grabbed at my hand, then Archer's, and started pulling us along. The penguin house was empty when we finally reached it, save for an exhausted-looking mother with three little boys. Rosie immediately raced up to the glass that separated the penguin exhibit from the concrete bleachers where visitors sat, pointing to each of the penguins in turn.

Archer and I took a seat on the first row of bleachers, watching as Rosie babbled away in excitement, and Archer slumped into his seat with an exaggerated sigh.

"Lighten up, won't you?" I said, nudging him with my elbow. "So you don't like penguins, big deal. That should make it a little more worth your while, though."

Archer's eyes fixed on Rosie as I pointed to her; she hadn't stopped giggling from the moment we walked into the penguin house. It made me smile. And though I knew Archer was doing his best to hide it, he was smiling too.

Rosie rushed up to me then, clutching at my knees, all smiles. "Aren't penguins cool?" she gushed. "Look at how they waddle around like that! They're my favorite animal!"

"Mine too," I said, grinning. "And you know what they say about penguins, right? It's kind of cool too."

A confused look crossed Rosie's face. "No, what?"

"Yeah, Hadley," Archer said, smirking at me. "What do they say about penguins?"

"Well, some penguins spend ages searching for the perfect pebble on the beach that they want to give to the penguin that they really like. Sort of like a proposal, when two people are in love and they want to get married, and the guy gives the girl a ring? So the girl penguin keeps it, and then they spend the rest of their lives together. Just the two of them."

I'd always loved that fact. Penguins were one of the few animals in the world that practiced monogamy. In this day and age, I knew there were more than a few people who could learn from penguins when it came to relationships.

"*Oh.*" Rosie looked excited. "I like pebbles. I hope I find my penguin one day."

So do I, I silently agreed.

"Tell me, Hadley," Archer said as we left the penguin house, on our way to the reptiles. "Have you found your penguin yet?"

His tone was teasing, and I felt my face flood with color at his jab, now embarrassed that I'd even brought up that story.

"No. I'm only sixteen," I said, refusing to meet his eye. "I've got plenty of time."

"All the time in the world," Archer agreed.

"What about you?" I asked. "Have *you* found your penguin?"

"No." His answer was firm. "I'm not sure I have one."

I refused to believe that. Everyone had their own penguin, including Archer. If he managed to open his eyes just a little bit, he might possibly find that *maybe* his penguin was right in front of him.

CHAPTER 16

A Little Holiday Shopping—
13 Days Until

I stood in the kitchen in Mama Rosa's, at attention beside Archer, waiting for orders from Victoria. She was staring down over the rims of her glasses at a grocery list she had scribbled onto a piece of yellow paper a mile long, and was using the pen in her hand to make corrections. The stern expression on her face wasn't out of character, but it made me nervous nonetheless.

I'd never really worked under Victoria before. By the time I showed up for my shifts, she usually had already signed out for the day and was with Rosie somewhere.

"Grandma, we've been standing here for ten minutes," Archer said. "Any chance we can leave this year?"

Victoria's eyes flashed as she glared at Archer. "You watch your mouth, boy. You'll leave when I say you can leave."

Archer tipped his head back and sighed loudly as he rolled his eyes. I bit my lip to hide my smile. I'd always been under the impression that girls tended to be more dramatic, but Archer was totally changing my perspective on that.

"And don't you roll your eyes at me."

The woman obviously saw everything. It took another few minutes before Victoria finally folded up the grocery list and thrust it at Archer, along with an envelope I presumed to be full of cash.

"I want you both to go to D'agostino's and buy everything on this list," Victoria said. "No more, no less, and absolutely no substitutions. Do I make myself perfectly clear?"

Archer snapped a perfect military salute. "Ma'am, yes, ma'am."

Victoria moved with surprising speed for someone her age as she snatched a wooden spoon off the counter and whacked Archer across the knuckles with it. "Don't you sass your grandmother, boy."

I had to clap a hand over my mouth and turn away to keep from bursting out laughing.

"Now get out of here," Victoria said, brandishing the spoon at us. "I expect you to be back in three hours."

"Of course, Mrs. Incitti," I said before grabbing Archer's arm to pull him from the kitchen.

Archer snagged a few cloth shopping bags off the hooks by the back door, and then we were heading through the alleyway and out onto the sidewalk in front of the coffeehouse.

"Does preparing for holidays normally go like this in your family?" I asked.

"What, my grandma bossing everyone around?" Archer said. "Hadley, that's every day. My grandmother is the matriarch of the family. She's seventy-nine, but I swear she's been keeping herself alive off espresso and pure spite all these years."

As we walked to D'agostino's, Archer listed off a few of the meals that would be prepared for Thanksgiving dinner. By the time he was describing the desserts his mother and aunts made, my mouth was watering at the thought of getting my hands on a few cannoli or some tiramisu. The more he talked, the more I began to feel disappointed. I had nothing to look forward to but a day of takeout, alone in the apartment by myself.

It took us almost a half hour to reach D'agostino's. It was a rather large grocery store, but it had that homey feeling of a business that had remained in one family for a long time—sort of like Mama Rosa's.

Archer folded up the piece of yellow paper Victoria had given him and tore it in half, separating the list, then handed me one of the pieces.

"Here. We'll divide and conquer. Grab your own shopping cart, and let's meet up at the registers in a half hour."

I did my best to replicate his military salute, grinning. "Sir, yes, sir."

I was still smiling as I grabbed a shopping cart and made for the dairy section. The first few items on my list were approximately nine different types of cheese.

I had no idea what Victoria could possibly need that much cheese for, but her orders earlier had been very specific. I did not want to be subjected to her wrath if I didn't get every block she'd asked for.

Strolling through the aisles, plucking things off the shelves, and sorting through the fruits and veggies was a mindless sort of task, and as I went, I thought about Archer. We only had thirteen days to go, and I sensed I was finally getting through to him. Yesterday we'd gotten more personal in our conversations than we ever had before. I didn't even talk to Taylor about my parents the way I talked to Archer. My weird family dynamic was something I'd kept bottled up for so long, but for some reason I knew I could share that side of my life with him.

And I was so relieved Archer was showing me glimpses into his own private world and the thoughts that always seemed to be swarming his mind. He was not an open book by any means, but I got the feeling he trusted me—or was at least starting to.

Maybe this was what Archer had needed from the very beginning. For somebody to say hello, to be persistent and show him they cared. To do something small and simple to show him he mattered. Small things could make a difference.

"Excuse me. Do you need some help with that?"

I started at the voice that had spoken quite literally out of nowhere, and glanced over my shoulder to see a very tall, very elegant-looking man standing uncomfortably close. He was dressed in a perfectly pressed gray suit, and his blond hair was slicked back in a way that didn't seem popular anymore. I placed him to be at least in his thirties, but he held himself in a way that made him seem older than that.

"I'm sorry, Hadley," the man said in a smooth English accent. "I didn't mean to give you a fright."

He smiled at me with his head tilted to the side, and I realized when I got a good look at his eyes—one a deep blue, the other black as pitch—that this was no ordinary man. The little time I'd spent with Death gave me the ability to recognize that much in a person. A shiver of fear raced down my spine as I wondered how in the world he knew my name.

"Oh, no, I . . ." I sounded as if I had just been punched in the gut. "I'm . . . I'm fine. I've got it."

The man raised an eyebrow, and there was an unsettling glint in his mismatched eyes. "Really, it's not a problem."

Before I had time to object, he moved closer, reaching up to grab at a large can of artichoke hearts. "Four cans, yes?"

He had to have read the grocery list placed on a box of pasta in the cart, because I knew for a fact that I hadn't voiced any of the items I needed to collect. The man pulled down four cans of artichokes and then turned to me, resting his hand on the side of my cart.

"There. That wasn't so difficult, was it, Hadley?"

I was about to demand this man tell me how knew so much, but was prevented when Archer's voice called, "There you are, Hadley. I've been looking all over for you."

Whatever was written on my face—panic, most likely—as I stared at the stranger before me seemed to immediately set Archer on high alert. His grip on his own cart tightened when he noticed the man standing so close to me, and Archer's back was ramrod straight as he approached.

My visitor didn't move, instead turning his smile on Archer as he came to a stop in front of us, saying, "Oh, hello," in that eerily smooth voice.

"Hello," Archer said. He left the cart and came to my side, forcing the man to take a step back as Archer slid an arm around my waist.

It was a possessive gesture, one that made it seem as if there was something more than just friendship between the two of us—but I suspected that was what Archer intended. The look on his face confirmed it.

"I was just giving Hadley a hand here," the man said. "Couldn't reach the top shelf, bless her."

"Is that so?" Archer said. "Very nice of you."

The man smiled again, although this time his eyes were

tight. "Oh, I always try to be nice." The way he pronounced the last word sounded anything but.

I opened my mouth in an attempt to intervene, or at least come up with an excuse on the spot for Archer and me to escape, but Archer gave my hip a hard squeeze—a clear sign that said, *Let me handle this.*

"Don't see that much anymore in this day and age," Archer said.

"No," the man agreed. "I don't suppose you do. But it's a small world. I suspect we'll be seeing each other again."

He winked at me as he backed away, giving another one of those smiles, and then turned and sauntered off down the aisle.

The moment the stranger was out of sight, Archer let go of my waist and took a step back. A sigh of relief escaped me as I leaned against the shelves, a hand at my chest.

"Who was that?" Archer asked. He'd fixed his gaze on the end of the aisle as if he were expecting the man to return.

"I . . . have no idea," I said slowly. "But he was definitely . . . *freaky.*"

"I don't like the way he was looking at you," Archer finally said, glancing over at me. "Like you were something to eat."

I had been more focused on the man's eyes, the way he seemed to be able to see straight through me, rather than his expression. I was starting to worry that he was one of the *things* Death had warned me about, back when I signed the contract. The *things* that didn't like when the order of the world was disrupted, something I had definitely done when I went back in time to try to save Archer's life.

And even if Archer didn't know the truth about the

unbelievable secrets I carried with me, he knew enough to tell that there was something wrong with that man.

"Well, he's gone now," I said.

"Let's go," Archer said, reaching for the cart. "It looks like we have everything, and I don't want to stick around and risk running into that creep again."

I wholeheartedly agreed.

It took us about fifteen minutes to work our way through the checkout line and place everything in the shopping bags, and it took us almost another hour to lug everything back to Mama Rosa's. Archer had been adamant that a cab was "too expensive," despite my repeated offer to pay for one, so by the time we reached Mama Rosa's, my arms were aching from having to carry the heavy shopping bags for numerous blocks.

"Good. You're back early," Victoria said as Archer and I hefted the shopping bags up onto the kitchen counter in the coffeehouse. "Now unpack everything."

I fought back a groan as I slumped against the counter, massaging my forearm.

"Okay, fine, but let me at least make us some drinks," Archer said. "It's freezing out there."

"Fine." Victoria waved a hand at Archer as she started rummaging through the shopping bags. "Just be quick about it, boy."

I shot Archer a grateful smile as he left the kitchen, and then turned to help Victoria sort through the mess of groceries on the counter. Archer returned a few minutes later with two hazelnut lattes, one that I eagerly took, exhaling in relief as the hot drink began to warm me up.

I was still jittery from the encounter with that man in

D'agostino's, so downing a large amount of caffeine probably wasn't all that smart, but I hardly cared. I didn't want to think about what his presence in my life meant, not here with Archer. I'd have to save freaking out for another time.

When the monstrosity of unloading the groceries was finally done and over with, I had a definite reason as to why I never wanted to work with Victoria Incitti again. The woman made even the toughest drill sergeant look like a pansy. Archer had probably learned all his bossiness from her. I was actually a little relieved when I was given the go-ahead to leave, just so I could go home to a place where no one was yelling at me.

I had pulled on my coat and was in the process of slinging my bag over my shoulder when Archer turned to me and said, "Oh, by the way? You're coming to Thanksgiving dinner."

He said it so casually, like he was mentioning something about the weather, that I sort of stood there and stared blankly at him.

"What?"

"You heard me." Archer didn't seem to notice my shock as he swung the refrigerator door shut. "You're coming to Thanksgiving dinner. I meant to tell you earlier, but I forgot."

I was utterly baffled.

"I am?" I said. "Since when?"

"Since right now," Archer told me. I couldn't tell if he was smiling or smirking. "I know you don't have any other plans. So you're coming to Thanksgiving dinner with us. Or you're fired."

I was unable to keep back the wide grin that broke out across my face.

CHAPTER 17

Thanksgiving, the Incitti Way— 12 Days Until

I was wide awake at what felt like the crack of dawn on Thanksgiving morning. I knew the second I opened my eyes that I wouldn't be able to go back to sleep; I was far too antsy already thinking about dinner later that day. So I dragged myself out of bed and to the kitchen to make a pot of coffee (using beans I'd bought from Mama Rosa's) and toast a few frozen waffles. Breakfast in hand, I settled down in front of the TV, resigning myself to a morning of watching cartoons while I waited for the afternoon to come. It was a better alternative to fretting about that creepy man who had shown up in D'agostino's yesterday afternoon. I didn't want to think about that on a holiday. I knew he had to be connected to Death *somehow*, but I forced myself not to focus on that just yet. Given the way I'd taken up excessive worrying, I figured he'd circle back around in time. And then I could properly freak out.

Around two in the afternoon, I left the couch for the shower. I spent a good half hour standing underneath the flow of hot water before I stepped out and wrapped myself in a towel, only to stand in my closet for what felt like another half hour. I wasn't one of those girls who spent ages in front of the mirror every morning getting ready for the day. But when I was faced with the prospect of meeting Archer's entire extended family, things were a little different.

In the end, it took me another forty-five minutes before I was finally able to consider myself appropriate to leave, clad in a pair of jeans, a nice brown blouse, and boots. By then it was half past three, and there was no way I'd be able to ride the train and get to Mama Rosa's on time. A cab would be impossible thanks to the Macy's Thanksgiving Day Parade, so I was going to have to wait it out on the train and hope Archer's family would be understanding about my tardiness.

Out in the chilly afternoon, I wished Hanson the doorman a Happy Thanksgiving before booking it down the block to the nearest subway entrance.

I was on the edge of my seat, twisting the ends of my coat between my fingers the whole ride. I had never been to a family gathering like this before, sad as that sounded, and had no idea what to expect. My mom's parents had passed away when I was little, and she was an only child. The majority of my dad's side of the family were all down south in Tennessee and weren't fans of the city, which made get-togethers rare.

"All right, Hadley," I muttered to myself, heading up to the front door of the coffeehouse when I arrived. "You can handle this."

The drapes were drawn tight over the front windows of the shop, so I didn't get the chance to see inside before I raised my hand and rapped my knuckles on the door.

I heard the locks tumble, then the door swung open and

I was face-to-face with a boy who had the same familiar features the Incitti family seemed to share, with the hazel eyes and dark hair. From the way his eyes glinted and the impish grin that curled his mouth, I got the impression this boy lived for mischief.

"Well, hello there," he said, wiggling his eyebrows at me. "You must be Hadley. I'm Carlo DiRosario."

"Nice to meet you," I said, shaking his offered hand.

"So, are the rumors true? Are you really dating my cousin? I didn't think he could ever—"

"Carlo, what are you doing?"

Carlo was shoved to the side a second later, and then Archer was standing in the doorway, frowning at the two of us.

"Hey, coz," Carlo said enthusiastically. "I was just saying hello to Hadley here. You didn't tell me she was—"

"Shut your mouth, Carlo."

Archer pulled me across the threshold and slammed the door behind me, twisting the locks home again.

The coffeehouse was the most crowded I had ever seen it before—even on the busiest of days. There was a large group of people buzzing around the long row of pushed-together tables in the middle of the floor, all chattering loudly, mostly in Italian, as they set out plates and cutlery and poured large glasses of wine.

And then there was an assortment of children running around, screaming and giggling, playing some version of tag.

This was Archer's extended family?

Carlo was rocked back onto his heels as he watched me look around, a wide smirk spreading across his face. He said something with gusto to Archer in Italian that made Archer immediately hit him upside the head and say with a scowl, "Do us all a favor and shut up, won't you?"

I opened my mouth to tell Archer I was going to head to the back to drop off my things, but a loud bark of "Carlo!" beat me to the punch.

A short woman with dark hair pulled back into a tight bun marched over to us, hands on hips, eyes narrowed.

An apprehensive look crossed Carlo's face as he quickly took a step back, holding up his hands in a surrendering gesture. "Hi, Ma, I was just—"

"Don't lie to me, Carlo. Quit antagonizing your cousin," the woman scolded.

"And don't be rude, Archer," Regina said, suddenly appearing.

Both boys were red in the face as they mumbled out various apologies.

"Oh! Hadley!" Regina smiled brightly when she finally noticed me, and then reached out to hug me tightly. "It's so good you could come."

"Thank you for inviting me," I said with a smile of my own. And if I hadn't been invited—or rather, told to come by Archer—I would've spent this day alone, shut up in the apartment.

"This is Hadley?" the other woman said in surprise before pulling me into a hug that was just as tight. "Oh, it's so nice to finally meet you! I've heard so many good things about you."

I stammered out a thanks while the woman held me at an arm's length, examining me closely.

"*Oddio*, you're beautiful," she said with another smile. "I can see why Archer likes spending so much time with you."

"*Zia,*" Archer muttered, shooting the woman a reproachful look. "Come on."

I felt my cheeks flushing with color. "Um, thank you?"

"I'm Karin, Archer's aunt," the woman said, ignoring her nephew. "And you've already met my son Carlo."

"Everyone!" Carlo shouted, throwing his hands in the air. "This is Hadley!"

Silence fell for a moment as several pairs of hazel eyes fixed on me, and then there was a loud shout of "HADLEY!" before I was attacked with so many hugs and kisses, I thought I was going to suffocate. By the time I had been squeezed and had my cheeks kissed about a hundred different times, I was finally introduced to all of Archer's family in the room.

Victoria and her late husband Cesario had had four children—Karin, Sofia, Regina, and Vittorio—and between them, they had fourteen more children. Karin and her husband, Art DiRosario, had eight: the twins, Stefan and Augustine, who were the eldest of all the grandchildren and attending college in Upstate New York; Carlo, a freshman in high school; Lauren, who was fourteen-year-old; and then Maria, Georgiana, Joseph, and Gina, who were all anywhere from ages three to eight.

Sofia and her husband, Ben Orsini, had three: Mia, a seventh grader; Stephanie, who was nine; and then William, who had just learned how to walk.

Then there was Regina, with Archer and Rosie.

And the last Incitti, Vittorio, had an adorable three-month-old son named Isaac with his very pretty wife, Anna.

"Hadley! Hi, Hadley!" Rosie came skipping through the kitchen as I hung up my coat and bag on the hooks in the backroom, and she was followed by a group of kids whose names

I had just been told but couldn't put a face to. "Wanna play sardines?"

"Yeah! Wanna play sardines?" a little girl with dark curls asked, attaching herself to my leg. "Sardines is so much fun!"

I had no idea what kind of game sardines was, so I said instead, "But aren't we supposed to be having dinner soon?"

The little girl currently swinging from my arm stuck her lip out in an outrageous pout. "Come on! Please?"

"Yeah, please?"

I was then suddenly mauled with hugs and loud pleadings to play whatever sardines was.

"You guys, really, we're about to eat dinner!" I managed to force out through bursts of laughter.

"But there's always time for sardines!" one of the boys—Joseph, I think—said loudly.

"All right, enough!" A girl with her midnight hair done up in braids came marching through the kitchen, a hand on her hip, looking suspiciously like a younger version of Archer's aunt Karin. "Leave Hadley alone. It's time to go wash up for dinner."

She was met with instant protests. "Aw, come on!

"Do we really?"

"But it's sardines!"

"No buts!" the girl ordered, jabbing a finger toward the water closet—sized bathroom in the corner. "It's time to wash up for dinner. Now."

The group of kids obediently stomped their way over to the bathroom, grumbling and complaining under their breaths.

The whole scene was just too cute, I was unable to resist calling, "But I promise I'll play sardines with you all later!" after them, to delighted bouts of giggles.

"Sorry about them," the girl said with a sheepish smile, walking up to me. "They can be a little overwhelming sometimes."

"No, not at all," I said quickly. "I don't mind."

"I'm Lauren," the girl said, sticking out a hand for me to shake. "We met just a few minutes ago."

"That's right," I said. "Nice to meet you again."

Lauren smiled again, showing off bright-white teeth. "You know, at first I was expecting you to be a total Blair Waldorf wannabe. It's nice to see that you're not."

I was stunned into silence. "Um . . ."

"Archer told me your family was rich," she explained. "I figured if you live in New York and you have money . . ." She trailed off, letting me fill in the blanks.

"Sorry to disappoint," I said with a grin.

Lauren shrugged. "Nah, it's not a bad thing. If you weren't cool, Archer would never be seen with you. I don't know if you've noticed, but my cousin is kind of a hermit. The select few people he graces with his presence are normally pretty important to him."

I wanted to believe that what Lauren said was true, that I was important to Archer, or at least that I was getting close.

"Wanna help carry out the food?" Lauren asked, jabbing a thumb over her shoulder to the fridges and the counters with trays and plates of dishes stacked a mile high. Regina, Karin, and Victoria had already begun to carry out a few.

"Sure," I said. "I'd love to."

For the past few years, I had spent my Thanksgivings either at the dining table at Taylor's apartment or by myself with a meal I'd ordered from some restaurant. So, really, I'd never had what one could call a "traditional, sit-down, family-packed Thanksgiving dinner."

To say I was surprised by the display of food spread out across the tables would be putting it lightly. I was absolutely dumbfounded.

There were plates upon plates of succulent roast turkey, honey-glazed ham, potato salad, buttery rolls, stuffing, steamed vegetables, cranberry sauce, and then every classic Italian dish you could think of. I wanted to try it all.

"All right, everyone!" Victoria said loudly over the chattering and laughter. "Sit down. It's time to eat."

Everyone immediately scrambled for a seat.

I managed to grab an empty chair by the plate of ham I had my eye on, eager to grab a few slices, and Archer ended up dropping into the seat to the right of me, Carlo on my left.

"Bow your heads for grace," Victoria said.

I bit the inside of my cheek, determined not to blush as Archer took my hand lightly in his own, looking anywhere but at me. Grace was in Italian, which I didn't even attempt to understand, so I just silently said a quick prayer of thanks of my own.

"Well, what are you all waiting for?" Victoria said once the prayer was finished. "Dig in."

Archer quickly dropped my hand, and I busied myself with piling a few slices of ham on my plate, thankful for the distraction.

The table settled into a lull of conversation as everyone began to eat. Regina and her sisters had dived into conversation about their children and their antics, not caring that their children were sitting just a few seats away. Vittorio and his brothers-in-law were engaged in some animated talk about poker. The younger kids, toward the end of the table, just seemed to laugh the entire time.

"So, Hadley." Sofia leaned across the table toward me, smiling, the moment I finished the rest of the mashed potatoes on my plate. "Tell us a little about yourself."

I felt my cheeks warm as several pairs of eyes flicked over to me.

"Um . . ." I bit my lip, embarrassed to be put in the spotlight so suddenly. "I'm not really sure what to say."

"Anything," Sofia said. "I'm interested in knowing how you met Archer."

"Oh, well, we—"

"We had freshman English together." Archer cut me off briskly as he cut up pieces of turkey for Rosie. "End of story."

"Fascinating," Vittorio said, joining in. "But what's the deal with you two?"

I felt my stomach drop. I had to remind myself this was bound to come up sooner or later. "I don't . . ." I cleared my throat nervously. "There's no deal."

Of course there actually was a *deal*, but I was pretty sure Vittorio knew nothing about the contract I'd signed with Death.

Vittorio looked unconvinced. "Really."

"We're not dating, if that's what you're getting at," Archer said flatly. "We're just friends."

My heart did this little jump, because that had been the first time Archer had ever called me his "friend," but I quickly added, "Right. Just friends."

"Wait. You two aren't dating?" Carlo eagerly jumped into the conversation. "Does that mean you're on the market, Hadley? I've always had a thing for brunettes."

I choked on a breath of air, my face flaming hotter as I turned horrified eyes on Carlo. Was he trying to mortify me?

"Carlo!" Half the table shouted in protest. "Show some respect!"

Archer's arm shot out so quickly to smack Carlo on the head that I never actually saw the action, just Carlo wincing and rubbing at his scalp. By this time, I'd sunk down so low in my seat that I'd almost disappeared underneath the table.

"Boys!" Victoria's sharp voice carried down the table to us. "You'd do best to watch your mouths. Your cousins and siblings are down there. Set a good example. As punishment, you two can go ahead and get started washing dishes."

"Oh, come on, *really*? I—"

"Get to it," Victoria barked. "You listen to your elder, boys."

Archer shot Carlo a glare before he shoved back from the table and stood, grabbing at empty plates. Carlo followed suit, snickering under his breath as he carried off an armful of wine glasses to the kitchen.

"I apologize for my son's behavior, Hadley," Karin said, giving me an exasperated look. "He gets his foot in his mouth more often than not."

Ten minutes passed of Archer and Carlo stomping back and forth from the kitchen to the tables, clearing away the dishes, and when the last handful of forks and knives and cups had finally disappeared, one of the younger ones said timidly, "So is it time for dessert yet?"

A round of cheers went up at the mention of dessert, which was apparently the pinnacle of any dinner with the Incittis. Besides, I found that sugar helped brighten any get-together.

It took almost five minutes to cart all of the desserts out of the kitchen. The plates and trays had barely been set down before the tables were swarmed, hands snatching at any dessert they could reach. I had to squeeze my way in around a few of the younger kids just to grab a handful of Italian cookies and one chocolate cannoli. I quickly retreated to the sidelines while the desserts continued to be devoured, a little worried that I might sustain bodily injuries if I accidently got in someone's way. When I finally took a bite of my cannoli, I almost groaned.

Archer hadn't been kidding about his family's desserts. I could only come to the conclusion that God had gifted the Incitti family with the ability to make the best sweets possible. I chowed down my cannoli and finished it in about five seconds flat, and I'd finished two of my cookies before I caught sight of Archer lounging on the bench in front of the old upright piano in the corner of the coffeehouse.

I sighed when I took note of the frown on his face. What was he thinking about now that made him look so pained? More importantly, why was he always doing that—stepping off alone? I wandered over and plopped myself down on the bench beside him.

We sat in silence for a few minutes as we finished off the rest of our cookies, taking in the scene of pleasant chaos around us. There seemed to be a never-ending supply of laughter and jokes everywhere, just as it had been during dinner. I didn't think I'd ever felt anything like it before. And I didn't want it to end, because I didn't know if I would get the chance to feel it again.

"Thank you," I said to Archer, glancing over at him. "For inviting me. This has been amazing."

"I'd say my mother forced me to invite you, but I'd be lying," Archer said, his gaze fixed on his shoes. "I'm glad you could come."

For a moment, I didn't know what to say. A part of me had suspected Regina told Archer to ask me, because I'd told her about my parent's ridiculous work schedules and that it wasn't unusual for me to spend a holiday or two alone. Yet Archer was the one who invited me.

And that made me very, very happy.

"They've certainly taken a liking to you," Archer said, almost grinning as he watched his relatives, who remained crowded around what remained of the desserts.

"Well, I like them," I said. "They're great."

Archer scoffed as he quickly finished the rest of his cookie and dusted off his hands on his jeans. "Yeah, they are. But they can also drive me nuts."

My cell phone rang before I could respond. Despite the fact that it was Thanksgiving, and so I should've expected it at some point, it was still a bit of a shock to see that the incoming call was from my mother.

"Hello?" I answered, getting to my feet, moving off to the side to find what little privacy I could. I tried to ignore the way Archer's eyes followed me, suddenly feeling very self-conscious.

"Happy Thanksgiving, Hadley," my mother said, her voice warmer than usual.

"Happy Thanksgiving," I said. "How are things going with you and Dad?"

Obviously ,we were both choosing to ignore the fact the

last time we'd seen each other hadn't been under the best of terms, but at least she'd called. She told me a little bit about what was going on with their case and how it should be cleared up in just another day or two, then passed the phone off to my dad.

"Sounds a little loud on your end," my dad said after wishing me a happy Thanksgiving. "Are you still at your boss's for dinner?"

"Yeah," I said. I'd texted them the night before to tell them about my change in plans. "Regina has a big family, and they just brought out the desserts, so the little kids are excited."

"That's nice," he replied. "Are you having a good time?"

"Absolutely," I answered without thinking. "I was a little nervous about meeting everyone, but they . . . they're great. I'm kind of wishing I'd taken two years of Italian instead of Spanish, but I'm having a really nice time."

I could almost hear the smile in my dad's voice when he said, "That's really good, kiddo."

I hung up with my parents after another minute or two of chitchat and returned to the piano bench where Archer was still seated. "Sorry about that," I told him. "It was my parents. They just called to wish me a happy Thanksgiving."

Archer looked like he was concentrating very hard on something when he spoke, picking at the cuff of his button-down shirt. He was always fidgeting with one thing or another if something made him uncomfortable. "You and you parents . . . I know we talked a little about them the other day. Am I right in guessing you don't spend much time with your family?"

"Yeah," I answered. "My parents are always busy, and the

few cousins and aunts and uncles I do have live out of state. We don't get together too often."

"So . . . it's mainly just you, then, isn't it?" Archer said, finally meeting my gaze.

"Mainly," I said, growing more and more confused by his line of questioning. "I mean, I've got Taylor and Brie and Chelsea and everybody else, you know, but . . . yeah. It's just me most of the time."

I felt very lonely then, saying those words aloud and realizing it to be true.

There was a difference between being lonely and being alone. I thought I didn't mind being alone because it was what I was used to. I just hadn't realized how lonely I actually felt until I was welcomed with open arms by Archer's family and treated like I was one of their own. I hadn't known it was possible to miss something you'd never had.

"No need to look so worried," Archer said, nudging me with his shoulder. "They like you, so you're stuck with us. If you're not at every holiday meal from now on, they'll have my head."

I burst out laughing, immediately pleased by the thought. "Archer, I'll gladly come to every meal your family has if that means no more takeout or TV dinners."

Archer looked stunned for half a second before he laughed, causing his aunts Sofia and Karin to cast curious glances in our direction.

And that was when there was a loud crash from the kitchen, something like the sound of glass shattering.

I was on my feet and sprinting for the kitchen in a flash, Archer hot on my heels. I skidded around the front counter, through the kitchen door, only to come to a screeching halt.

My hands flew up to cover my mouth.

I could feel Archer freeze where he stood behind me, and heard his sharp intake of air. "Mom?"

Regina was curled up on the floor, her back against the cupboards, and the shattered remnants of what looked like a glass serving bowl lay scattered around her. She was trembling from head to toe, and her face was deathly pale.

She looked . . . Well, she looked as if she had just seen Death.

Regina looked up at the sound of Archer's voice, and a gut-wrenching sob flew past her lips as she tried to scramble upright. "Archer, thank God, it's Chris, something—something— It's . . . Y-you've got to . . ."

It was in that moment that the walls Archer had spent years building to keep people out came tumbling down. Emotion was written across his face like a blinding flash of light. He looked distraught. Confused. Hurt. Angry.

For those few short seconds, I saw the boy who tried to act like nothing bothered him only because he needed to be strong for his family, because he felt as if he had to be the one to keep them all together, giving little thought to himself and ignoring his own needs. I saw everything I had ever suspected about him, and more.

Then just as quickly, the wall was back up again, and nothing remained but a boy whose thoughts were only for his mother.

"Mom, everything's fine, you have to listen to me, it's okay," Archer was saying, reaching out to Regina. "It's okay, Mom, I'm here, you—"

But Regina was past being able to be consoled. She had

her arms around Archer, sobbing into his shoulder, and I kept hearing her saying Chris's name over and over again in a voice that broke my heart.

"What is going on in here? I thought I heard— Oh, God."

Victoria stood in the doorway, surveying the situation with a look of shock. She immediately seemed to know what was happening. A second later Vittorio appeared, closely followed by Sofia and Karin.

"Not again," Vittorio muttered, moving to Archer's side and reaching out to place a hand against Regina's face. "She's still taking her medication, isn't she?"

"Of course she is," Victoria snapped. "Every day." Even though Victoria was being her usual snippy self, I could tell by her hardened expression that it caused her pain to see her daughter like this.

"I swear she hasn't had a flashback like this in years," Karin said, sounding distraught. "Not since after it happened."

Flashback? I didn't understand what that meant exactly, but I could put two and two together easily enough. Regina was reliving the night Chris died, and nobody but her could see it. It had been years since Chris was killed, but it was obvious that Regina never recovered from it. And seeing her like this . . . I doubted she ever fully would.

"Take her upstairs, Vito," Sofia said, and it sounded as if she was crying. "The kids don't need to see this."

Vittorio scooped Regina up into his arms and made for the back door. The way her head seemed to loll against his shoulder made me think she had fallen unconscious. Victoria, Karin, and Sofia immediately rushed them.

I made to follow suit without thinking, to see for myself

that Regina was going to be okay, but Archer threw out a hand and caught my arm when I'd taken only a few steps.

"Stay here," he said, lowering his voice.

"Archer, I—"

"Please."

I wanted to ignore him and go upstairs with the others despite what he said, but I forced myself to stay put. Everything about Archer screamed that he was hurting, even if he was going to deny it. I didn't want to make it any worse.

"Okay," I said softly. "Okay. Just . . ."

Archer seemed to understand, even if I wasn't sure what I had been trying to say.

He gave a short nod, and then he was out of the kitchen and up the stairs after his aunts and uncle. I watched him go, feeling even more hopeless than I had moments before.

"Hadley? What's going on?"

I turned and saw Lauren and Carlo hovering in the doorway, each with anxious expressions on their faces. I wondered if they knew the extent of what happened that night all those years ago and just what it had done to their aunt.

"I . . . don't know," I said. "She's . . ."

"She'll be okay," Lauren said with a nod, trying to convince herself. "*Zia* Regina. She'll be fine. She's strong."

I wasn't expecting Lauren to throw her arms around me in a hug, but I hugged her back. Carlo gave my shoulder a comforting squeeze when I pulled away from Lauren, followed by a tight smile, then turned and left the kitchen. Lauren and I stood in the kitchen for a few tense, silent moments, not knowing what to say. What was supposed to happen now?

I knew what I wanted to do—go upstairs to try and help

Regina. No wonder Archer was so protective of his mother. I couldn't even begin to understand how Archer had shouldered the burden of protecting his family for so long.

"We should go," Lauren said, glancing over at me. "Play with the kids or something. Standing around won't help."

It took a second for me to come out of my distracting reverie and return to the present. "The kids," I said. "Sure. That . . . It's probably best."

Lauren nodded, and we left the kitchen together, coming back around the front counter to where the rest of the family was settled. The younger ones didn't seem to notice that anything was amiss. They were running around and screaming and laughing, no doubt on a sugar high from all of the desserts they'd just consumed.

Karin, Sofia, and Vittorio's significant others—Art, Ben, and Anna—were huddled off to the side by the fireplace, their heads together as they talked quickly and quietly with one another, already aware of what had happened. I took a seat on one of the overstuffed chairs by the couch while Lauren and Mia—Sofia's daughter—tried to keep the younger ones from running back to lick the dessert plates.

I heard the sound of approaching footsteps on the creaky, hardwood floors, and when I looked up I saw Art DiRosario standing in front of me, a concerned expression on his face.

"I take it you didn't know about Regina," he said bluntly, getting straight to the point.

I shook my head. "No. I mean, I knew what happened to Chris and everything. Archer told me, but not about . . . about this. Has Regina . . . always . . .?"

I was struggling to come up with the right words, but Art

seemed to get what I was trying to say. He perched himself on the edge of the couch a few feet away, sighing as he said, "Yeah, Regina's always had a rough time with her PTSD."

"PTSD?" I repeated, frowning.

"Post-traumatic stress disorder," Art clarified. "It can cause some pretty nasty flashbacks."

I immediately thought back to my psychology class last year. My teacher, Mr. Hathaway, told us soldiers returning home from overseas often experienced post-traumatic stress disorder—and it wasn't too pleasant of a condition. Your husband's murder would surely stick with you long after the fact.

"Does Regina have flashbacks often?" I asked Art.

He frowned in thought. "You know, not much anymore. It used to be a lot worse right after it happened. It didn't help that she was pregnant with Rosie at the time. Even the smallest things would set her off, like seeing some of his old clothes or smelling his cologne. I can't imagine what would have caused one now."

My heart ached for Regina all the more. It wasn't fair that someone as kind hearted and good as Regina Morales would have to deal with something like this. It wasn't something *anybody* should have to suffer with.

"Isn't there anything we can do to help?" I asked Art. "I mean, Karin said she's taking medication, but can't we do something else?"

Art gave a small, grim smile. "There's not much we can do, Hadley, when she refuses to go to counseling."

"But why?" I said, confused. "There's nothing wrong with counseling. I bet it'd help if she tried."

"Believe me, we've brought it up more than once, but she

pretends not to hear every time. She just likes to put on a happy face and act like nothing's wrong. And Archer's no better."

"What?" I said, taken aback. "What do you mean, Archer's no better?"

Art exhaled, shrugging again. "Archer inherited more than just his mother's looks. He's about ten times as stubborn as she is. He likes to pretend his own problems don't exist."

"And I bet he won't go to counseling either," I said, already knowing the answer.

"I think Archer would rather gouge out his eyes than talk to a shrink," Art said.

He paused for a moment. "On a lighter note, it does seem like spending time with you is doing him some good. We were very surprised when Regina said Archer's friend would be joining us for dinner."

"Is it really that unusual?" I asked. Surely they had met one of Archer's friends before.

Art wasted no time saying, "Yeah, it is. Archer doesn't like getting close to people. My guess is because he's afraid something will happen to them, like Chris."

A lot of things were clicking into place tonight. No wonder Archer pushed people away. I couldn't imagine how lonely Archer must have been. He'd profusely deny it, but that wouldn't make years of isolation go away. You couldn't just close yourself off from the rest of the world because you were afraid of getting hurt. Some people were worth the hurt.

"I hope this doesn't change your opinion of them," Art said, watching me with a curious expression on his face. "Archer and Regina, I mean."

"Absolutely not." I didn't intend to sound as severe as I did, but it got my point across. "Some days Regina is more of a mother to me than my own mom, and Archer is a great friend."

Art smiled, looking pleased with my little outburst. "Glad to hear it. Stick around, okay?"

"I'm not going anywhere anytime soon," I assured him.

He got to his feet and reached over to give me a friendly clap on the shoulder. "At any rate," he said before going to join his brother-in-law, "it sure is good to hear that boy laugh again."

CHAPTER 18

You Don't Understand

We ended up keeping the kids entertained with games of tag and hide-and-seek for more than hour, and by the time their parents came back downstairs to cart them home, almost all of them were half asleep. I helped as best I could, rounding the kids up to get them into their jackets. While it would've been an exaggeration to say it was a tearful farewell, I felt a little sad, saying good-bye to all of Archer's extended family. I wasn't sure if I would ever see them again, and that was a depressing thought. Literally *everything* depended on how the next twelve days went.

I didn't want to go home without having at least one small scrap of reassurance that Regina was okay, so, looking for any excuse to stick around, I headed to the kitchen to start cleaning. Ignoring the perfectly functioning dishwashers, I cleared out one of the sinks, filled it with hot, soapy water, and got to work on the dishes. As I cleaned, my mind kept wandering back to that scene I would never forget in my entire life, no matter how long I lived.

Despite my best efforts, I could not comprehend what happened. One sophomore psychology class did not make me an expert on mental health. I knew psychological disorders were generally unpleasant. But Regina had been somewhere else entirely—a dark, frightening place that only she knew about. It was locked away in her own mind, and when it made itself known, it became reality to her. I couldn't help but wonder if Archer felt the same way. He had been there that night. He had seen everything, things no eleven-year-old ever should.

Because of that night, he'd spent so long pushing everyone away outside his family—and even then I suspected he was never entirely upfront with his relatives about how he was feeling. Why would he be, when he clearly thought they mattered more than he did? Archer wouldn't want anything to happen to his family, not like what happened to Chris, so he put them in front of himself. That kind of self-sacrifice was amazing to me, but I knew it also had to be so hard on Archer.

"What are you still doing here?"

I let out a shriek at the unexpected sound of Archer's voice behind me, and spun on my heel, splashing soapy water everywhere. "*Archer!*" I gasped, clutching at the counter behind me, my heart racing a mile a minute. "I swear you should carry a bell with you or something. Don't you make noise when you move?"

Archer ignored me as he glanced around, leaning up against the doorjamb. "Why are you still here?" he repeated. "I heard everyone leave a while ago."

"Uh, yeah," I said awkwardly. I bit my lip, turning back to the pile of dirty plates and cups still stacked on the counter beside the sink. "I just, um, wanted to help out with the dishes since there's so many, and . . . uh . . ."

Archer stared blankly at me while I struggled to come up

with an excuse as to why I hadn't gone home. His hair was a mess, like he'd repeatedly been running his fingers through it, and his eyes were bloodshot. I didn't think he'd been crying, but he obviously wasn't okay. It was painful to see him like this.

"We have dishwashers."

"Um, right," I said quickly. "I was going to put everything in the dishwasher, I was just, um . . . making sure that all of the food had been scraped off the plates."

Archer raised an eyebrow, his lips pressed together in a tight line, clearly not buying it.

"Okay, fine. I'm still here because I wanted to see how Regina was doing. And you too. I was worried."

"Well, thank you for your concern, Hadley, but my mother and I are just fine."

I did not believe for one second that was the truth. And I think Archer knew I didn't believe it. I crossed my arms in a defiant gesture, staring expectantly at Archer. He glared back in return.

"Archer, I'm not as stupid as you seem to think I am," I told him. "I know you're definitely *not* fine."

"What I don't get," Archer said loudly, ignoring me as he picked up a stack of silverware and dropped it into the sink, "is why you're *still* acting like any of this matters to you. This isn't your family, and it's not like we're dating. What does it matter to you whether or not I'm *fine*?"

"I know your family isn't my family," I said, hurt he would even insinuate such a thing. "Of course I know that. I just . . ."

"Come on, Hadley," Archer said, rolling his eyes. "You barely know me. You don't need to act like I matter to you."

That one comment was finally enough for me to say what

had been on the tip of my tongue for some time now. How could he think that I wouldn't care about anything that he thought or felt or did?

"Has it ever crossed your mind that I *care* about you?" I said, trying to fight back the swell of emotion rising in the pit of my stomach. "I get that maybe you're not used to this, having a friend, but if you think I'm pretending—pretending to care about you and your family—then maybe you need a good old-fashioned reality check, because you're obviously not seeing something."

Archer remained silent as I spoke. I could see the tension in his shoulders and by how tight he was clutching at the counter behind him. He was refusing to meet my eyes, and he kept looking to the kitchen door, like he was contemplating making a break for it. It wasn't enough to keep me from saying what I did next.

"You don't get to decide who's allowed to care about you or worry about you or make sure you're okay. Life doesn't work that way. I know I don't understand everything that's happened to you or your family. And maybe I never will. But I don't have to understand to care."

I sucked in a deep breath, feeling unsteady on my feet as Archer finally lifted his gaze from his shoes. He was staring at me with this expression that I couldn't describe—like he was actually seeing me for the first time.

"Archer, I'm not lying when I say you're my friend," I said, telling myself not to stop now. "And you can hate it as much as you want, spout off as much as BS as you want, but I'm not going anywhere. Maybe next time, before you go making assumptions about how I feel, just try talking to me, okay?"

I hadn't realized how much I'd wanted to say those words until they finally left my mouth. And still, Archer said nothing. He took a step closer, and my heart immediately skipped a beat as he bit his lip, a determined look in his eyes.

"I . . . I'm actually . . ." I swallowed hard, stumbling over my words. "I'm actually a good listener if you'd just give me a chance."

"You're really not going to let this go, are you?" Archer asked quietly. He seemed resigned, but also a little bit pleased. Like maybe he didn't want me to let him go in the first place.

"No, I'm not," I said firmly. "You should know by now I'm always stubborn."

He opened his mouth, clearly wanting to say something, but nothing came out. We stood there in the middle of the kitchen for several moments, neither of us speaking. I was unsure if there was anything else I could say that would get my point across further. I'd known from the beginning that Archer was stubborn and hardheaded and wasn't open to change in his life. But was it really too much to hope for that Archer was *finally* okay with being my friend?

"I'm . . . I'll just go now, then," I said shakily, reaching over to pull the stopper in the sink, grabbing at a dishtowel to dry my hands. "I'll still be here tomorrow at six, but I—"

"Wait."

I was halfway through putting on my jacket as I turned back to give Archer a questioning look. "What?"

He stepped closer, too close, gripping the fronts of my jacket, gently backing me up against the wall.

"What are you doing?" I squeaked, distracted by how close he was. Too, too close. His hands were on either side of my head, against the wall, and he was leaning closer. My thoughts were racing a mile a minute. I only realized Archer was about to kiss me when his lips were just a few centimeters from mine. He was holding still, waiting for my reaction, whether or not I would shove him away or close the distance between us.

And for some insane reason I didn't entirely understand, I wanted that distance gone.

"Archer." I sucked in a breath, attempting to steady my breathing. "What are you doing?"

He pulled back far enough to where our eyes locked. He gave a small sigh, biting his lip again, and I had the sudden, uncontrollable urge to be the one biting his lip. "I don't know," he admitted, his voice barely above a whisper.

Neither of us knew what to do next. We were just there, in that moment. It was as if every awful little thing that happened earlier today disappeared, and the rest of the world was breaking apart into little pieces and falling away.

I took a deep breath, forcing myself to say the words *maybe I should go home*, because what were we doing? Was I really about to kiss Archer?

"Before you open your mouth to say this is a bad idea," Archer said, his fingers hovering over my neck, "don't."

I reached up to lace my fingers through his hair to pull him toward me, and just as we were finally, *finally* about to kiss, I heard a loud, gruff, "*Ahem.*"

Archer and I jumped apart so quickly, I smacked my forehead against his. Much to my horror, it was Victoria standing right beside us in the doorway, and she did not look amused.

"When you've finished up in here, make sure you lock up, boy," she said to Archer. "I'm going to bed." She disappeared upstairs without so much as sparing me a second glance.

As soon as she was out of earshot, Archer turned to me, saying, "Hadley, we need to—"

Too embarrassed to do anything but run, I said, "I really should just be going now. You were right, it's getting late. See you tomorrow!"

I left through the back door as quickly as I could without tripping over my feet and landing flat on my face.

And Archer didn't follow after me.

A Breach of Contract— 11 Days Until

I stumbled my way out of the apartment at half past five the next morning, barely able to keep my eyes open. It felt as if I'd gotten about two minutes of sleep before I was woken by my alarm. It was Black Friday, and Mama Rosa's needed extra hands to keep up with the slew of people who were expected to be grabbing coffee and pastries in between stores.

The night doorman managed to flag a cab outside to take me to the coffeehouse. I wasn't so sure I'd be able to make it to the subway without falling down the stairs and passing out.

I still wasn't able to completely wrap my mind around everything that had happened last night. I had enough difficulty trying to understand Regina's unexpected flashback, but then I had almost kissed Archer Morales too?

My face burned bright red when I remembered the hard, intense look that had been in Archer's eyes when he had backed me up against the wall and lowered his head toward me, so close I could almost feel his lips against mine. It wouldn't have been my first kiss, but it would have definitely been a kiss worth remembering—that, I was sure of.

But what had come over Archer to make him want to kiss me? He hadn't ever shown any inclination that he thought of me in that way. Whatever the reason, I had to get my head in the game. I couldn't afford to be distracted by thoughts of the "almost-kiss incident" today—not if I wanted to remain unscathed while attempting to make coffee and handling food.

The lights were blazing in the kitchen as I slipped inside. I pulled off my jacket and scarf and hung them on a hook by the back door before cautiously heading to the kitchen.

Victoria was at one of the ovens, pulling out a fresh tray of cinnamon rolls. She looked up and gave me an acknowledging nod as I walked in. I felt myself flush as I nodded meekly in return. I doubted I would ever be able to look Victoria in the eye again, let alone speak to her. How could I when she had walked in on me about to kiss her grandson?

Archer stood at the kitchen sink, scrubbing out a few coffee pots with soapy water. He gave me a cursory glance and a small nod. I stopped in front of him, my mouth open, wanting to say something, but Victoria spoke up before I could.

"Hadley, get a start on wiping down the tables, if you don't mind, and then help me fill the pastry case."

"I . . . I'm . . ." I bit back a sigh. "That sounds good."

I quickly went about wiping down the tabletops, and then assisted Victoria in assembling the assortment of pastries in the pastry case.

By then, Archer had already cleaned the grinder and espresso maker, stocked the small fridge up front with milk, half-and-half, and whipped cream, and was now counting the change in the till.

"Archer, go open up," Victoria said, striding out from the kitchen. "It's six."

Archer acquiesced, heading to the front door.

When I had been told that Black Friday was going to be tough, I was a bit skeptical. How bad could one day with a little extra work be? Mama Rosa's was a coffee shop, not a department store. I was sure everyone had just been exaggerating.

Sadly, I was mistaken. Very mistaken.

By eight, my feet were aching and my arms were sore from hefting so many trays full of breakfast sandwiches, drinks, and pastries. Apparently, Mama Rosa's really was quite a popular place to stop for food and a drink while catching a break from shopping; we were packed from opening, with a short break in the late afternoon, straight until closing.

Waitressing gave me a better workout than any gym class ever could, and the fast-paced work proved to be a distraction. There was barely any time to even think about the events of Thanksgiving. And apart from the time where I almost dumped a latte down my front, things went as smoothly as they were capable of—which was more than I could've hoped for. It had been a miracle that Victoria, Archer, and I managed to make it through the day without any extra help. I kept expecting Regina to show up to assist us later on in the day, but she didn't, much to my dismay.

I let out an exhausted groan as I flipped off the neon *open* sign and twisted the locks home on the front door a little after seven in the evening. "Remind me never to make my career in retail or the food industry."

Victoria let out a bark of laughter as she counted the day's earnings at the register. "You say that now, girl. Just wait. In this day and age, you take what you can get."

Victoria gave orders to sweep and mop every inch of the coffeehouse, to make sure the kitchen was cleaned spotless, and that the leftover pastries were wrapped and set aside for the deliveryman stopping by tomorrow morning. As soon as she finished issuing instructions, she marched off, presumably upstairs.

I grabbed the bin behind the counter and got to work collecting dirty cups, bowls, and plates left on the tables. I'd cleared off nearly half of the tables before I looked over and saw that Archer was leaning against the counter, eating a sandwich.

I frowned. "Aren't you going to help?"

Archer grunted out something that sounded like, "When I'm done."

"Gee, thanks."

He shrugged and strolled off into the kitchen without another word.

So I flipped on the old handset radio on the counter by the till, which was set to some classic station, then finished clearing the dishes off the tables. After I disinfected the tabletops and rearranged the chairs, I carefully wrapped each pastry in plastic wrap as instructed and set them neatly in a box for the deliveryman.

I took a break just long enough to make me a quick cup of chai tea—I needed all the extra caffeine I could get my hands on—and pulled out the broom and dustpan and got to sweeping.

I was heading to the kitchen for the mop and bucket after sweeping when I realized that the radio wasn't playing music anymore.

There was something about the silence in the place that was . . . strange. Not right. I was hit with a sudden rush of cold air that made me shiver and wrap my arms around myself.

There had been a fire crackling away in the grate all afternoon to help combat the frigid temperature outside, which had given off warmth and a pleasant smell of chestnuts, but now the room felt as cold as a glacier.

I headed over to the fire grate and grabbed a poker, hoping that if I shifted the logs around enough, I'd get some heat back in the place. I crouched down beside the grate and started jabbing at a few logs.

"Hello again, Hadley."

I spun on my heel, throwing out an arm to grab hold of a nearby chair when I almost lost my balance.

The man from the grocery story was lounging casually on the sofa. He gave me a lazy smile, legs crossed and arms tucked behind his head.

"What . . ." My voice cracked when I tried to speak. "Who are you? What are you doing here?"

The man's smile widened, though it seemed as if he was baring his teeth instead of smiling. A shudder of fear ran through me.

"No need to look so frightened," the man said in his polished English accent. "I assure you, I'm not here to cause you any trouble . . . At least not yet, of course."

"How . . ." I looked over to the front door. The locks were still in place. "I just locked the doors. How did you get in here?"

If he had snuck in through the back, surely Archer would have seen him. Unless Archer had followed his grandmother upstairs, leaving me behind to do all of the work. The thought that I was alone with this man, whoever he was, had my palms sweating and my stomach churning.

The man wiggled his fingers at me, still smiling. "I have my ways."

As he moved his hand, I saw the awkwardly shaped, criss-crossing black symbols tattooed all over his fingers, running up the sleeve of his suit. They were eerily similar to the ones on my own forearm, except that they didn't form any numbers.

"You work with Death."

No other explanation made sense.

He gave a graceful shrug of his shoulders. "Oh, I wouldn't say I work with Death, but of course I do know the old chap. He and I go way back, you see."

There was something about the smirk that twisted his lips as he said Death's name that was not comforting. Whoever this man was, I got the feeling he wasn't on Death's side.

I tightened my grip on the fire poker, almost brandishing it. "I think it might be a good idea if you leave."

"But why?" The man was pouting now. "I've only just gotten here. I was hoping we could have a little chat."

"Sorry," I said. My hands were starting to shake. I wasn't sure if I would be able to keep from fainting if I stayed in close proximity with this man any longer. "I'm not interested."

"Oh, it's nothing too unpleasant, dear girl, I promise. It'll be quick and painless." He patted the space on the couch beside him. "Have a seat."

A sliver of ice slipped down my spine as he said *quick and painless*. "I'm fine where I am, thanks," I managed to say.

The man shrugged again. "So be it. I hope you will forgive me for not beginning the introductions sooner," he said, as if readying himself for what was to be a very long conversation. "I was merely so excited to finally have the chance to speak with you earlier. And now that I've gotten a better look at you, I have to say . . ." The man rubbed his jaw with a large hand, tilting his head to the side as his eyes traveled me up and down. I held the fire poker closer to my chest. "I'm not all that impressed. You're very ordinary, aren't you? I can't imagine what Death sees in you."

"Well, then," I said, my voice shaking. "Maybe you should take that up with Death. Or maybe you could, you know, leave."

The man laughed, loud and jovial. I looked toward the kitchen, desperately hoping that Archer was there, that he had overheard part of the conversation and would come to investigate. This guy wouldn't try to pick a fight with me if Archer was there, would he?

"Now why would I do that?" he said. "I haven't even gotten to the reason why I came for a visit. In fact, I haven't even introduced myself."

"Then say what you need to say and get out of here."

"Oh, my. You're not very nice, Hadley. Somebody should teach you some manners." The man rose to his feet, and I took an immediate step back when I saw how he towered over me at an alarming height. "First of all, my name is Havoc. And fortunately for you, I'm willing to overlook your rudeness because I'm here to help you."

"Well, f-forgive me if I don't believe you," I stammered out.

"Of course you don't." Havoc made a pitying click with his tongue, shaking his head. "You've got it all wrong. What you're doing. It isn't right."

Somehow, he knew about Archer. "I'm not doing anything—"

"Don't play stupid with me." Havoc's voice had changed abruptly, becoming deeper and much harsher. "You know exactly what I'm talking about."

I swallowed hard, another shiver of fear washing over me. "And if I do?"

"Listen to me very closely, Hadley." The man moved closer, and my back hit the mantel of the fireplace as I tried to move away.

"I've been watching you from the very beginning, you see. Your every move. Figuring out what really makes you tick. It's my job."

"Why? Why are you doing this?" I demanded.

"It's simple, really. I need you to leave Archer Morales alone," Havoc said curtly. "I need you to let him end his life."

I swore my heart stopped beating. "What?"

"You heard me." Havoc gripped the mantel on either side of me, leaning closer. "You're playing a dangerous game, Hadley. You're messing with things that aren't supposed to be meddled with. Changing a person's fate, preventing them from dying . . . that's very serious business. Not something a mere human should ever concern themselves with."

"Archer didn't just die," I forced out with a sudden rush of bravado. "He killed himself."

"That's exactly my point," Havoc said smoothly.

It felt like my throat was closing up, making it difficult to breathe. I couldn't speak.

"You can't mess with time like this," Havoc continued, lowering his voice. "There is an order to the universe, and therefore there are consequences for every action you take. There are consequences for every second Archer Morales spends alive when he should be dead. And these consequences aren't something I'm so sure you're prepared to deal with."

I wanted to shout and scream at the top of my lungs at this man, tell him that there was absolutely no reason whatsoever that a person should ever feel like they had to end their life, but I couldn't muster up the strength to say anything.

"People kill themselves," Havoc said bluntly. "That's the way it's been since the beginning of time, and that's the way it's always going to be."

"Not here," I managed to say with a choked breath. "Not now. Not ever. People . . . people matter. Archer matters. You can't make me believe that's not true."

Havoc looked down at me for a moment, his head tilted to the side, and then he started to laugh. He laughed and laughed, and it seemed like he was never going to stop.

"Hadley, have you finished up out there yet?"

A sob leapt up my throat at the sound of Archer's voice shouting from the kitchen, but Havoc clapped a hand over my mouth before I got the chance to form any words.

"Yeah, just give me a few minutes," he called out in a voice that was disturbingly similar to my own. "I'm almost done."

Havoc kept his hand over my mouth as he leaned closer, his nose almost skimming across my cheek as he lowered his voice to a whisper. "Think of me as a debt collector, Hadley," Havoc said. "Every death is a debt that needs to be paid to restore the balance you've disrupted. And I really don't think you want to be the payment for Archer's debt, now do you?"

Then he was gone.

The fire poker slipped from my grasp and landed on the floor with a loud clatter. I managed to make it to the couch before my legs gave out. I was trembling from head to toe, and there were tears painfully burning my eyes, but they wouldn't fall.

If this man—*Havoc*—was telling the truth, then I could be endangering Archer just as much as I was trying to help him. I'd seen enough sci-fi movies to know that there were always drawbacks to people messing with time. The thought had crossed my mind when I'd first met Death, when I signed the contract, but I'd been too fixated on saving Archer to worry about what changing the past would mean. Now it seemed like there would be an immense price to pay.

What had I done to Archer? To his entire family? To myself?

I heard loud footsteps, and then Archer's voice was saying, "Hadley, is everything okay? I heard something drop, I thought— Wait. What are you doing?"

I lifted my head from my hands and saw Archer crouched down in front of me, a look in his eyes I hadn't ever seen before.

"Sorry," I muttered, rubbing at my cheeks. "I just stopped to take a break. I'll be finished in a few minutes."

I got to my feet, brushing past Archer to grab a mop from the kitchen as I'd originally intended. Archer got the picture that I wasn't up for sharing what was really on my mind, and I was glad, for once, he was giving me space.

CHAPTER 20

Late-Night Quandaries— 10 Days Until

I hadn't been able to sleep after my confrontation with Havoc. I was afraid to close my eyes, worried that I would see his unsettling smirk sketched on the back of my eyelids. It was fortunate that I wasn't scheduled to work the Saturday following Black Friday, because I was afraid I would've wound up fallen asleep while taking orders or trying to make a latte.

After a night of staring up at the ceiling, trying to think of anything but my encounter with Havoc, Archer, and how I only had a little over a week before my deal was up, and massaging the numbers etched onto the skin of my wrist, I rolled out of bed and journeyed to the kitchen. It was just after seven in the morning, and the sun was steadily rising over the tops of the buildings, throwing a pinkish light off windows up and down the street just outside.

I was making a pot of coffee when I heard the front door opening and noise coming from the living room.

"Hadley, is that you?"

My mom appeared in the kitchen doorway then, followed

by my dad. They looked exhausted and travel worn, but they both smiled when they saw me.

"Mom! Dad!"

It was a little out of character for me to throw my arms around both of them, but I was happy to see them. After so much time with the Incitti family, I was sort of desperate to fix my own.

"What are you doing up so early?" my mom asked as she shrugged out of her coat and draped it across the back of a dining room chair. "Do you work today?"

She said this so easily that I figured she must have had time to process the whole my-daughter-has-a-job situation while away on her business trip, and had finally come to terms with it.

I shook my head. "No. Just couldn't sleep, that's all."

"Well, I'll take some of that coffee," my dad said, grabbing a mug out of the cupboard. "I swear I'm done taking red-eyes."

I pulled some eggs out of the fridge and set about scrambling them while my mom lent a hand grabbing some bacon from the freezer to fry. We had thrown together a simple little breakfast in a few minutes, which we then carted to the dining table.

"How was your trip?" I asked as I dug into my eggs.

"Dreadful." My mother exhaled deeply as she sipped at her coffee. "I've always said Clinton needs to be careful when doing cold calls to potential clients. He picked a real winner this time."

I didn't totally understand what my parents were talking about as they described the events of their trip, but they were hopeful the case would have a positive outcome and would be wrapped up soon.

"How was your Thanksgiving?" my mom asked.

"It was nice," I answered, trying to keep my story simple. "I was happy that they invited me. Archer said they'd all be upset if I didn't come to every holiday dinner from now on."

My dad smiled as he polished off the rest of his bacon. "They sound like good people."

"They really are."

And that was what was going to make this so difficult, if Havoc decided to make good on his promise to intervene. I wanted more than anything to save Archer, but not at the expense of anyone else.

In a move uncharacteristic of my parents, they retired to their bedroom to clean up and relax for a while. It was Saturday, so their offices were closed, but usually they were out and about running errands or meeting with clients. I couldn't remember the last time they actually spent a Saturday at home.

I cleaned up the breakfast dishes, grabbed my homework from the bedroom, and brought it back to the living room. I dropped everything onto the coffee table and settled down on the couch, reaching for the TV remote. I needed to do something to keep my mind occupied, and by occupied I meant not dwelling on what Havoc may or may not do. Or worrying about Archer too incessantly. There was still that part of my brain that was constantly nagging at me to check in Archer, maybe send him a text or two, but he was hardly a talkative person via cell phone. The few times we had texted, he was very monosyllabic.

I was still on the couch, slugging my way through a worksheet on parliamentary procedure, when my parents emerged from their room, looking much better after a few hours of rest.

"Have you moved at all?" my mom asked from the kitchen as she poured herself a cold cup of coffee.

"Not really," I answered. "Well, actually, I made a few waffles around lunchtime."

My dad laughed, sitting down on the couch beside me. "You and your waffles."

I was kind of pleased he was teasing me about my obsession. It meant he'd noticed.

"Why don't you call Taylor or one of the girls?" my mom asked, seating herself in the recliner by the windows. "You know, celebrate the last of Thanksgiving break."

"Yeah, maybe," I said.

The funny thing was, I didn't really want to leave the apartment. Yeah, part of that was because I was still a little freaked out by yesterday's events, but most of it was because I hadn't had quality time with my parents in forever. And since I now was tangled up in some scary Tilt-a-Whirl with Death, Havoc, and Archer, I thought it might be a good idea to hang with my parents. I might not get the chance again.

I spent the rest of the day lounging around the apartment with my mom and dad, which was an unnatural occurrence with more than a bit of awkwardness, but at the same time, it was really nice. We ordered some Chinese takeout for dinner from a place a few blocks over, and after watching a marathon of old sitcoms, they decided to head to bed early.

I was exhausted from a night without sleep, but even then I wasn't sure I was ready to close my eyes. My parents were only a few feet down the hallway in their own bedroom, and it was reassuring to know they were so close, that I wasn't alone. However, it still didn't erase the fear that Havoc would somehow worm his way through the locked door into my room.

I couldn't stand the sight of my ceiling any longer after lying in bed, wide awake, until one thirty in the morning. I abandoned my bedroom for the kitchen and rummaged quietly through the cupboards, looking for some teabags to make myself a cup of tea. I paused on my way to fill a mug from the water cooler, catching sight of a dark shape in the dining room out of the corner of my eye. I waited anxiously for the shape to move, make a noise or something, but I failed to see any movement.

Maybe it was because I'd already had a run-in with some obviously supernatural being with a burning vendetta against me, or maybe insomnia had made me bold, but I immediately marched over to the light switch without sparing my safety a second thought. If it was Havoc again, I wanted to see his face rather than worry about him skulking in the shadows.

When my eyes adjusted to the light, I was shocked but ultimately relieved to find that *Death* was seated at the dining room table. His hands were clasped before him, and he smiled pleasantly as I stared at him. My breathing slowly began returning to normal.

"Well, good morning, Hadley."

"How long have you been sitting there?"

"Oh, not long."

"Because that's not creepy *whatsoever*." I shuddered. Even though Death was better than Havoc, I didn't exactly like the idea of him spying on me.

Death shrugged.

"You could've said something, you know," I spat, pulling out the chair across the table from him and taking a seat.

"I don't believe I'm the one with all the questions," Death said.

My eyes narrowed as I examined Death. He didn't look quite as unsettling as he had the first night I met him, or at the church. He was still unnaturally pale, with that skeletal appearance, and smiling still didn't really suit him, but something was different this time. Probably because Havoc had replaced Death as the most frightening thing I'd ever seen.

"What are you doing here?" I asked Death, curling my fingers around the empty mug. "I didn't ask you to come."

Death pursed his lips, looking uncomfortable as he drummed his fingers on the tabletop. "I will admit that this *is* unusual on my part."

"What, randomly showing up at people's apartments in the middle of the night and sitting in the dark?"

"No, that I do quite frequently, actually."

I slumped backward in the chair, releasing a sigh. "Are you trying to be funny?"

"Not at all."

From what I'd seen, Death didn't just show up out of the blue. Well, apart from when he was offering people contracts or confronting people in churches. But he definitely didn't appear whenever I had questions or needed help. He had to be here for a reason, but he was skirting around the issue. And I knew as well as he did that issue was Havoc.

"Did you know he'd show up?" I asked as I looked at Death, jumping right to the point.

Death understood what I was asking without having to

explain myself further. "I always hope he won't be a problem, but . . . yes. To be fair, though, I *did* warn you."

"Oh, right," I said with a snort. "Like telling me *there are things that may not be happy with you disturbing the natural order* is a good enough warning. That's about the least specific thing you could have said."

"It was true. I can assure you, Havoc certainly isn't happy you're trying to change things," Death said.

"Yeah, I figured that much out for myself, thank you," I snapped. "So is everything he said true? Is he some kind of debt collector that's going to kill me if Archer doesn't die like he's supposed to? One of those life-for-a-life kind of things? Because that's what is sounded like to me, and I'm not going to lie, I'm pretty freaked out."

Death looked momentarily uncomfortable. "Sounds about right, yeah."

"Then what are you doing here? Just going to tell me you can't help me again?"

"Not this time." Death shook his head, still tapping away on the tabletop with his fingers.

I was taken aback by this. "Sorry?"

He brushed this aside with a wave of his hand, and said, "I just want to talk."

"The last time you said that, you offered me a contract. I really, really don't want to be signing away on the dotted line again."

Death leaned forward, propping his elbows up on the table, a very serious look in his eyes. It was unsettling to see his face missing his trademark smirk. "Havoc is . . . complicated. He thrives on the misfortune and pain of others, and he'll do anything he can to make sure that keeps on rolling. *The way of the world*, I think he's called it before. Just his name alone instills chaos, and he's willing to upend the world and cause all kinds of turmoil so the darkness that exists in this world doesn't disappear. He wants to keep that balance. So *good* never has a fighting chance."

"Why didn't you tell me this sooner?" I hissed, feeling sick to my stomach at this new piece of information. Throwing out things like *darkness* and *good versus evil* was far beyond my understanding. It sounded too Hollywood to be real, but ever since this started, the impossible was starting to become the norm for me.

"I didn't want to bring Havoc to your attention, of course," Death said, like this should've been obvious. "Thought it might scare you off. But now that he's introduced himself . . ."

"Everything's messed up," I finished for him.

"But you knew it would be from the beginning."

"Yeah, but that doesn't make it any easier."

"Is anything in life ever easy?"

I gave a disgusted groan and slumped forward in my chair, resting my forehead on the table. I wanted to be done with this. I was suddenly very, very tired, and nothing sounded more appealing than my bed. Definitely not staying up, listening to Death speak in riddles and rhymes.

"Anything else you want to share with the class?" I asked miserably. "Maybe a helpful hint or two about how to deal with this guy?"

As Death began to speak, there was something in the tone of his voice that made me sit up. Caution. Maybe a little guilt.

"There are things about the world you don't understand,

Hadley. Bad things happen out there, but bad things happen in here too," he said, tapping a finger to his forehead.

"What's that supposed to mean?" I demanded.

"What Havoc does . . ." Death's face was far too expressionless to be normal, like he was trying to keep himself in check. "It's not always out there for your eyes to see. You might find that it's more . . . inside your head."

My heart skipped a literal beat. "What's that supposed to mean? I'm going to go crazy?"

Death gave a slight shake of his head, but the pause in his response was enough to send me spiraling into panic. What if Havoc made me go crazy? What if he made Archer go crazy? Crazy enough to do something insane like hurt himself?

"He's going to make Archer do something bad, isn't he?" I started listening off all the possibilities of what could happen, my voice taking on a hysterical note. "He's going to hurt his family, isn't he? He's going to—"

Death held up a hand, cutting off my rapid flow of questions. "My advice to you, Hadley, before you start hyperventilating, is to keep a clear head."

I stared expectantly at him, waiting for more advice. Death returned my gaze with that same blank expression.

"That's it?" I said flatly. "*Keep a clear head*? How am I supposed to do that?"

If the last two weeks were anything to go by, that wasn't something I was very good at.

Death sighed, clasping his hands together on the table before him. "I don't have all the answers, Hadley."

"Would you stop saying that?" I snapped. "There's got to be

something you can do to help me! You're Death, right? You can time travel! *Please!* Just tell me how to stop Havoc!"

"Sorry, kid."

My parents were asleep just down the hallway, and I had to stifle a frustrated scream when Death disappeared with a tight smile and an annoying little wave. I threw myself back in the chair, scrubbing my hands over my face, trying to fight back the fresh wave of tears threatening to pull me under.

Confessions— 8 Days Until

I was anxious to return to school after Thanksgiving break. I wanted to jump back into my normal routine of classes, and homework would help take my mind off the growing sense of dread making a home in the pit of my stomach. I took an early train, eager to get out of the apartment, and I was one of the first to arrive at school. I thought about finishing up the last bit of American Government homework I'd tossed aside, but instead I wound up wandering aimlessly through the halls.

I hadn't seen any trace of Havoc since he'd introduced himself Friday night. But just because I couldn't see him didn't mean he wasn't there. For all I knew, he was hiding around the corner, waiting for the perfect opportunity to strike. The fact that I didn't know *how* he was going to mess with my life was confusing and horrifying at the same time. I'd had enough to worry about from the beginning, and now those fears had only increased tenfold, and it sure felt like Death's *advice* wasn't going to be of any use.

The odd thing was that, in retrospect, things were looking up in every other area of my life. I'd spend an unheard of full day with my parents, and I hadn't been itching to make a break for it. Archer wasn't pushing me away every chance he got. And now the time had come for me to make amends to one last person, and to make a confession that was well overdue.

After days of trying to squish any thought of it, I was done denying it. I was going to explode if I didn't confess, and soon. It had to be done. I was going to spill my guts, which was far more appealing than obsessing over Havoc. I found Taylor at her locker a few minutes before the first bell of the day.

"I like Archer."

Taylor was struggling to shove a notebook into her bag as she swung her locker shut, and barely spared me a glance. "Sorry, what?"

I let out a loud groan, squeezing my eyes shut. I didn't want to say it again, but the embarrassment wasn't anything less than what I deserved after being such a crappy friend lately. It was the first day back at school after Thanksgiving break, and I'd kept this bottled up long enough. I wasn't sure I'd ever gone this long without admitting some sort of secret to Taylor. It had been hard enough keeping *every* secret I had under lock and key, and she deserved my honesty.

"You were right," I repeated. "About Archer. I like him. I feel . . . *something* for him. I'm just really not sure what it is."

This much was true. The things I felt for Archer . . . they were there, and they weren't going to go away. They just had yet to be defined.

Taylor whipped her head up so quickly that I thought she was going to break her neck, and then she started grinning. "I knew it. I *so* knew it! You have a thing for Archer Morales!"

"Taylor, be quiet," I snapped, making a shushing motion with my hand. "The entire student body doesn't need to know!"

Taylor gave me a pitying look, shaking her head. "I'm pretty sure the entire student body already knows, honey. You don't exactly hide it all that well."

"Well, congratulations then," I said. "You were right all along."

"I'm always right," she said smugly. "At least where boys are concerned."

"Sure." I guessed I could give her that.

"So. What's the deal with you two?"

"What deal?"

Taylor gave this exasperated little huff, staring at me with an *are you really as stupid as you seem* expression. "I mean, are you dating or what? You spend practically every day together. You work at his family's coffee shop!"

"We're *not* together," I answered firmly.

I was trying to convince myself of this just as much as I was Taylor. Besides our almost kiss, there had been no sign that Archer was interested in me. He definitely hadn't asked me to be his girlfriend. In fact, on more than one occasion, he had been pretty adamant that we were just friends.

"Yeah, like you expect me to believe that," Taylor scoffed. "You're so hiding something. Spill."

"We almost kissed the night of Thanksgiving," I blurted, unable to hold back the words any longer.

"*What*? You waited until *now* to tell me that?"

"Nothing actually happened!"

"How could you say *nothing happened*? He kissed you!"

"*Almost* kissed me," I corrected, and I could feel my face getting hot just thinking about it.

"Well, what stopped him?" Taylor demanded, now gripping my forearm, practically shaking me for information.

I sucked in a breath, gnawing on my lip. "His . . . grandmother walked in on us."

She cracked up at this. "Oh, no. Please tell me you're joking."

"I wish I were."

Taylor had no idea how badly I'd wanted that kiss to happen. I was still trying to come to terms with it myself.

"And what? No repeat performance?" she pressed earnestly, eyebrows raised.

"I don't know," I admitted. Every part of myself definitely wanted one. "We never even talked about it. I can't think about that right now, not until he brings it up."

Taylor's face fell. She stared at me for a moment, her head tilted to the side, frowning, and said, "Of course you can. You like him."

"I know that," I muttered. "It's just . . . things are different with us."

"Not so much that you can't admit your feelings for each other, right?" Taylor hinted.

"I'm not really sure about that right now," I said. I knew that it was going to come up, though. Archer wasn't stupid. He was going to figure out how I felt about him eventually. But I had more important things to worry about when it came to Archer than his feelings toward me.

I took a deep breath. The second half of my confession to Taylor was an apology. "Look . . . I need to go to class. But I just wanted to say I'm sorry. For being such a crap friend lately and bailing on you and the girls. I promise it's not going to be forever."

At least I hoped so.

Taylor didn't say another word about Archer, but I could tell by the look on her face that this conversation was by no means over.

"It better not. But you're forgiven," she said, giving me a playful jab to the shoulder. "But if you're going to wander off because of a guy, at least make sure that guy likes you too, okay? Because if he doesn't, he's clearly an idiot."

I laughed. "I'll do what I can."

I kept my head down as I walked to chemistry, thinking about what Taylor had said. I was beginning to mentally prep myself for a repeat conversation with Chelsea during class. Taylor was probably right and the whole student body already knew I had a thing for Archer, but Chelsea and Brie were going to need to hear the confession from me. And even though I didn't like admitting I was wrong, I had to say it felt good to be talking to my friends again.

I didn't see Archer until after the final bell, and I was a little worried it was because he'd found out I was blabbing about my feelings all over school. But then again, I had to skip lunch in order to sit in the library to work on yet another paper on *The Great Gatsby* for my English class. Neglecting some of the homework I'd been assigned over Thanksgiving break was not the smartest idea I'd ever had.

I made my way from the ceramics room to the second floor where Archer's locker was, hoping I would find him there. I stood on my tiptoes, peering over the crowd in the stairwell until I spotted him. "Hey, Archer!"

He glanced up when I called his name, and there was this small, barely there smile on his face. So even if he did know I had a crush on him, at least he wasn't completely freaked out by it. "Hey. Don't forget you about your shift tomorrow—"

But his words were lost on me. Without warning, I suddenly lost my footing and went tumbling backward down the stairs. It was as if someone ripped the floor out from underneath me, even though I was sure I'd been standing firmly on the top step. I had already gained too much momentum to be able to throw out my hands to find purchase on the stairs in order to stop myself from rolling.

I kept hearing my head smacking against the steps, one after the other, and the sound was ringing in my ears. When I finally landed in a heap at the bottom of the stairs, I was afraid to open my eyes and encounter a spinning ceiling.

"*Hadley!*"

I somehow recognized that voice—Archer's voice—through the white noise popping and crackling in my ears, and then I felt large, warm hands gently turning me over. "Hadley, are you all right?"

I carefully opened my eyes and saw Archer hovering over me. "Hey," I said. "I fell."

"Yeah, I know. I saw."

I tried to pull myself up into a sitting position, but it proved to be impossible with the way everything flipped upside down and shook. Archer slowly and surely came into focus, and his eyes were wide, as pure shock had taken over his face. One of his hands pressed against my cheek, the other at my waist, and our close proximity made it even more difficult to collect my thoughts. I did my best to get up one more time.

"Hey, no— Wait a second, will you?" Archer's hand moved to grip my shoulder, keeping me from rising to my feet. "Just sit still. You hit your head pretty hard."

"Yeah, I'm feeling it already," I said, squeezing my eyes shut.

I sat there at the bottom of the stairs for several minutes and didn't open my eyes until my breathing finally evened out. Having Archer so close beside me made that a challenge, though. He was still touching me, and it was comforting. Safe. But also a little exhilarating.

"Can you move everything?" Archer asked as I looked over at him. "Nothing broken?"

I wiggled my fingers and toes. "So far so good."

"Okay. You wanna give standing up a try?"

"Yeah. Gimme a second."

I gripped his arm tightly and hoisted myself to my feet. I stumbled a little bit, but I eventually managed to stand upright.

Archer squeezed my hand. "Are you sure you're all right?"

"Yeah, I'm okay," I told him. "But since when have you had two heads?"

He sighed heavily, looking defeated. "Since always." Archer took my bag from me and hefted it up on his shoulder. "Come on."

"Wait, where are we going?" I said as Archer wrapped an arm around my waist and gently started leading me down the hallway.

"I'm taking you to the office," Archer said. "The nurse probably already left, but I'm hoping we can get you a bag of ice or something. You've already got a bruise the size of an egg on your head."

I reached up and tentatively ran my fingers over my fore-head, wincing when I found the aforementioned bruise. "Ow."

Archer gave another disgruntled sigh. When we reached the main office, the receptionist was just closing up for the day, most of the lights already off, her bag ready to go as she messed with the keys on her keychain. She looked up as we entered.

"Sorry," Archer said quickly. "She just fell down the stairs and hit her head pretty hard. Could we maybe get some ice for her? I really hope she doesn't have a concussion."

I really hoped I didn't have a concussion too. My head was starting to throb painfully, and the edges of my vision were a little too black.

The receptionist went through a door into the back, and I heard her opening and shutting drawers, then the sound of ice being scooped up and dumped into a bag. She appeared a moment later and thrust the bag of ice at me, saying, "You need anything else?"

"No," I said. "But hey, thanks. You're a peach."

Archer quickly steered me out of the office and promptly burst out laughing the second we were out of earshot. "I'll get you a cab," he said, and my favorite grin was still in place. "Probably best that you don't ride a bus that purposely goes over potholes."

"Yeah, I'd appreciate that."

We had to walk a block over, away from the mess of buses and parents still waiting around to pick up their kids from school, before Archer was able to flag down a cab for me.

"You sure you're going to be all right?" Archer said as he held the door of the cab open for me. "You'll be pretty banged up in the morning."

"I'm well aware, thanks," I said as I slid carefully onto the seat. "But I'll be fine."

"Look, my afternoon shift starts soon, but I can always call to get it off and take you to the ER just to—"

"Hang on there," I said quickly, cutting him off midsentence. "Nobody needs to go to the ER here. I'm *fine.*"

Archer didn't look convinced and was about to start protesting again, but before he could, I told him, "Seriously, Archer. I appreciate your concern, but I'm okay. You don't need to miss work over me."

"It's not that big of a deal," Archer said with a scoff. "My mom can survive one afternoon without me."

"If I didn't know you any better, I'd say you were worried about me, Archer Morales," I said, and it was difficult to keep from sounding smug.

A splotchy pink color dotted his cheeks, and he went from looking concerned to uncomfortable in half a second. "I just watched you take a nosedive down a flight of stairs. Of course I want to make sure you're okay."

"Fair enough," I reasoned. Was it wrong I felt elated Archer was worried about me? "But I really am fine. I promise I'll call if I need you."

"Okay." Archer continued to hold the door open, watching me as I buckled myself in. "Let me know if you'd rather not come in for your shift tomorrow."

"Don't worry about it," I said. "I'll be there."

I couldn't let one lousy headache and a few bruises stop me from working when I actually enjoyed what I did.

"Yeah?"

"Yeah."

"Are you two goin' to keep jabberin' out there, or are you goin' to shut the door so I can drive?"

"Yeah, sorry," Archer said to the cab driver, not sounding sorry at all.

He shut the door and stepped back onto the sidewalk, and the cab pulled away from the curb and into traffic. I glanced out the window in enough time to see Archer give a two-fingered wave, and then head off down the street.

I settled back against the seat, still holding the bag of ice against my bruise. My head did not stop spinning until we'd already traveled several blocks, and I slowly began to piece together what just happened. Despite the headache, one thing was clear.

I hadn't fallen down the stairs because I'd lost my balance and slipped. My feet had been firmly planted on the ground, and I had been gripping the railing tightly. Nobody had knocked me over. No, something else had happened—it felt like I had been shoved down the stairs by something that wasn't there.

I couldn't be positive, but the sinking feeling in the pit of my stomach made me think that this could have something to do with Havoc. I would admit to being a klutz, sure, but I'd never lost my balance like that.

I was anxious to get out of the cab and into the safety of my apartment, where I could examine what my suspicions might mean and the possible consequences. I paid my fare when the cab pulled up to the curb outside the apartment complex, and thankfully, Hanson the doorman was there to help me out.

"That's one nasty bruise," Hanson said as he led me to the doors. "You feeling all right?"

"I've been better," I admitted. "Nothing a nap and some Tylenol can't fix." I hoped that was true.

I made way across the lobby and rode up to the seventh floor in the elevator. I managed to keep the bag of ice on my forehead as I fumbled around in my bag for my keys, then unlocked the door to 7E.

My bag hit the floor, and the mess of melting ice followed when I walked inside and saw the words scrawled in an elegant script in black Sharpie across the windows in the living room.

Time is ticking, ticking, gone
You'll be seeing me before too long
But never mind, how'd you like that fall?
Next time you won't be the only one to lose it all.

CHAPTER 22

Revelations—
7 Days Until

Regina was wiping down the front counter with a cloth as I stepped through the door of Mama Rosa's Tuesday afternoon, bringing in a flurry of snow with me.

"Hadley." Regina flushed as she looked up at me. "Hi."

"Hi," I said, shrugging out of my coat. "Sorry I'm a bit late. The weather really sucks, and . . ."

Something about Regina's expression made me immediately shut my mouth.

Her gaze was fixed on the counter as she scrubbed with more force than necessary, her shoulders a little hunched over as she worked.

"Is . . . something wrong?" I asked hesitantly.

"No," she said quickly, looking up. "No, not at all. I probably should have called earlier. You shouldn't have come in. It's a bit slow tonight."

I looked around. A bit slow was an understatement. The place was as empty as a graveyard.

"That's okay," I said. "I'll . . . Just don't put me on the payroll tonight, then."

"Hadley, really. You can go home," Regina said, attempting

a smile. "Archer's out running errands right now, he'll be back soon. He can help close up then. I won't hold it against you if you leave."

The thing was, I didn't want to leave. I didn't want to go home to an empty apartment, where haunting words had been scribbled across the window in black marker, words I still saw after spending hours scrubbing them away. The last thing I wanted was to be alone.

"It's not a problem at all," I told Regina sincerely. "Really. I'd like to stay."

She finally gave in a moment later with a small chuckle, and then gestured a hand toward the kitchen. "Well, if you insist."

I hung up my jacket and bag on a hook in the back room, slipped on an apron, and joined Regina at the front counter. She now crouched down in front of the pastry case, taking out a few old muffins and scones and placing them in a box.

This was the first time I had seen Regina since Thanksgiving. I hadn't had a shift since Black Friday. I wanted to ask her if she was all right after what happened Thanksgiving night, but the subject of her PTSD was obviously taboo. I was still having difficulty understanding what it was like for Regina, living with the fear of possibly having a flashback at every wrong turn hanging over her head.

"Look, Hadley."

I stopped wiping down the register and looked to Regina as she stood up straight, setting the pastry box on the counter. "Yes?" I said.

Regina took a deep breath, brushing back her hair over her shoulder. "Listen, I'm . . . I don't want you to think that . . . that

I'm always like that. What you saw on Thanksgiving. Because I'm not. It's . . . complicated. I—"

I cut her off before she could get any farther.

"Archer already told me what happened. It's okay."

I wanted to say I understood, but who was I kidding? I had no idea what it was like to go through what Regina and her family did. That kind of pain and hurt . . . I never wanted to know what that was like.

"He did?" Regina looked stunned. "Archer told you?"

I nodded. "Yeah. He did."

It took her a moment to completely rid herself of shock, and when she did, she sighed, crossing her arms tightly over her chest. "I suppose that makes this . . . a little easier, then."

"Regina, please don't apologize for anything," I said before I could stop myself. "There's nothing you need to be sorry for."

She attempted a smile that was marred by the fact her eyes were brimming with tears. "I swear we're not as messed up as we might seem."

"Not messed up," I agreed quickly. I was a little hurt that she would even think her family was messed up. Her family was beautiful. "Sometimes unfortunate things just . . . just happen. And we can't really do anything about them. But it's not your fault. Please don't think that."

"Unfortunate," Regina repeated with a bitter laugh. "I suppose that's the right word for it."

"Regina, you have a beautiful family and you're the best mother I've ever seen. Rosie absolutely adores you, and I know Archer doesn't show it, but he does too. He needs you. They both need you. And if your husband were here, I know he would think the same thing—that you're a strong woman who can do anything."

I believed what I just said, but what right did I even have to say those words?

"I'm sorry," I murmured after a moment. "I'm sorry, I shouldn't have—"

"It's all right, Hadley," Regina said. "Really. Thank you for saying that."

"I should be the one thanking you instead," I said. "You've sort of taken me in as your own, offering me a job, letting me come to family dinners, and . . . Well, it's nice for a change."

Regina gave my shoulder a comforting squeeze and smiled. Really smiled. I could see why Chris Morales had fallen in love with her. She was beautiful, inside and out.

"You don't need to thank me, Hadley," she told me. "You've brought my son to life in more ways than one. It's only natural you would be a part of our family."

"How . . . What do you mean?" I asked, fixated on my shoes.

Regina thought about her answer for a moment or two before she spoke slowly, thoughtfully.

"After Chris was killed, it was hard on all of us. But Archer . . . it was especially hard on him. To him, Chris was his father. And afterward . . . well, Archer sort of shut down. He stopped doing all the things he enjoyed. Stopped talking, stopped laughing. There were days where he would just lay in bed and not do anything, just stare at the wall in this sort of daze because he didn't want to face anybody. And then after what he went through at school, getting picked on, beaten up, being told he was going to end up a murderer like his father . . . You have no idea how badly that tore me up, how much it broke my heart, seeing my baby hurting and not being able to do anything about it."

Regina stopped to take a deep breath, gnawing on her lip.

"That's why Archer got held back a year in school," she continued, running her fingers through her hair. It was something I'd seen Archer do before. "He'll be nineteen when he graduates. He didn't want to go because of what people said, what they did to him. And how could I let him after all that happened?" Her eyes were full of a pain only a mother could feel for her child, and it made my chest constrict with a pain of my own. "Hadley, you make Archer smile. And after years of not seeing my boy smiling at all? Of course I'm going to want the reason for his smile around as much as possible."

I couldn't comprehend just how awful it must have been for Archer over these past few years. How often had he been given a load of crap like what Ty Ritter had confronted him with the other week?

"That's why you offered me a job, isn't it?" I said. "Because of Archer. I know it's not because I'm an extraordinary barista."

Regina looked slightly embarrassed. "I wasn't trying to be a matchmaker and set you two up, if that's what you're thinking. Archer just needs a friend. And you are his friend, Hadley."

"A friend," I repeated. It was difficult to keep back a smile. "That I can do."

"Good," Regina said, giving a smile of her own. "I'm glad."

The atmosphere seemed lighter now. Not so suffocating.

I was thankful I had been able to talk to Regina about this. It had put several things into a new perspective.

A blast of cold air blew through the coffeehouse as the door swung open and some guy who looked frozen to the core wandered in. I took his change while Regina quickly made him a caramel mocha. He left looking considerably happier.

Regina and I fell into a discussion about how our days had gone. Compared to what we had previously been talking about, it was a relief to talk about something considerably lighter.

"No, really, I'm terrible at geometry, I swear," I said as Regina laughed loudly. "If it weren't for Archer helping me, I totally would have failed that test!"

"Did he really say that, though?" Regina demanded. "'You butchering your math is giving me hives'?"

"Yes! I'm not joking! He—"

The outdated phone beside the cash register started ringing before I could finish speaking.

Regina took a second to collect herself and then answered with a polite, "Mama Rosa's Coffeehouse, how can I help you?"

There was a beat of silence as the person on the other line spoke.

"Yes, this is she."

Genuine fear started to grip me like a vice when Regina's face began to drain of color, turning the color of a sheet. She sucked in air through her teeth, almost like a dying person taking their last breath.

"Well, are they all right? Can I speak to Archer?" Her voice sounded hollow, dead. "Is there— No, I'll be there as soon as I can. Have you called Karin DiRosario? Well, do it again until you get ahold of someone! Right. Okay. Good-bye."

She slowly set the phone back on the receiver and grabbed at the counter behind her.

I was afraid to know what happened, because there was no way on this earth it had been something good.

"Regina?" I reached out to squeeze her hand. "Is everything okay?"

She shook her head. It was several moments before she said anything. The silence stretched on with an almost suffocating intensity.

"There's . . . been an . . . accident," she said slowly, her voice cracking. "Archer and Carlo . . . There was a . . . They were on a bus, a-and . . . it crashed."

CHAPTER 23

Accidents

I had misheard Regina. There was no way what she just said could possibly be true.

"You're . . . no. That's not . . . that's not right," I said.

During my encounter with Havoc, he made it plainly clear something bad was on the horizon. His note of *next time you won't be the only one to lose it all* was self-explanatory. If this really was the next time, if he had done this . . .

"Hadley, we have to go." Regina squeezed my shoulders, bringing me back to painful reality. "Now."

I yanked off my apron and made a mad dash through the kitchen to grab our jackets from the back room as Regina made a quick phone call to Victoria, who was with Rosie at Karin's house.

"They're both at Bellevue," Regina told me as I passed over her jacket. "It's not too far from here."

"Taking the train is going to waste too much time," I said, heading for the door. "We need to take a cab."

Regina switched off the open sign and locked up as I stood on the curb, flagging down a cab. I jumped into the first one that pulled over to the sidewalk and was quickly followed by Regina. I watched her carefully as the driver navigated the streets to Bellevue, worried that she might suddenly break down like she had on Thanksgiving. But she didn't. She stared blankly ahead, her hands twisted together in her lap.

It felt as if a lifetime had passed before the cab finally pulled to a stop outside the emergency room entrance at Bellevue. I paid the fare before Regina could object, and then we were both scrambling onto the sidewalk and sprinting through the doors into the hospital.

"Excuse me?" Regina made a beeline for the information desk, slipping through the clumps of people milling around, with me right on her heels. "Excuse me!"

The woman wearing green scrubs sitting behind the desk looked up from her computer. "Yes?"

"Archer Morales and Carlo DiRosario were just brought in. I need to know what room they're in," Regina demanded.

The woman raised her eyebrows. "Are you family?"

I took a step back when an angered expression crossed Regina's face, so out of place with her soft, pretty features. She slammed her hands down on the counter and leaned closer to the woman, lowering her voice. "Look, lady. This is my son and nephew we're talking about. You've got another thing coming to you if you don't tell me where they are right now."

The woman turned visibly pale and leaned back in her chair, then quickly nodded, tapping around on her computer.

I almost cheered. *Go, Regina!*

"Carlo DiRosario is straight through those doors," the woman said, pointing her finger to the doors to our right. "Third room on the left. Though I'm not seeing any Archer Morales here."

"What?" Regina and I gasped in unison.

"I'm sorry, but if he's not in the system, he hasn't been brought in," the woman told us.

We didn't stick around to hear what else she had to say.

I burst through the swinging doors on our right, Regina at my side, as we sprinted down the hallway, which bustled with nurses and doctors heading every which way. I skidded to a stop outside the room the nurse mentioned and wrenched back the green privacy curtains without warning.

Carlo was propped up on a mountain of pillows. Numerous shallow cuts decorated his face, and nasty bruises were already beginning to form across his forearms and neck, but he was alive and breathing. He seemed quite surprised to see Regina and me standing at the foot of his bed.

"Where's the party?" he said, grinning.

"Carlo, thank God you're all right." Regina rushed over and threw her arms around him, squeezing him tightly. "I was so worried."

Carlo's face whitened and he scrunched his eyes closed while awkwardly patting Regina on the back.

"I'm fine, *zia*, but, um . . . you're suffocating me."

"Oh." Regina pulled away quickly, rubbing at the tears staining her cheeks. "Sorry."

Carlo glanced around Regina toward me then, and his grin returned, wider than before. "Good to see you again, Hadley."

"I'm not going to lie, Carlo, it's great to see you too," I admitted, coming to the bedside to give his hand a gentle squeeze. "How are you feeling?"

"Well." He heaved a dramatic sigh, settling back against his pillows. "Other than the fact that it hurts to move, I'm flipping fantastic."

"*Caro*, what happened?" Regina took a seat on the edge of

the bed, placing her hand over Carlo's. "I swear I nearly had a heart attack when I got that phone call."

"I have no idea, *zia*," Carlo answered after a moment of thought. A pained expression crossed his face again as he thought back to what just happened. "One minute I was just sitting there in my seat, with my headphones in, and then there was this loud screeching noise, and then the bus started tipping, and . . ."

He couldn't finish his sentence.

"Your mom will be here soon, sweetheart," Regina told Carlo, squeezing his hand. "I'm so sorry."

"I know, *zia*, I just—"

"Where's Archer?"

I hadn't meant to cut Carlo off, but the question had been bubbling at my lips since the moment I first walked into the room. I usually wasn't one for dramatics, but I doubted I would be able to think properly until I saw Archer with my own eyes. Saw for myself that he was alive, and breathing, and that he was going to keep breathing. That I would make sure he kept breathing.

"Dunno," Carlo said. I didn't like the way he was smiling at me. Like he knew something I didn't. "He's gotta be around here somewhere. He was here when they brought me in. Why don't you go find him?"

Regina looked like she was about to protest as she opened her mouth, but Carlo winked discreetly at her, and she stopped short. "Go ahead, Hadley," she said while giving Carlo a curious look. "I'll stay with Carlo until Karin gets here, and then I'll be along in a minute. I want to find a doctor and figure out what's going on."

I didn't need to be told twice. I turned on my heel and left the room, anxious to find Archer as soon as possible. It was almost impossible to make out any sign of him with the hallway so crowded with nurses and doctors, as well as carts full of medical equipment and beds lining the walls. I maneuvered my way down the hallway as best I could without accidentally bumping into someone, and turned left.

When I saw him standing in the middle of the hallway, cell phone at his ear, talking quickly and quietly, I felt a great wave of relief wash over me. Fear still radiated through me straight down to my toes, but he was here, alive, and that suddenly seemed like the only thing that mattered.

"Archer?"

He looked around at the sound of his name, and a confused expression crossed his face. "Hadley? What are you doing here?"

A sob left my lips when he said my name. I leapt at him before I really knew what I was doing. He gave a startled gasp when I threw my arms around him, his cell phone falling to the floor with a clatter as he caught me to keep us from toppling over.

"*Hey*," he huffed out as I threaded my fingers through his hair, breathed in his familiar scent. "What are you doing?"

I started babbling. "I thought something terrible happened to you, I thought—"

"Hadley, stop. *Stop.*"

He gently slid my arms from around his neck and moved me back a step, firmly gripping my shoulders. "I'm fine, all right? Nothing happened to me. I wasn't even on the bus. I was waiting for Carlo at the next stop."

My shoulders sagged as I gave another sigh, a hand at my chest. This seemed too good to be true. "Thank God," I mumbled. "I swear, I thought I wasn't going to be able to . . ."

"You thought you weren't going to be able to do . . . what?" Archer said uneasily, clearing his throat.

My fingers loosened their iron grip on his jacket, and I took a step back.

"I thought . . . I thought I wasn't going to be able to ever . . . fight with you about geometry again," I finished lamely, even though we both knew I meant so much more.

We had barely spent that much time together in the grand scheme of things. There was still so much we didn't know about each other. I didn't want that chance ripped away from us.

Archer looked at me, a conflicted expression on his face, and then moved forward without warning, grabbed my face in his hands, and kissed me.

I was so shocked, I just stood there for several seconds until I managed to respond. My fingers clutched at his jacket, whether to shove him away or pull him closer, I wasn't sure. I could feel his heart pounding wildly against his chest, and my legs had begun to shake, but neither of us pulled away. We were kissing as if we were both desperate, grappling for something we couldn't quite reach. It definitely wasn't perfect, but this was us. I didn't want it to end.

I hadn't realized Archer had backed me up against the nearest wall until I felt myself slump against it when he pulled away, his hands falling to his sides.

We stared at each other for several moments, tension wavering between us.

"I'm . . . sorry," he finally said, sounding winded. "I didn't . . ."

"No," I said. "Don't be."

There was no denying that kiss hadn't just complicated everything a thousand times over. I didn't regret it, though.

"I shouldn't have . . ." Archer released a shaky breath, turning away from me.

"Archer." I grabbed his forearm and tugged him around to face me. "I kissed you back, didn't I?"

Archer stared down at my hand gripping his arm for a few seconds, then gently shook himself from my grasp, bending down to grab his fallen cell phone.

"I'm going to head back to Carlo," he said, not meeting my gaze as he spoke. "If you're here, I'm guessing my mother is too?"

"Yes, she's—"

"It's getting late. You don't need to stick around. You should probably go home now."

I didn't even get the chance to say anything in response before Archer started off down the hallway toward Carlo's room. He didn't once look back.

24

Clearing the Air—
6 Days Until

The next morning, I woke an hour before my alarm was set to go off, after only getting two hours of fitful sleep during the night. I padded my way down the hall, through the living room, for the kitchen. I wasn't surprised to see two empty coffee cups in the sink, along with the morning's newspaper spread open at my mother's chair at the dining room table. I'd heard my parents come in the night before, but I had been too exhausted to get out of bed to greet them. I smiled a little when I saw a sticky note on the fridge in my mom's handwriting that said "Have a great day!" next to a lopsided smiley face I knew was from my dad. They were still as busy as ever, but I could tell they were trying.

I got a fresh pot of coffee brewing before sitting down at the dining table in front of the newspaper. I nearly spat out a mouthful of coffee when I saw the small article tucked away toward the end of the current events section, barely fifty words. The first line read:

James St. Pierre, 36, previously convicted of first-degree homicide, is appealing his sentencing.

Archer's biological father, the man who killed Chris Morales almost six years ago, was requesting an appeal for his case. Now, I wasn't even remotely an expert when it came to how American government worked, but even I knew enough to know that this couldn't be good.

For the hundredth time since I'd gone to bed last night I replayed the events of yesterday evening, going over the discussion I'd had with Regina at Mama Rosa's and then the events at the hospital with Carlo and Archer. And not once did it seem as if Archer or his mom had received life-altering news like the fact Regina's ex-husband, a convicted murder, was trying to get out of prison.

Because maybe they didn't know.

I took a deep breath. Contrary to my mom's note, this was *not* going to be a great day.

There were a few early birds wandering the halls when I arrived at school an hour later. I marched to my locker and pulled out the texts I would need for the day, along with leftover homework. Homeroom wasn't set to start for another half hour or so. At the very least, I could look over my lab write-up for chemistry or review my notes for American Government for the surprise quiz I knew was coming. That was the one good thing about traveling back in time. I could prepare for pop quizzes I'd already taken.

I hunkered down in the library, going over my homework, and was the first one to make it to homeroom. It was a struggle to keep focused when the whole time I was wondering if Archer had seen that article in the paper yet. And if he hadn't, if I would have to be the one to tell him.

Despite my own concerns, I paid extra attention in American Government during fourth period. Mr. Monroe's lecture on the amendment process was somewhat interesting, if you took into account the changes the United States had undergone over the centuries, but I had something a little more pressing on my mind. When the bell rang, signaling the start of lunch, I didn't race out the door like I normally would have. I took the extra time to pack my bag carefully, and then approached Mr. Monroe, seated at his desk, a little warily. He was perfectly aware that I held little interest in his class, but I thought I had been doing a better job of trudging through his lessons.

"Um, excuse me. Mr. Monroe?"

He looked up from a test he'd been marking up with a red pen and seemed startled to see me standing in front of his desk. "Miss Jamison," he said in a crisp voice. "Is there anything I can do for you?"

"Actually, I had a question," I said. "And I was wondering if you would be able to help me."

Mr. Monroe's eyebrows shot up his forehead, and he looked even more baffled now. I rarely, if ever, asked questions in his class. "Of course," he said after he composed himself. "I'd be happy to assist in any way I can."

I decided to lay it right out on the table. "What are someone's chances of being granted an appeal after their trial?"

"Well, that depends," Mr. Monroe answered carefully, taking off his glasses and setting them on his desk. "The circumstances of the trial matter, and also on the severity of the crime. However, every person has the right to appeal their sentence. Whether or not they're actually granted that appeal depends entirely on whether or not new evidence has been found to even warrant a new trial. Besides, double jeopardy goes into play after their sentencing as it is. Does that answer your question?"

It took a moment to absorb what Mr. Monroe had said. I didn't know the exact details of St. Pierre's trial, but surely someone convicted of first-degree murder wouldn't be taken lightly. Mr. Monroe had said that every person had the right to appeal his or her sentencing, but why had St. Pierre waited six years to do so? What was so important about right now?

My first thought was Havoc. Could he be behind this too? Since he and I had talked in Mama Rosa's, everything that could go wrong had gone wrong. I was starting to believe nothing was a coincidence anymore.

"Yeah," I said, finally remembering to answer Mr. Monroe. "That did answer my question. Thanks."

It was with caution that I approached Mama Rosa's, anxious about what was waiting for me on the other side of the door. I was thankful I had another shift this evening before my day off tomorrow; otherwise, I wasn't sure if I would have been able to muster up the courage to come to the coffeehouse on my own. Archer managed to avoid me at school—if he'd even been there, that is. Maybe it was because of our kiss, or maybe it was because he'd likely seen that little story in the paper by now. Either way, he might need someone to talk to. *I* was that someone.

The drapes on the front windows were pulled back, the open sign was lit and flashing, and all appeared as if it were business as usual. The front counter was currently unmanned, and there were only a handful of customers seated at the tables and on the couch in front of the fireplace.

I made my way around the counter and into the kitchen, intent on hanging my stuff up in the back. Archer was at the industrial-sized sink, rinsing dishes, but he didn't look up as I entered.

I cleared my throat loudly to make my presence known, not wanting to startle him, and said, "Hey, Archer."

For some reason, all I could think about was how he'd kissed me in the hallway at the hospital. And yet that didn't even come close to being at the top of the list of what was important right now. Archer had probably forgotten about the kiss already, and I couldn't deny the fact that it might be better that way. He had bigger things to worry about than me.

Archer glanced over his shoulder as I spoke, and unless it was a trick of the light, his cheeks looked a little pinker than usual. He set down the bowl he'd been scrubbing out and grabbed at a dishtowel, turning to face me.

"Hey," he said, his voice oddly quiet. "Is, uh . . . everything okay out there?"

"Yeah," I said as I slipped out of my jacket and hung it and my bag on a hook by the back door. "There's no line at least."

"Okay. Cool. You can help me with the dishes, then?" He said it more like a question than a statement.

I grabbed a clean apron and slipped it on, rolling up my shirtsleeves as I went to the sink. We worked in amiable silence for a few minutes as he scrubbed the dishes clean, and I rinsed them and stacked them in the dishwasher.

"How's Carlo doing?" I asked, trying to make conversation.

"Good," Archer said briskly as he washed another bowl. "He had a mild concussion, so they kept him overnight just to make sure he was fine. He was discharged this morning."

I began to breathe a little easier hearing that. "That is good, then. I'm glad."

He gave a noncommittal grunt as he passed off a plate to me.

"And, um . . . how are you doing?"

Archer dropped the plate he was holding into the sink with a loud clatter, turning to me with a tight expression on his face. "You know, don't you?"

I was taken aback at his rather abrupt outburst. "I'm sorry?" I said.

"You know," he repeated forcefully. "Don't you? You know about the appeal. Of course you know. How?"

I let out a defeated sigh, grabbing the plate Archer had dropped and cleaning it myself. "There was an article in the newspaper this morning."

"What?"

"And when you weren't at school today, I figured that's why you were probably here, with your family."

I knew enough without asking that both Archer and Regina weren't in the best of conditions right now. I would tell him everything was going to be fine, that St. Pierre's chances of actually being granted the appeal were slim, but it wouldn't have meant anything to him. I only knew what Mr. Monroe had briefly told me. My dad was one of the city's top defense attorneys, but I knew shockingly little about law.

"Just . . . can you just go stand at the counter or something?" Archer said, returning to the pile of dirty dishes, not meeting my concerned gaze. "I'm sure you know the drill by now."

"Okay," I said. "I can do that."

I left him in the kitchen, even though I wanted to stay exactly where I was. We didn't need to talk or even acknowledge each other's presence. I just wanted him to know that I was there. He didn't always have to be alone—especially now. After spending the past two weeks with him, it was becoming easier and easier to tell when he needed space.

Business picked up at about five o'clock, as people began to make their way home from work, and Archer was forced to join me up front, though he didn't say a word. I took the orders and made change while Archer worked with smooth efficiency, making drinks and warming up sandwiches and soup for customers.

We were five minutes from closing, and I had already begun the routine of shutting down for the night, when the door swung open and someone strolled inside, bringing with them a flurry of unexpected snow.

I looked up from wiping down a table, beginning to say, "Hi. Someone will—"

My voice trailed off into nothing as the man who'd just walked in unwrapped the scarf from around his neck, shaking snow out of his stylish, graying hair.

"Mr. Van Auken?"

My father's business partner glanced in my direction at the sound of his name and broke into a surprised smile. "Hadley? Wow! Look at you! How long's it been?"

"Um . . ."

I had no idea what to say. I'd seen Rick Van Auken only a handful of times since he'd made partner with my dad back when I was thirteen. I was surprised he even remembered Kenneth Jamison had a daughter. From what I knew of the man, he had more money than King Midas. And yes, Mama Rosa's was in Manhattan, but in a considerably less posh part than what Mr. Van Auken would have been used to. I had no idea what would bring him to this neck of the woods.

"You work here?" Mr. Van Auken said, approaching me.

"Um, yes?" I said awkwardly.

"Great, great," he said, sanding his gloved hands together. "Is Regina Morales here by chance?"

I found this even more confusing than Mr. Van Auken coming into a place like Mama Rosa's. How did he know Regina? People like Mr. Van Auken and Regina Morales lived in circles that usually never touched unless the universe decided to throw humanity a curveball.

"Uh, yes, I think so," I said slowly. I didn't actually know. I hadn't seen her since the night before. "Hang on a second, would you? Hey, Archer? Archer!"

"Yeah, in the kitchen!" I heard him shout back.

"You think you could come out here for a second?"

Archer came walking out of the kitchen a moment later and frowned when he saw Mr. Van Auken.

"Is your mom around by chance?" I asked him nervously.

"Who's asking?" he said bluntly.

He didn't look all that happy to see someone in the shop so close to closing, asking for his mother, no less.

"Rick Van Auken," Mr. Van Auken said, striding forward with an outstretched hand. "You probably don't remember me, but I used to work for the district attorney's office. I prosecuted your father."

I stood there with my mouth open, wide enough to catch a few flies. Rick Van Auken, my father's business partner, had prosecuted Archer's father for first-degree murder.

"I heard about the request for an appeal. I know it's a little unusual for me to be making a follow-up with you," Mr. Van Auken continued, "but I remember this case. It wasn't . . . easy. I'd like to speak with your mother about possibly representing you if need be."

Archer took a deep breath, opening his mouth as if to speak, but all that came out was this huffy sort of noise. Instead, he gestured behind him toward the kitchen. Mr. Van Auken seemed to understand that Archer was having difficulty speaking and made his way around the counter, following him into the kitchen and up to the apartment.

I flopped down onto the couch, feeling clammy all over. I closed my eyes, wishing my mind would stop swarming with thought for just one second. I gave a jolt of surprise as Archer sunk down on the couch beside me a few minutes later, looking as surly and stone-faced as ever. I wondered how long I'd been sitting there.

I knew better than to ask, "Is everything okay?" so instead I settled for, "How is Regina?"

"Surprised," Archer said stiffly, leaning forward to rest his elbows on his knees, hands clasped beneath his chin. "Fine. I don't know. I'm pretty sure we'd all forgotten Van Auken was in charge of the case. But I think she's relieved to see him," Archer continued. "Somebody to clear everything up. He even said he would do the case pro bono. Guess he needs to do a certain number of hours or whatever, but still."

"Then that's good," I said slowly. "Good."

Archer glanced over at me, a frown tugging at his mouth. "You look like you're about to puke."

"No, no, I'm fine." I shook my head. "I'm fine."

"Yeah, you don't look fine. What's eating you?"

"Rick Van Auken is my father's business partner. They've co-owned the firm Watson & Bloomfield for the last couple of years, ever since the original owners retired."

If Archer was shocked, he kept his face a perfect mask of indifference. When he spoke next, his voice was just as monotone. "You're joking."

I shook my head, holding in a heavy sigh. "No," I said. "I never knew that Mr. Van Auken used to work for the district attorney. He comes from old money. I guess I always thought that he'd been as high up as he is now. It's . . . odd."

"Odd," Archer repeated. "Odd that your father's business partner just so happened to be the one who prosecuted my father in his murder trial? No, that's just freaky. How could you not have known?"

I shrugged. "It's not like I spend quality time with Mr. Van Auken, and my father certainly doesn't discuss any of his cases with me. I didn't even know about your dad until you told me the other week."

"Do you trust this Van Auken guy?"

I barely knew him. "All I can tell you is that he's one of the best. Your mom is in good hands."

Archer sighed, running his fingers through his hair. "I hope so. The last thing my mother needs is to hear is something bad about the appeal."

"Every person convicted of a felony crime is allowed the right to appeal his case, but that doesn't mean he'll get out, let alone actually get his case heard by the courts."

Archer stared over at me with a baffled expression on his face. "Since when do you pay attention in American Government?" he asked incredulously.

"Since I decided I wasn't happy with my B in that class," I said, also thankful that I'd stopped to talk to Mr. Monroe after class earlier. I'd thought about talking to my dad, too, but I couldn't think of a way to bring up the subject of the appeal without having to bring Archer and his family's past into the mix. "And look how useful it's proving to be."

Thinking back, I probably could've asked my dad for extra help, but that would have been one insanely awkward tutoring session. I was scraping by well enough on my own.

"People find ways to manipulate the law all the time," Archer pointed out. "Who's to say my father won't get lucky?"

"I wouldn't be so sure of that."

Archer and I both jumped at the sound of Mr. Van Auken's voice and turned to see him standing in the kitchen doorway, Regina beside him.

"What's that supposed to mean?" Archer said, somehow managing to keep the cynicism out of his voice.

"St. Pierre won't be getting out. I'll make sure of it."

Despite Mr. Van Auken's confidence, Archer did not appear to be placated. "And where's the proof?"

"Archer," Regina said admonishingly. "You shouldn't—"

"Because," Mr. Van Auken said. "The evidence against

your father was airtight. Fingerprints on the murder weapon. Copy of the house key in his pocket. Bloodstains on his clothing matching Christopher Morales's. If there was somehow a discrepancy in the case that would cause the courts to grant your father an appeal, he'd have to have an extremely good lawyer on his side. But there's not. He's going to be denied."

He turned to Regina before Archer had the chance to respond and said, "You have my card. You know how to reach me if you have any questions or concerns, al right?"

"Right." Regina gave a nod, a tight smile. "Thank you, Mr. Van Auken."

"Call me Rick, please. I'll keep you updated as much as I can, but I'm confident this will have a positive outcome."

Mr. Van Auken shook Regina's hand, gave me another smile and a curt nod in Archer's direction, and left the coffee shop, out into the still-falling snow.

The three of us looked at each other as the door swung shut.

"So, um . . ." Regina took a deep breath, crossing her arms tightly over her chest. She was pale and her face had this pinched look, but she seemed . . . okay. *Okay* was the best word I could come up with. "Well, that wasn't too pleasant of a conversation, but it wasn't awful. Things might be fine."

"Well, that's just fantastic," Archer said sarcastically. "But, hey, did you know that Van Auken is Hadley's father's firm partner?"

"What?" Regina looked at me in shock. "Really?"

I couldn't keep back an aggravated sigh, shooting an annoyed look at Archer. "Yes, but they made partner years after St. Pierre's trial."

"That's . . . quite unusual," Regina said, frowning. "But rather convenient, I suppose."

"*Exactly*," I said, giving Archer a pointed look. "I could help, if you needed me. Find out more about what's going on, maybe."

"He's not taking this very well, is he?" I said, looking over to Regina as Archer walked back into the kitchen. I heard dishes being dumped into the sink louder than necessary.

She shook her head, taking a sip of her tea. "No. Anything to do with his biological father sends him over the edge. It makes him . . . very angry."

That much was obvious. But I could hardly blame him for that. He had every right in the world to be angry at St. Pierre.

"And as much as I despise even thinking about my ex," Regina began with a sigh, "Mr. Van Auken brought up valid points. It's going to be hard to convince myself of it, believe me, but . . . I think the chances of him getting out really are slim to none."

"Good," I said, forcing myself to smile. "I'm glad."

Regina's face took on a wary expression as she set her mug of tea on the counter, turning to the cash register. "Well. We should probably get to closing, then."

It was clear Regina had no desire to continue the conversation, so we got down to closing, working in silence.

This time I didn't feel the need to break the silence with a never-ending flow of questions. I could only hope that tomorrow would be a better day and everything having to do with St. Pierre's trial would be all but forgotten. Mr. Van Auken was one of the city's most prestigious lawyers. He knew his stuff. He wouldn't have come all this way just to dash Regina's hopes. The evidence was all stacked against St. Pierre. Even Havoc couldn't mess with something as firm and unshakeable as the truth.

CHAPTER 25

A Sudden Test— 5 Days Until

Archer was quiet most of the next day. He barely talked at lunch, keeping his head buried in a book. He didn't even eat any of my fries. I couldn't blame him for being so distant. I suspected his thoughts still remained with his family and the fact that his father was trying to get out of prison.

I was actually looking forward to discussing *The Great Gatsby*—which I still hadn't finished—in sixth-period English, if only to get my mind off everything else. But when I got to class, the room surprisingly was empty. I checked the time on the clock above the door and saw that there were still five minutes to go before class started. But shouldn't at least one person be here by now? Like perhaps my teacher, Miss Graham?

I pulled my copy of *The Great Gatsby* and my notebook out of my bag, wondering why I was the first one here. That never happened. Usually I beat the tardy bell by seconds. I flipped to a clean page in my notebook and started doodling with my favorite purple pen.

Surely only a minute or two had passed, but I found myself growing tired, like I was being dragged beneath the surface of some thick blanket of fog the more I covered the page in doodles. The nights I spent tossing and turning were finally catching up to me. All I wanted to do was close my eyes and rest my head on my desk and sleep for a very long time. I felt my head begin to droop, my eyes were sliding shut, and then I was abruptly yanked back to the present when a hand descended on my shoulder, a quiet, silken voice murmuring, "Well, hello, my dear Hadley."

I let out a yelp at Havoc's proximity, and I tried to scramble up out of my seat to get away from him, but his grip on my shoulder was impossibly tight. I looked around, wondering why no one seemed to notice Havoc hovering over me, but the desks were still empty, as if my classmates had never showed up. Nobody else was in the room but the two of us.

"What are you doing here?" I snapped, my voice trembling despite how hard I was trying to appear calm. "Let me go!"

Havoc ignored me, making his way around to lean across the desk, still tightly gripping my shoulder. "I came to offer you a chance to reconsider your deal with Death," he said in polite tones. "Because you've had an eventful week, haven't you?"

That was an understatement. This had been the most confusing, frightening week of my life.

"It's been . . . okay," I said.

"Okay? That's not the word I would use. You know what my favorite part was?" Havoc said, his lips pulling up into an eerie smile. "Watching you trip and hit that pretty little head of yours when you fell down those stairs. Seeing the look on Archer's face when he thought you were *seriously* injured. Did you like my little note I left for you?"

"Loved it," I said, forcing myself to be calm.

"What's it going to take to change your mind, hmm?

Perhaps a little mishap the next time Victoria takes the train? Maybe a gentleman who just can't help but think Regina is *so* pretty? Oh, and Rosie is such a sweet little girl, isn't she? How well do you think Archer would take it if something happened to his sister?" He leaned even closer. "Because someone *is* going to die, Hadley. You can let that someone be Archer, or I can make it be someone else. Really, it makes no difference to me."

The words were out of my mouth before I could stop to consider the consequences of what I was saying. "If you're going to talk like that, I should be the one you're coming after. Not Victoria. Not Regina. Definitely not Rosie."

Havoc raised an eyebrow, looking pleasantly surprised at this. "Is that so?"

Since I'd already said it, and I couldn't take the words back—I didn't even want to. I nodded, gritting my teeth.

"Well, I do believe you've just given me permission to raise the stakes," Havoc said pleasantly. "At first I didn't understand why Death would offer a little girl like you a contract, but I'm beginning to see it now. You do put up a fight, don't you?"

I tasted blood in my mouth, and I realized I'd been biting my lip. "I'll never stop putting up a fight, either," I said when I finally found my voice.

"Oh, I'm counting on that," Havoc said, and there was a disturbing glint in his eyes. "That's what's going to make this so much fun."

I didn't get the chance to respond.

I blinked, and the next second I was watching Miss Graham scribbling out a plot diagram on the board, chattering away about the complex relationship between Jay Gatsby and Daisy

Buchanan. My classmates were seated around me, only one-third of them paying attention. It was just like any other class on any other day.

"Um. Miss Graham?" I tried raising my hand, but my arm felt too heavy to move.

Miss Graham stopped in the middle of her sentence, glancing over her shoulder at me. "Yes? Hadley?"

"Can I, ah, be excused please? I don't feel very well."

There must have been something in my face that showed I was about to puke, because Miss Graham immediately nodded, waving her book at the door. "Go ahead."

I shoved my things into my bag and bolted for the door. There were a few girls hanging out in the girls' bathroom down the hall, but I paid them no mind and raced for the nearest stall.

I didn't throw up like I thought I would, and instead slipped to the floor when my legs gave out. I stuck my head between my knees, sucking in air, wishing my stomach would stop rolling.

"Hey, are you all right?" I heard knocking on the stall door I was still leaning up against. "You've, um, been in there awhile. We heard groaning."

"Yeah, I'm good," I called out weakly. "Just a little sick to my stomach."

The stranger said a few words wishing me well, and then I heard the sound of footsteps and the bathroom door swinging shut.

My head spun as I pulled myself up to my knees, grabbing at the toilet paper dispenser for support. I gave myself a few moments to get my breathing steady again before grabbing my bag and leaving the stall.

I had no desire to return to Miss Graham's class. I didn't want to ever step foot in that room again. So I wandered down the empty hallway, thankful the period hadn't let out yet. When I reached my locker, I wished I actually had decided to go back to class. I read the four lines written in black Sharpie on my locker door, my pulse racing.

Since you liked the first note so much,
I thought a second one would be just the touch.
Accidents often happen in a city like this,
And we both know there are people you're going to miss.

Archer was snapping his fingers in front of my face, and I realized he'd been saying my name over and over for a good minute now. "Hadley, are you even *listening* to me?"

"What? Oh. Sorry."

My voice sounded faraway, exactly where my thoughts were. I'd taken a short shift at Mama Rosa's tonight, just about three hours, and it was turning out to be my worst one yet. I'd been unable to concentrate at all, still reliving my confrontation with Havoc at school. I even went as far as to go snooping around the coffeehouse just to make sure he wasn't here.

I had a hard time tearing my eyes away from Archer. I watched his every move as he worked, repeatedly telling myself that he was alive, perfectly fine, going about his evening just like everybody else, and that it was going to stay that way.

When Victoria had shown up a while ago, I'd given Rosie a big hug and had been afraid to let her go for several moments.

It'd been hard not to throw my arms around Regina when I first saw her too. Havoc's warnings had burned themselves into my mind, impossible to remove. I couldn't stand the thought of being the cause if something were to happen to a little girl as sweet as Rosie—and the same went for the rest of Archer's family.

"I told you to take these muffins out of the oven ten minutes ago," Archer was saying, wrenching open the oven door, using an oven mitt to pull out a tray of obviously ruined blueberry muffins. "What is with you tonight? I swear, you're even worse than usual. And would you quit tugging at those things!"

He dropped the tray of muffins on the counter and snatched at my wrist. Before I could even protest, he was unraveling the ghost beads, revealing the twisted little number 5 on my wrist. There were electric little pinpricks dancing across my skin at his touch, making me squirm. Whatever he'd been about to say died in his throat as he looked at me in confusion.

"What's so important about the number five?" Archer asked quietly.

Five days to make sure you don't kill yourself come next Tuesday, I nearly said.

That's all I had left. Five days to make sure Archer was still with me when my contract was up. And now with Havoc in the picture, I couldn't bring myself to think of the future without wanting to burst into tears. But I also couldn't see myself abandoning this now. It was impossible, not even an option. Come hell or high water, I was going to see this through. I *had* to.

"That's how long I need to study each day for finals," I blurted, snatching my arm back, quickly slipping the ghost beads back around my wrist so the number 5 was hidden.

"Oh, come on." Archer snorted. "You really expect me to buy that? What is it really for?"

"Kids, up front!" Regina's voice carried into the kitchen. "We have customers!"

"Try not to burn the place to the ground," Archer threw out as he moved past me out of the kitchen.

"Let's hope not," I muttered.

CHAPTER 26

Potluck Smarts— 4 Days Until

Archer was reading a dog-eared copy of *Hamlet* at lunch the next day and didn't look up until I slapped my geometry test down on the table in front of him.

"Behold," I said. "Observe my brilliance."

Archer glanced away from *Hamlet* long enough to give my geometry test a cursory glance, and then did a double take. "*You* got an A?"

"Told you I could do it!" I exclaimed, feeling a little offended at the disbelieving look on his face.

A slow smile started to work its way over his face as he flipped through my test, checking over my answers. "And you even used the right formulas too. That's my girl."

I immediately felt my cheeks flood with heat as I sat down, unwrapping my roast beef sandwich. It took Archer only a second to figure out why my face was now the color of a brick, and he quickly tossed aside my test and pulled my tray of fries toward him. I was pretty sure Archer was incapable of blushing, but he did look slightly embarrassed.

He'd just called me *his girl*. I had the sudden, uncontrollable urge to start giggling.

"Think you could wait until I actually sit down next time before you steal my food?" I said, eager to steer the conversation in a different direction.

"Yeah, yeah," Archer said distractedly as he picked up *Hamlet* again. "You never finish your fries anyway."

"Because I leave them for you, you dope."

He looked up from his book, a startled expression on his face. "What?" The way he seemed so surprised by this was odd.

"What do you mean, what?" I said, frowning. "Did you not forget that I pay you in fries in exchange for geometry tutoring? And, anyway, I'm trying to expand your diet. Gotta give the lunch meat and cherry Danishes a break, right?"

Archer kept silent as he ate a few more fries, his shocked look turning into an amused one. "Fries are bad for you."

"Yeah, like cherry Danishes are so much better," I said, taking a sip of my water.

"Obviously cherry Danishes are better." Archer set aside *Hamlet*, snatching another bunch of fries. He chewed for a long moment before he spoke. "Hey. What are you doing tonight?"

"Nothing," I answered slowly. "Why?"

"My family is apparently just dying to see you again," Archer said, "so I was told to tell you that you should come to a potluck dinner at our parish tonight."

He spoke in a rush, trying to get it over with as soon as possible, and it took me a moment to process what he said.

"You were told . . . Wait, what?" I pushed my sandwich to the side, my attention focused solely on Archer now. "You want me to come to a church dinner tonight?"

"You have no idea the impression you made on my relatives."

What a golden opportunity. I hadn't been scheduled to work tonight, so now I didn't even have to coerce Archer into hanging out after school.

"Archer, I would *love* to come to a church dinner with you," I said, trying and failing to keep the grin off my face.

"Okay, yeah, you don't need to look so smug about it," Archer said, looking skeptical.

"What? I don't look smug," I said, biting the inside of my cheek to keep from laughing. "I love church and I love dinner. And I'm just happy to see all of your cousins again, and I—"

"You somehow managed to squeeze a job out of my mom, and now you're finally going to steal my family away from me, is that it? Was that your plan all along?"

"Hey! Sharing is caring!"

He took a handful of fries and grinned. "If you say so."

I was excited to go to the potluck at Archer's church. I really did want to spend more time with the Incitti family, and it sounded like fun. When I pestered Archer for more details, he told me the parish had this annual potluck in December to raise money for local charities during the Christmas season. Apparently, it was quite the event—Mama Rosa's was closing early for the day, and there would even be a live band there.

Not wanting to look frumpy, I pulled on a simple red dress with black leggings and ballet flats, followed by my jacket. I appraised my reflection in the mirror for a few moments before I decided I looked okay enough, then snatched my bag off the desk and left.

"Having a night out on the town?" Hanson asked as I walked out of the apartment building.

"Potluck dinner with a friend," I said.

"Is this the same friend you've been spending all your free time with?" he said with a wink.

"Yeah," I said, grinning. "Turns out we have a lot in common."

Maybe Archer and I didn't have the same interests—I would never do math for *fun*—but there was one major thing we both shared: we were both willing to do anything for the ones we loved. It hadn't taken me too long to figure that out.

Hanson flagged down a cab, and I quickly buckled myself in, giving the driver the church's address. I was meeting Archer and his family there, in the church gym. The event wasn't officially set to start until six, but with the way traffic was tonight, I doubted I would arrive on time.

When I got to the church, the gym doors were thrown open, light spilling out onto the pavement and a jazzy, fast-paced tune filling the night air. A few people were milling around by the entrance, soda or coffee drinks in hand as they greeted one another. I got a few smiles as I approached the doors. I purchased a ticket from the elderly couple sitting at a table just inside the doors, and walked farther into the gym, taking in the sights.

Numerous strands of Christmas lights were strung across the ceiling, casting a dim, golden glow over the floor. An array of brightly decorated Christmas trees were set up in a far corner, stacks of presents piled beneath them. Long rows of tables had all sorts of plates and crockpots and trays full of food set on display, and people were lined up to get their share.

I made my way through the tables of families laughing and eating together, searching for any familiar face. I was almost to the food line when I caught sight of Lauren DiRosario rushing toward me, a smile on her face.

"Hadley! I'm so glad you could come!" she said excitedly, gripping my shoulders. "I swear, I thought I was going to go insane if there wasn't another girl around."

I laughed. "Glad to be of help."

She linked her arm through mine and led me over to two tables that were occupied by the entirety of the Incitti family. Just like on Thanksgiving, I was bombarded with another round of squeezes and kisses and, "It's so great to see you again, Hadley!"

The only ones that were not present were Sofia, Ben, and their three children, who lived three hours away in Albany.

Archer didn't stand to greet me, but at least he smiled. He was slouched in his seat, picking at a plate of chicken and rice in front of him. I could tell by the expression on his face that his mind wasn't totally in the present.

"Hey," I said, dropping into the empty seat beside him.

He glanced up from his plate of food, opening his mouth to say something, but nothing came out. His eyes traveled me up and down for a moment, and he raised an eyebrow, saying, "Nice dress."

"Um." I yanked on the edges of my dress, suddenly feeling self-conscious. I was starting to wonder if I should have stuck with jeans and a T-shirt. "Thanks."

Archer blew out a sigh, dropping his fork, turning in his seat to lean closer to me. "After we eat, would you want to—"

"Hadley, c'mon! Come get some food with me!"

I was pulled out of my chair and tugged toward the food line with Rosie and Lauren before Archer would even finish his sentence. I shot a look at him over my shoulder, but he just gave me a smirk in return. One of the ladies working the food tables handed me a plate, and I piled it full with chicken and rice, mashed potatoes, biscuits, and a few scoops of fruit salad.

I was forced into a seat beside Lauren and Karin, a few chairs over from Archer, who was now having an animated discussion with Vittorio and Art about the Italian national soccer team. I listened to the easy chatter around the table as I ate, trying to put all that had happened over the past few days from my mind.

When I was with the Incitti family, it was easy to forget what brought me to Archer in the first place. It felt like I belonged here, with these people who treated me as if I were actually a member of their family. More to the point, I *liked* being with them all. I liked being with Archer. It was entirely screwed up that it had taken him ending his life to bring us together. If I had just gotten over my nerves and hadn't been such a wimp in freshman English, then maybe this wouldn't have happened at all.

"Attention, everyone!"

I looked up from my plate as Regina got to her feet, wine glass in hand, and the chatter around the table immediately died down. I didn't know what kind of announcement Regina was about to make, but I wondered if it had something to do with her ex-husband's appeal.

"So, I'm pretty sure it's no surprise that these have been a rough couple of days," she began, taking a deep, steadying breath. "Carlo was in an accident, and we found out my ex-husband made a request to appeal his sentencing."

"I hope that *jerk* never sees the light of day again," I heard Lauren mutter under her breath.

"Well, after speaking with the former assistant DA who oversaw the trial," Regina continued, beginning to smile, "we are very hopeful that the chances of my ex-husband being offered an appeal are slim to none."

Cheers and applause erupted around the table, loud enough to garner attention from half the people in the gym. It was well deserved, I thought. I glanced over at Archer as Regina took her seat after leaning over to hug her sister Karin. I could see he had a white-knuckled grip on his fork as he picked at the mashed potatoes on his plate, but the expression on his face was actually relaxed. That had to be a good thing.

Archer looked up then, catching my gaze, and the smallest of smiles pulled at his lips. Definitely a good thing.

When I'd eaten everything on my plate, I excused myself and made off in the direction of the desserts. When in doubt, always go for dessert. I grabbed another plate and dumped a handful of cookies on it, followed by a few squares of brownies, and a big piece of vanilla cake with pink buttercream frosting. This would absolutely upset my stomach, but Taylor liked to live by the saying *calories don't count during the holidays*, and I was definitely in agreement.

I forked off a bit of the cake and happily munched away as I returned to my seat. I only made it a few steps before Carlo suddenly appeared in front of me, a somewhat mischievous smile on his face. There were yellowing bruises on his face, and those dozen cuts were angry and red, but he otherwise looked as if he was well on his way to making a full recovery from the accident the other night.

"It's good to see you out of a hospital bed," I said, grinning. "How're you feeling?"

"Well, I'm just fabulous, Hadley, thanks for asking," he said before reaching over to snatch my desserts. He dumped the plate on a nearby table and wrapped an arm around my waist, steering me toward the dance floor.

"Carlo!" I yelped, gripping his forearm tightly. "Hey, wait! I wanted to finish that cake!"

"It can wait. I want to dance."

I gave up trying to make an escape, and instead let Carlo take the lead, placing a hand on his shoulder, my other hand in his own. "What are you doing?" I asked him, trying not to trip over my feet. "Trying to embarrass me?"

"Not at all," Carlo said smoothly. "Just trying to make my dear cousin jealous."

"He wouldn't get jealous over me," I insisted. I wanted to get off this dance floor as quickly as possible. "It's not like that."

"His girl dancing with another guy? Who wouldn't that make jealous?"

"I'm not his girl," I said, though I couldn't help remembering how Archer had just used that term at lunch earlier today.

Judging by the look on his face, Carlo obviously knew I was lying through my teeth. Then he gave a small sigh, and an unusually serious expression came over his face. I found it disconcerting that his charming smile wasn't in place. The cuts and bruises from the other night weren't helping.

"What is it?" I pressed when he remained silent.

"I'm not trying to sound rude, Hadley, but you don't know Archer like the rest of us do. You don't know how happy he used to be before Chris was killed."

I was taken aback by the abrupt change in conversation. Why was he bringing this up? "I know that," I said hesitantly. "Regina said the same thing."

I would never know that side of Archer, and I found it strangely painful. The person Archer had been back then was long gone. I doubted he would ever return. It was an unusual feeling, missing someone I'd never known.

"Because she's right," Carlo said. "You don't see the change in him that we're seeing. He's different. He's . . . happy. You should have seen the look on my grandma's face when she heard Archer laughing on Thanksgiving."

I kept my eyes fixed on my feet, trying to keep my mind from jumping to ridiculous theories about Archer and his happiness. It wasn't working. "And you think . . . you think I'm the reason he's happy?"

"I think you're playing a big part in it."

Wasn't that what I'd been trying to do from the very beginning of my twenty-seven days?

"Don't doubt yourself," Carlo said, tugging me away from my distracting thoughts.

"I don't—"

"I just wanted to tell you that you shouldn't doubt what you are to Archer. Because you are something. And I love my cousin. I like seeing him happy. We all do."

A smile tugged at the corners of my mouth before I could stop it. I liked Carlo. He was typical for a guy his age the majority of the time, but he was also pretty perceptive. I could see myself being his friend.

"You see things," I said.

His devilish smirk returned. "So do you."

"But . . . Archer doesn't," I said as an afterthought.

"No," Carlo agreed. "He doesn't. But he sees you."

The song ended, and couples broke apart, clapping politely for the band. I stepped away from Carlo, and we both joined in clapping.

"Thank you, Carlo," I told him. "For the dance."

"Thank *you*, Hadley." I froze when he moved forward and pressed his lips against my cheek in a surprisingly affectionate gesture—one that didn't seem right for a fifteen-year-old guy. "Stick around, won't you?"

He shot me one of his special grins and wandered off, leaving me behind on the dance floor. I wasn't completely sure of what just happened, but I was glad I had gotten the chance to talk to Carlo. It was difficult to doubt the sincerity of his words. I was going to do my best to take them to heart.

I had to force myself to move and leave the dance floor when the next song started and couples began to dance again. I went on a hunt for the bathroom, only to run into Archer the moment I stepped out into the small hallway off the side of the gym.

"Sorry," I said, taking a step back. "I didn't see—"

"Dance with me."

That was the last thing I was expecting him to say. I didn't dance. He didn't dance. Did he? "What?"

"Dance with me," Archer repeated. The expression on his face was completely serious.

I couldn't wrap my mind around it. Why would Archer want to dance with me? Had Carlo actually succeeded in making him jealous?

"You'll dance with my cousin, but you won't dance with me? Gee, thanks, Hadley."

I laughed without thinking. "I'll step on your feet," I warned him. "Just ask Carlo."

Archer's lips turned upward in a grin. "I've got big feet."

He laced his fingers through mine and pulled me through the hallway, back to the gym and out onto the dance floor while I spluttered in embarrassment. The band had struck up a slow, sweet tune that sounded as if it had come straight out of the forties.

Archer wrapped an arm around my waist and pulled me closer, taking my hand in his free one. It was distracting how warm his skin was against mine. I was positive he could feel how hard my heart was pounding from our close proximity. I'd already tripped over his feet twice, but I was going along with it. It was nice, even. We were together, and for that moment, it was enough.

It Happened
One Night

27

It had already been snowing for quite some time when I walked out of the gym after saying my good-byes to the Incitti family. Archer and I had only danced that one dance, but I couldn't help the giddy feeling that bubbled up inside every time I thought of his hand in mine. I raised my arm to hail a cab, but stopped when I heard a voice call my name.

"Hadley? Wait up a second! Hadley!"

I glanced over my shoulder to see Archer jogging toward me. "Did I forget something?" I said as he came to a stop in front of me.

"Yeah," Archer answered. "Me. I'm going to take you home."

For a second, I thought I misheard him. "You're going to take me home," I repeated.

"Last time I checked, you're not in need of a hearing aid," he said dryly. "You heard me. I'm taking you home."

I didn't protest. Even if I wanted to, I wouldn't have been able to find the words.

"You know, this is feeling awfully like a date, Morales," I said as we began to head down the street in search of a cab. "Having dinner, you asking me to dance, and now you taking me home."

Archer laughed. "When I take you on a date, Jamison, my family isn't going to be involved in any way whatsoever."

I somehow managed to put one foot in front of the other, even though my heart gave a ridiculous leap in my chest and my breath caught in my throat. He said *when* I take you on a date. Not *if.* It was impossible to squash the feeling of hope washing over me.

"Well, regardless," I said, hoping my voice sounded normal. "Thank you."

Archer shrugged, tucking his hands into his pockets as we walked along. There were hardly any cars driving by on the street, or other people out on the sidewalks, and it seemed almost unnatural that there was such a lack of noise in New York. Snowflakes were falling in soft waves, blanketing the city in a cover of white. It was like a dreamland.

When we finally did catch a cab, we had walked three blocks. I gave the driver my address, and Archer and I settled in for the ride. It passed faster than it would have had there been traffic, and for that, I was thankful. I was anxious to get out of the car. I let my hand rest on the seat beside me, and it was growing increasingly difficult not to just reach over and lace my fingers through Archer's.

I let Archer pay the fare, noticing the dirty look he shot my way when I reached for my wallet, and stepped out onto the sidewalk. Hanson had already gone home for the night, otherwise I would've enjoyed introducing him to Archer.

The night doorman pulled open the door of the apartment complex for us with a polite nod, and we walked across the lobby, toward the elevator. I kept a watchful eye on Archer as we rode up to the seventh floor. I couldn't help but feel as if there were unsaid things in the air between the two of us. What exactly did tonight mean? Something had obviously changed. He had to know that as well as I did.

I pulled my keys out of my coat pocket as the elevator doors slid open, and Archer and I walked down the hallway to 7E in silence.

"So." My hand stilled as I slid the key into the lock. I was too nervous to look over my shoulder at Archer. "Thanks . . . for, um, taking me home," I said weakly.

"I'm not a total jerk," Archer said teasingly. "My mother raised me to be a gentleman, thank you very much. I know better than to let a girl walk home alone at night."

I glanced over at him with a wide grin. "Could've fooled me. Do you want to come in?"

The words flew from my lips before I even knew what I was saying. I didn't want this night to be over just yet, and even if it meant throwing myself out there and possibly making a fool of myself, I'd do it just to spend more time with Archer.

Confusion was plastered across his face. "What?"

I sucked in a deep breath and did my best to smile. "Do you want to come in? There's always some good movie on one of the classic channels this time of night."

It took a moment of thought on his part, and in those seconds I thought for sure he was going to say no, but then he grinned. "As long as you have popcorn."

"I'm sure that can be arranged."

I unlocked the door and pushed it open, reaching in to turn the lights on. Archer followed cautiously after me into the apartment, peering around with a shrewd look in his eyes. He'd barely stepped over the threshold before he was saying, "You're joking."

"What?" I set my bag on the coffee table, looking at him curiously. "Is there something—"

"You live *here*?" He gestured around at the living room, the leather couches and the flat-screen TV, the floor-to-ceiling windows, as if that was the only explanation I needed.

"Um, yeah," I said uncomfortably. "My mom has a flair for decorating. Sometimes I wonder why she went into business instead of interior design."

Archer continued to stand just past the doorway, long enough for me to worry that he was actually going to make a break for it, his eyes still roaming around the apartment. "Well," he finally said, sounding awkward. "I guess you really do work for us because you like us. Not because you need the money."

Finally, I thought, feeling elated. *I like* you, *you idiot*. I was hoping he recognized that little difference in the equation.

I made two bags of microwave popcorn as requested, and we settled on the couch together, the black-and-white film *It Happened One Night* playing on the TV. It might not have been what our classmates were doing on a Friday night, but I didn't think either of us cared. We'd definitely gotten the better end of the deal.

When I opened my eyes, the movie was still playing on the TV. Archer was asleep on the opposite side of the couch, his head pillowed on his arm, the other covering part of his face, his breathing slow and steady. I sat up, pushing my hair out of my face, looking at the time on the cable box. We'd barely been out for half an hour, but I guess we'd both been more tired than we thought.

"Archer?"

He didn't budge.

"Archer?" I repeated, this time louder.

Nothing.

"Are you awake?" I said, moving up onto my knees to lean over him.

"I am now." He sucked in a heavy breath and opened his eyes, propping himself up onto an elbow. He took in his surroundings for a moment before glancing over at me with a frown. "We fall asleep?"

"Yeah," I said. "It's almost eleven."

"Huh," Archer said.

I was surprised at his uncaring attitude toward the hour. "Your mother and grandmother probably aren't going to be very happy with you."

"Probably," he said. But he smiled at me, this sort of breath-taking smile I'd never seen before. "They'll deal. They knew I was taking you home. Besides, it's not like I'm out in a shady part of town."

"Oh, yeah," I said, attempting a sarcastic laugh. "Because the Upper East Side is so exciting." I untangled myself from him and swung my legs over the side of the couch, getting to my feet. "But, um. Unless you'd like to meet my parents, it'd probably be a good idea if you head for home."

"Hmm." Archer pulled himself to his feet, ruffling his hair as he stretched his arms above his head. "They that bad, huh?"

"No," I said, taking the time to think about it. "But I think they just assumed that if I hadn't brought a guy home by now, I never would. I'd rather avoid that awkward conversation, if you don't mind."

"Oh." Archer looked a little uncomfortable. "Right."

He slipped on his shoes and pulled on his jacket, making his way to the front door. I followed after him, hands clasped behind my back, unsure of what to say. "I guess . . . I mean, I'll see you tomorrow," he said, his hand on the doorknob as he turned back to me.

"Yeah," I said. "At noon, when my shift starts."

"Okay, then."

I wasn't quite sure what made me do it. Before I could think that maybe it wasn't a good idea, I stepped closer and wrapped my arms around him, hugging him tightly.

He didn't immediately pull away, like he had that night at the hospital. Instead, he slowly and carefully slid his arms around my waist in return, his cheek pressed against my hair. His stance was still awkwardly rigid, and I got the feeling he wasn't used to physical contact, but this was a much better hug under much better circumstances.

Our embrace might have gone on a little longer than necessary, and eventually I had to remind myself to let him go and take a step back.

"Ah, right. Um." Archer cleared his throat, his eyes fixed on the ceiling, like he was too embarrassed to look at me. That was new. "See you tomorrow, then."

I seemed to have lost the ability to think rationally, and I decided to go along with it. I didn't want to analyze my every action right then, like I'd been doing since my twenty-seven days first began.

My fingers curled into the front of Archer's jacket, and I gently pulled him toward me, closing the distance between us. It was obvious what my intentions were. I was going to kiss him, and he did nothing to stop me.

This kiss was nothing like our first in that hallway in the hospital the other night. I didn't think either of us were particularly skilled, but every ounce of uncertainty we'd shared before had disappeared. It became all the more difficult to breathe when Archer's hand slid around the back of my neck, tilting my face up to his.

I couldn't say that I'd kissed many guys before, but Archer had to be the best. I was sure of it. There was this weightless sort of feeling bubbling under my skin as we kissed. I could feel my pulse thrumming in my ears. Had it not been for the sound of my parents' voices on the other side of the front door, I doubted I would've stopped kissing him anytime soon.

"*Crap.*"

I quickly pulled away from Archer, sucking in deep breaths as I ran my fingers through my hair, attempting to smooth the tangles his fingers had caused. Archer was watching me with an expression that was both amused and horrified, and whispered, "Is that your parents?"

"Yeah," I muttered. "Sorry, but it looks like you'll be—"

My apology was cut short when the locks tumbled and the front door swung open, and both my parents strolled inside. It wasn't uncommon for them to arrive home at the same time most nights; their offices were both fairly close to each other. They'd definitely never come home and found me with a boy, though.

"Hey, Hadley," my dad said, giving me a tired smile as he

pulled off his jacket, heading for the coat closet. He'd somehow walked past Archer without even realizing it.

"Hi, Dad," I said quickly. "This is—"

"I got your text from earlier. How was that potluck?" my mom asked, still glued to her phone as she dropped her purse on the coffee table.

"It was a lot of fun. Great food. But this is—"

Archer stepped forward at that moment, loudly clearing his throat, offering a hand to my mother. "Hi. I'm Archer."

My mom and dad stood there for a few beats of tense silence, staring first at me, then at Archer, confused expressions on their faces. Up until this point in my life, I was positive I'd never experienced something so awkward. Now would have been a good moment for a hole to open in the floor and swallow me up.

"Nice to meet you," my mother finally said, sounding distant as she shook Archer's hand.

"You must be Hadley's friend from work," my dad said, moving forward to shake Archer's hand next.

"We met freshman year of high school, but yeah," Archer said. I was stunned at how smooth and confident he came across as, smiling politely at my parents. "My mom owns the coffeehouse we both work at."

"Is that so?"

My dad made polite chitchat with Archer for a few minutes about how the business was going, and my mom just stood there, as lost for words as I was. This was just *weird*. I had never imagined Archer ever meeting my parents. He belonged to an entirely different part of my life, and to have him suddenly introduced to my mom and dad, who seemed to live on a different planet more often than not, was just jarring, to say the least.

"Hey, Dad? Um. I think Archer mentioned a little bit ago that he needs to be getting home now," I interjected, finally having worked up enough nerve to say something.

"Oh, right," my dad said, checking the time on his cell phone. "It is getting rather late."

"It was a pleasure to meet you both," Archer said politely to my parents, smiling.

"You too," my dad said, shaking Archer's hand again. "You're welcome back anytime, of course."

I tried to rid myself of the shock I felt as I quickly pulled on my shoes, ushering Archer toward the door.

"Well, that was awkward," I said as soon as I shut the front door shut. "I'm so sorry, I didn't—"

"Nah," Archer said with a shrug. "Your parents actually aren't that bad."

I hadn't been expecting to hear something like that from Archer, but it was a relief.

"Your mom looks like she smelled something rank, though," he added as an afterthought, smirking.

"I know," I agreed. "She always looks like that when she's caught off guard. The corporate business life will do that to you, I think."

I accompanied Archer down the hallway to the elevator, suddenly feeling very nervous. Archer and I had more or less just made out, and neither of us were saying a word about it.

"Well, I guess I'll see you tomorrow?" I said as the elevator doors slid open and Archer stepped inside.

"Yeah," Archer said, clearing his throat. "I'll see you tomorrow."

He smiled—actually, genuinely *smiled*—as he gave me

a two-fingered salute, and then the doors slid shut and he was gone.

I returned to the apartment, anxious to get the interrogation that was sure to come my way over with. The second I shut the door behind me, my mother stood up from the couch and asked, "Are we going to need to have a talk about having boys in the apartment?"

It took everything in my power not to burst out laughing.

Human Weaknesses— 3 Days Until

CHAPTER

28

I was a little *too* early for my shift at the coffeehouse the next day. Probably because I didn't want to sit around doing nothing, but more likely it was because I was desperate to see Archer again. Rather than bracing myself for nightmares of Havoc before falling asleep last night, I played that kiss over and over again in my mind. It was a much better alternative. I was worried it would be a little obvious that I was only too eager to repeat the experience.

"You're a little early," Archer noted as I strolled through the back door and into the kitchen a half hour before noon.

"Just wanted to get out of the apartment, I guess," I said casually as I shrugged out of my jacket and hung my things on one of the hooks beside the door. "It's a nice day."

Archer peered out the small window above the kitchen sink. "It's snowing."

"Right."

He set the tray full of cold-cut sandwiches he'd been pulling out of the fridge on the counter and turned to me, crossing his arms over his chest. There was this mischievous-looking grin on his face. "That desperate to spend time with me, Jamison?"

It was a question he'd asked in jest before, to which I'd always answered with sarcasm or annoyance. Today, my answer was going to be a little different.

"Yeah," I said. "That sounds about right."

Archer looked momentarily caught off guard at my response, but then his grin returned full force, and he reached out to wrap an arm around my waist to pull me up against him. I wasn't sure who made the first move exactly, but the resulting kiss was glorious.

"Is . . . this going to become a regular occurrence?" I asked breathlessly when we broke apart.

He looked perplexed at the question, and his answer was slow and carefully thought out. "I don't know. I want it to be. I think you're the most annoying girl I've ever met, but I never thought kissing you would be so much— Did you seriously just *pinch* yourself?"

"Sorry. I wanted to make sure I wasn't dreaming."

I was relieved that this definitely was *not* a dream. Archer wanted me—so far as I knew just to kiss, but that was a start, right? It wasn't like I was complaining either.

Archer let me go with a huff of laughter. "I finally find a girl I like making out with, and she also likes to pinch herself. Lucky me. But since you're here, you might as well start helping."

I laughed too as I went to the sink, pushing up my sleeves so I could wash my hands while Archer carted the tray of sandwiches to the pastry case. I twisted off the faucet and dried my hands with a paper towel, watching the falling snow outside.

I just about leapt a foot in the air, swallowing a scream, when I saw black letters beginning to appear on the window in front of me, like someone invisible was crouched on the counter, writing out a note with a black marker.

It sounded like I was hyperventilating as I read the finished message:

I have to tell you, this has been fun
And soon we're going to be done.
So get ready to face all you fear—
The end of this game is drawing near.

This was clearly another message courtesy of Havoc, and, like the previous ones, I had no idea what it was supposed to mean, other than Havoc was going to ramp up his efforts before this was over. I reread the note what felt like a hundred times, mouthing the words.

"Hadley!" Archer's voice snapped me out of my reverie. "Could you possibly give me a hand out here?"

"Coming!" I hollered back.

I quickly scrambled for another paper towel, got it wet, and scrubbed at the window until the message was no longer visible.

An unsettling calm had descended over the coffeehouse.

It was quiet. The few customers we did have were lost in the separate worlds that their books or electronics provided and didn't say much. It should have been a relief not to be running around filling drink orders or doling out bowls of piping-hot tomato soup, and maybe accidentally ending up wearing some of it.

Instead I was feeling . . . uncomfortable.

When I wasn't pulling loose threads off my apron, I was rubbing my fingers beneath my bracelet and across the numbers tattooed on my forearm. Looking at the gaping space where my missing numbers were made me feel hollow inside. I was in the final countdown now—just three days left. And Havoc knew it.

I glanced over my shoulder when I heard footsteps on the tiles in the kitchen, and Regina came walking out, looking considerably happier than she had in days. She was wearing clothes that were a little fancier than her regular modest attire, and her hair was brushed to the side in a pretty twist.

"My brother and sister are taking me out," she said by way of explanation. "Keep my mind off things. Have some fun. Even my mother is coming."

"That's great," I said, smiling. "You deserve a night off."

Regina smiled and squeezed my shoulder, and then suddenly looked nervous. "You'll be all right here, won't you? Just you and Archer and Rosie?"

"Of course," I said. "It's almost closing time anyway. And Rosie usually listens if Archer is in charge."

"Stop fretting, Ma," I heard Archer say as he exited the kitchen, handing Regina her jacket and handbag. "You're supposed to be taking the night off. I've closed plenty of times. I know the drill."

Regina nodded as she slipped into her coat, but she still didn't look convinced. "Well, still. Call if you need anything. And make sure your sister is in bed by eight, okay?"

"Yeah, I know what time Rosie goes to bed too."

I heard a series of loud, stomping footfalls, and then Victoria appeared in the kitchen doorway, nudging Archer to the side. "Out of my way, boy. Are you ready to go, Regina?"

"Sure," Regina said, attempting a confident smile. "Let's go."

Rosie suddenly appeared, squeezing herself through Archer's legs to get to Regina, complaining that she hadn't said good-bye yet. We accompanied Regina and Victoria to the front door, giving hugs and orders to have a good time.

Archer glanced at the clock on the mantel as the door swung shut after Regina and Victoria. "Half hour till closing."

"I think we can survive until then," I said.

"Debatable," Archer said. "Would you like to start closing, or would you rather look after that little devil?"

He was referring to Rosie, who was currently attempting to grab one of the leftover sprinkled doughnuts out of the pastry case.

"I'll go ahead and start cleaning up," I said.

The customers began to trickle out as closing time drew near. I went around the tables, collecting dirty mugs and bowls, dumping them in the large plastic bin we kept behind the counter. Archer followed after me, wiping down each of the tables, while Rosie plopped herself down on one of the couches, trying to read a chapter book.

"Make sure those are left in the fridge for the deliveryman tomorrow," Archer said, pointing to a box of leftover pastries. "I'm going to get started on these dishes."

"Sure thing, boss," I said.

"Hey, wait for me!" Rosie called, leaping off the couch.

"You said I could put the soapy thing in the dishwasher this time, Archer!" She dashed around the counter after Archer, looking thrilled at the prospect of dish soap.

"You're right," Archer said. "I did say that. But you actually have to help me put the dishes in the dishwasher this time, Rosie."

Rosie sighed and grumbled, "Fine," under her breath, sounding a bit too much like her older brother.

After putting the box of pastries in the fridge, I went around the floor to flip the chairs upside down and stack them on the tables.

I was cleaning out the espresso grounds when there was a loud CRASH! from the kitchen.

It was like Thanksgiving night was happening all over again. A part of me expected to be greeted with the same awful sight of Regina sobbing into her hands as I bounded into the other room.

I surveyed the scene in front of me and put two and two together as quickly as possible. Rosie was a mess amongst a shower of broken glass on the floor. There were shallow cuts all over her hands that were leaking blood. She must have tripped on her way to the dishwasher and broken a few glasses on the way down.

"Sweetheart, are you okay?" I asked, bending down beside her, brushing shards of glass off her lap. "Did you fall?"

Rosie ignored me, looking up at Archer with tears dripping down her cheeks. "Archer?" Her voice came out as a whimper.

Except there was . . . something wrong with Archer. He was clutching at the counter behind him, his eyes wide and fixated on Rosie's bleeding hands. His face had drained of color and he was as white as a sheet, his lips trembling. I could hear his breath coming in short, quick gasps.

"Archer?" Rosie said again, reaching out a hand toward him.

She hadn't actually touched him, but Archer leapt back as if he had just been shocked. Rosie started crying even harder.

"Are you okay?" I said slowly, even though it was obvious he was not. "Archer, you . . ."

His eyes hadn't moved from Rosie's hands. It occurred to me then what was wrong: Archer couldn't stand the sight of blood.

When he finally spoke after moments of a near-suffocating silence, his voice was oddly high pitched. "I can't . . . Just . . . the blood . . . I have to . . . You need to . . ."

He turned and stumbled his way from the kitchen, through the back door, and headed outside, slamming the door shut behind him.

"Hey, Rosie, it's okay," I said, reaching over to scoop her up into my arms, grateful she was pretty light for a five-year-old. "It's fine. I'm going to get you cleaned up, okay?"

"But I don't want you," she sniffled into my shoulder. "I want Archer."

"I know, sweetheart, but Archer's not feeling too good right now," I said, choosing to ignore the lump in my throat that formed at hearing her say that. "You'll see him later, I promise. He just needs some fresh air."

I quickly made my way up the stairs and into the family's apartment, flicking on the hallway light as I neared the bathroom. I set Rosie down on the counter and started rummaging around in the medicine cabinet, looking for Band-Aids and something I could use to clean her cuts. I found a couple of stray Band-Aids and a tube of Neosporin that I set aside to use until after I managed to coax Rosie into washing her hands with warm water and soap.

She was still sniffling as I gently dried her hands with a towel. The cuts didn't look too bad once the blood had been washed away, and thankfully no pieces of glass had been left behind. I dabbed some Neosporin over the wounds and stuck on a couple of Band-Aids.

Then I carried Rosie from the bathroom to the living room and settled her on the couch, wrapping the thick afghan draped over the arm of the couch around her. I grabbed the TV remote and turned on some cartoons, hoping they would provide a distraction for a while so I could check on Archer.

"I'm going to get Archer," I told Rosie. "You just stay here and watch some TV. Yell if you need anything, okay?"

Rosie nodded, already hunkered down beneath the afghan and fully entranced in the show.

I left the apartment door open as wide as it would go and went back down to the kitchen. I didn't see Archer, but I hadn't expected to. He was probably still outside.

I decided to give it a few more minutes before I went to check on him.

Grabbing the broom and dustpan propped up against the fridge, I got to work sweeping up the mess of glass, dumping them in the trash once I was positive I had every last piece picked up. I made a cup of tea on impulse before heading outside in search of Archer. It seemed like something Regina would do, and it was freezing outside.

Archer was sitting on the curb beside the door, hunched over his knees, the fingers of his left hand laced in his hair.

It was oddly reminiscent of the night of my first shift at the coffeehouse, except everything had changed exponentially since then.

Archer didn't look over as I sat down beside him, placing the mug of tea between us. I settled myself back against the wall, folding my hands in my lap. I wasn't going to be the first one to speak. This had to be on Archer's terms. If he was even willing to talk about it, that was.

"You brought me tea?"

"It seemed like the thing to do."

"What are you, British?" His voice was strained, but I heard a note of gratefulness in there.

"Rosie's fine," I said, avoiding the subject of how he was doing. "She's watching TV."

Archer remained silent as he picked up the mug of tea and tossed back a swallow. His fingers curled around the mug tightly, shaking.

"So now you know, then, I guess," he muttered before taking another sip of tea.

"Know what?" I said softly.

"That all the rumors around school are lies. Big, bad Archer Morales isn't as scary as he seems. That he's actually just . . ."

"Human?"

"Human?" Archer let out a short bark of laughter, staring over at me in disbelief. "If being human means turning into a mess at the sight of blood, then sure, by all means, I guess I'm human, then."

"You say that as if it's a bad thing," I said. "Archer, people have fears. I think it'd be unnatural if you didn't."

"You don't get it, Hadley. It's more than that," he said with a groan, dropping his head back against the wall. "This isn't a fear. I'm not afraid of blood. It's me not being able to . . . to . . . It's like going back to that night when Chris was . . . You know what? I don't think I'm ever going to be able to explain what this is."

"Just try," I said before I could stop myself. "I want to understand, Archer."

He got to his feet and was tight-lipped for several moments.

"I never wanted you to see me like that. And especially not my little sister. She must hate me now."

I was quick to disagree. "Rosie doesn't hate you, Archer. She just wants you to make her feel better. You're her big brother. She could never hate you."

"Yeah, well, how can I even do that when I start hyper-ventilating from just seeing a few little cuts on her hands?" Archer's voice was steadily rising as he turned his back to me, still clutching the mug of tea. "What's going to happen next? Rosie'll fall and scrape her knee, and I'll have a panic attack because she just so happened to get a little bloodied up? Or I cut myself by accident cooking dinner one night and I pass out right in front of my mom? It's happened before."

I jumped in shock when Archer suddenly yanked back his arm and sent the mug hurtling toward the side of the coffee house. It smashed against the bricks, and the shattered pieces fell to the ground like tinkling glass.

The urge to pull him into my arms and never let go was stronger than I'd ever experienced, but I forced myself to stay still. When Archer turned back to face me, I saw that his cheeks were flushed and his eyes were oddly bright.

"Sorry," he muttered as he sat down beside me, resting his elbows on his knees, clasping his hands beneath his chin.

"Look, Archer . . ." I cautiously reached out to place a hand on his forearm, to give a comforting squeeze. "I know there isn't anything I can say that'll make this any better, but I think that . . . this, what you feel . . . it isn't totally strange. What you saw that night . . . something like that won't go away so easily. Maybe it never will. I mean, I'm not going to lie to you; I know that's probably the last thing you'd appreciate from someone. You just have to . . . to . . ."

I was floundering, trying to come up with something that would make sense, but I wasn't having any luck. But there was actually the faintest hint of a smile on Archer's face as he glanced over at me.

"Anybody ever tell you that you suck at the whole motivational speech thing?"

"Thanks," I said sourly. "I'm trying my best here."

"Must be, if you're still here after that little display."

I swallowed back the chuckle that almost escaped from me. "Maybe now you're finally getting that I'm here to stay?

Archer stared at me thoughtfully for a beat. "Maybe."

We sat on the curb in silence for a few more minutes, listening to the comforting sounds of the city all around us.

"We should probably head back inside," Archer said quietly. "At least check on Rosie."

"You're probably right," I agreed.

I got to my feet and bent down to scoop up the larger pieces of the broken mug, not wanting anyone to accidentally get hurt.

There was the sound of a car making its way down the alley beside the coffeehouse as Archer was opening the back door, and a van I dimly remembered belonging to Archer's aunt Karin creeped its way forward and came to a stop a few feet from us.

"*Zio* Art?"

Archer looked confused as Art DiRosario stepped out of the van after killing the engine, walking over to us.

"What're you doing here?" Archer asked. He sounded nervous.

There was a grim expression on Art's face as he stood before us, rubbing a hand across the back of his neck. "Something's happened."

Coincidences Aren't this Common

io," Archer pressed. "Please, just tell us what's going on."

Art took a deep breath, finally lifting his gaze to look us fully in the face. "Your grandmother. She's in the hospital."

I could've sworn I misheard him from how quietly he mumbled out those words, but there was no mistaking the horrified expression that took over Archer's face.

"You're joking," he said flatly.

"Victoria had another stroke," Art continued, getting it all out in a rush. "During dinner. They called an ambulance, took her to the hospital. And, Archer, things don't look very good."

Archer took a step back, still firmly in denial. "No."

I passed a hand over my face, holding in a heavy sigh. This couldn't actually have happened because Havoc had some personal vendetta against me, right? Could he really cause someone to have a stroke?

And if Victoria didn't recover . . . who would be responsible?

"We thought it would be best for the kids to stay together," Art said as I helped him unbuckle the younger kids from their car seats. "And Archer, I figured you would want to come to the hospital too."

Archer only nodded stiffly as he carried Gina toward the back door of the coffeehouse. I helped Georgiana up the stairs to the apartment while the others, Lauren and Carlo included, trickled along behind us. When Archer walked through the door, Rosie's face lit up and she promptly shouted at him. "Archer!"

"Hey, *bambina*," Archer said, heading over to the couch to crouch down in front of her. "How're you feeling?"

"Okay," Rosie answered. "Hadley put Band-Aids on my hands."

"Well, that's nice of Hadley," Archer said. "I'm glad you're okay. But, listen. *Zio* Art and I are going out for a bit. You're gonna stay here with Lauren and Carlo and everyone else, okay?"

Rosie's lower lip began to tremble, but she nodded solemnly, as if she already knew something was wrong. Archer and Art said quick good-byes to everybody present and then made for the door. I caught Archer's arm as he passed by me, wanting to at least say one word to him before he left. God only knew how long it would be before I saw him again.

"What?" he said, shaking his arm free from my grasp. He wouldn't even look me in the eye.

"I feel like I need to . . . Do you think I could . . . Can I come with you?"

"No," Archer said immediately, like a reflex. "You don't need to."

"Archer, please," I said. I didn't want to beg, but I felt like I was about to. "I'd like to make sure that Victoria is okay."

This was a much different Archer from the one I'd been

laughing with and teasing earlier. He looked like the world was about to fall apart—and I knew when he felt like that he started pushing people away. But I couldn't just *not* go with him.

Archer glanced over at Art and Lauren and Carlo before tugging me off to the side, and then he said, "Hadley, I care about you. You know I do. But there's no reason for you to come with me. No offense, but the truth is that you work for us. That's it. *You work for us.* And this is about my family right now. There's just too much going on right now, and I really can't just— We have to go now, okay?"

He turned and left without another word, only stopping to say good-bye to Rosie again before leaving with Art. The front door shutting after them echoed like a loud snap in the room. The TV had been abandoned, and everyone was staring at me. Even the little ones had quieted down and were watching me with wide eyes.

"Hadley." Carlo took a few steps toward me, his hand outstretched as if to comfort me. "Archer, he . . . he didn't mean that. He's just upset because—"

"No, Carlo, it's fine, really," I said, and my voice cracked. "He's right. I really should be getting home."

"Hadley, you don't have to go," Lauren said quickly, but I was already heading for the front door, ready to bolt.

"Tell me how Victoria is doing later, okay?" I said before stepping out, shutting the door behind me, racing down the stairs to the kitchen.

I snatched my jacket off the hook in the back and yanked it on, grabbed my bag, and left through the back door.

When I signed the contract with Death, I knew this wouldn't be easy. What I hadn't counted on was becoming so emotionally invested. I had been telling the truth at Thanksgiving when I told Regina I felt like I was part of the family. She had become a trusted confidant, someone I could rely on, much more than just my boss or my friend's mom. Rosie was just the sweetest little girl in existence, and I was beginning to see her as the little sister I'd never had. Even Victoria, with all of her surliness, had become a constant figure in my life.

And Archer . . . I could never tell exactly where we stood. He was my friend, but there was something between us. Something I couldn't let go of. The things I felt for him . . . they were frustrating and complicated, and yet at the same time, they felt *right*.

Somehow, despite everything, Archer had let me in. But my time was running out now, and I wasn't willing to step away. I couldn't. I needed to be with Archer until my countdown zeroed out. How else could I be sure he would be okay?

So just go to the hospital! a voice in the back of my mind screamed at me. *Who cares what Archer thinks right now?*

Before I could talk myself out of it, I managed to find a cab some ways up the block and jumped in, quickly telling the driver to take me to the hospital Art mentioned Victoria had been taken to. The driver pulled away from the curb with a grunt and slipped into traffic.

When the car finally came to a stop outside the ER entrance, I stumbled my way out, throwing a twenty at the cab driver before racing across the street. I'd jogged about five steps when I heard the sound of screeching tires peeling out on the road. I looked up to see a bright yellow sports car racing down the street, heading straight toward me.

I barely had enough time to register the fact that I was

directly in the path of the car, and then I was airborne. I didn't feel the impact when the car slammed into me, but I felt it when all air was ripped from my lungs.

I was sent spiraling backward only to collide with another car heading down the opposite side of the street. I heard the sound of the windshield cracking beneath my weight when I crashed into it and went tumbling down the hood of the car.

The result was this awful bone-shattering noise when I landed on the pavement, and my whole world was spinning so violently that I could barely see. I was flat on my back, and I'd lost the ability to breathe. A feeling of icy numbness was spreading through me at an alarming rate.

"Oh my. Looks like you got yourself into a spot of trouble, didn't you, Hadley?"

I couldn't move, but I still managed to move my eyes to see Havoc crouched beside me, a wide smile stretched across his very smug face. The medical personnel from the hospital across the street didn't seem to notice him as they ran toward me, shouting to each other in medical lingo I didn't understand.

It was difficult to focus on his face; splotches of black were dancing across my vision, distorting his features. I wanted to scream, but all that came out was this choked, gasping sort of noise. I felt blood staining my lips.

"To be fair, I did warn you," Havoc said, patting my cheek. "I tried to tell you what would happen, but you didn't listen." He released a dramatic sigh. "Oh, well. I suppose you're going to get your wish now. You're going to die the tragic hero, and maybe, just *maybe* your friend Archer will live. You can never really know what someone's thinking, can you? Such a shame. Say hello to Death for me, won't you?"

A Culmination of Events

When I was old enough to understand that death was inevitable, I wanted it to rain the day I died. It seemed symbolic somehow, washing away anything bad and dark about life and beginning anew. But it didn't rain as I felt myself being pulled under, at least as far as I could tell. I wanted to stay conscious, to prove to Havoc he couldn't beat me, but I was tired of trying to fight my way to the surface. Everything was beginning to fade away. And that was when I knew death was truly inevitable—not in sixty or seventy years but right at that exact moment.

It wasn't painful, like I thought it would be. It was easy, like falling asleep. I felt so much better when my eyes closed, knowing I didn't have to open them again.

The last thought that floated across my mind before it all came ticking to a stop was that if I had to die so young, then at least it was in the place of the people I loved. That had to count for something.

CHAPTER 31

In Between

You're going to have to wake up sometime. C'mon, kid. Wake up."

I wanted that voice to shut up. Before it had started talking, I'd been relaxed. Calm.

"You can't stay asleep for much longer, Hadley." The voice was moving closer, somewhere above my head. "*Wake up.*"

I let out an aggravated sigh and cracked open an eye, ready to shout at the voice, only to let out a shriek and bolt upright when I came face-to-face with Death.

"*Death?* What the—" My breath caught in my throat as I looked around, attempting to recognize where I was. "What are you doing here? What am *I* doing here? Where . . . *is* here?"

I was sprawled out on the floor of an enormous, cathedral sized room. The walls were white, the ceiling was white— *everything* was white.

"Take it easy, Hadley," Death cautioned. "You're fine."

I looked down at myself. I was wearing the same jeans, long-sleeve shirt, and jacket I remembered putting on that morning.

Except my shirt was ripped all over, my jacket was hanging off me in tatters, and my jeans were torn. And they were covered in blood. The patches of my skin I could see were bruised, and it looked as if I had been burned in some places from where my skin scraped against something. But nothing hurt. That was what frightened me the most.

"Death, I . . ." I looked up at him, the words catching in my throat. "I'm . . . Did . . ."

Death said nothing as he took a seat beside me on the floor, stretching out his legs in front of him.

I waited anxiously for him to say something that might give me an idea as to what had happened to me. His face was an expressionless mask.

"Death . . ." Tears started to splash down my cheeks without my control. "I'm . . . I'm dead. I'm dead, aren't . . . aren't I?"

Death nodded once. Something like pity might've flashed in his eyes for a second before it was gone. "Yes."

I'd been warned about the consequences of messing with time, and I knew trying to help someone who clearly didn't want to be helped would be difficult, but this wasn't something I could have ever prepared myself for. I never thought I would wind up *dead*, no matter what Havoc threatened me with.

I had saved Archer—I hoped. But I had lost the people I had come to know as my family. My friends. My parents. Archer. *Everything.*

I forced myself to take a breath, gritting my teeth as a fresh wave of pain crashed over me. The emotional kind, not physical. I was not expecting this to be what would hurt the most—the *what could have been.*

Part of what influenced my decision to sign the contract in the first place was because of all the things Archer unknowingly threw away. He needed to realize the importance of what he was giving up, even if he thought it wasn't worth it.

What he'd done had been a permanent solution to a temporary problem. His pain wouldn't have lasted forever. Nothing ever did. I wanted Archer to know that. I *needed* him to know that.

I hadn't had any idea of what the future would hold when I accepted the contract Death offered. Now I was never going to get the chance to find out. Despite all the odds, wherever our crazy, mismatched friendship might have landed us, a part of me knew Archer and I would've been together—the way it was supposed to be. Now it had been taken away from me, from us. And it hurt more than broken bones ever could.

I scrubbed at the tears my cheeks with the sleeve of my ruined shirt. I was on the verge of a breakdown, but I needed answers. "So . . . so where am I?"

"Think of this place as a . . . waiting room of sorts," Death told me. "Not heaven. Not hell. Just . . . here."

"What am I doing *here* if . . . if . . ." I swallowed back another wave of tears. "What am I doing here if I'm dead? Shouldn't I be six feet under in a coffin now or something?"

"That's what you're about to find out." Death got to his feet and reached down to offer me a hand. "Let's go for a little walk, shall we?"

I grasped Death's cold hand and he pulled me upright. I managed to take a few tentative steps forward, but my knees suddenly buckled. I would've hit the floor if Death hadn't wrapped an arm around my waist to keep me steady. I couldn't help but think how much nicer he seemed to be now that I was dead.

"The first few minutes are always the worst. This way," he said, nodding his head toward a door that suddenly appeared in the far corner of the room. I stumbled my way alongside Death until he pushed open the door, a massive wooden thing etched with intricate carvings of symbols and figures I couldn't make light of.

"Death, what are we— Oh."

I was standing inside a room made entirely out of glass.

Nothing was visible beyond the sheets of clear glass except a white fog that pressed up against the sides of the room, even the floor, making it seem as if I was tucked away right in the middle of a massive cloud. Placed in the center of the room was a long table that wouldn't have been out of place in a conference room, surrounded by large leather chairs.

"Why don't you have a seat?" Death said, gesturing to the chairs around the table. "We've got a lot to discuss, and we haven't got that much time."

"Why?" I asked. "I'm dead, aren't I? Don't I have all the time in the world now?"

"Do me a favor. Just sit."

Deciding not to push it, I took a few steps forward, and was relieved I didn't hit the floor again. I dropped into the chair closest to me and settled back, turning to Death expectantly.

He kicked back in his chair and propped his feet up on the table, tucking his arms behind his head.

"Consider this a . . . performance review," Death began.

"A performance review," I repeated. "Of what?"

"The execution of your contract, of course." Death reached into his jacket pocket and pulled out the stack of crumpled papers I remembered having signed without reading twenty-five days ago.

"Oh."

This didn't sound promising. Now that I was dead, did

that mean our contract was no longer valid? I hadn't survived the full twenty-seven days. Would the world snap back to that original timeline, the one where Archer had killed himself?

"No need to look so frightened," Death said, a wry smile twisting his mouth as he stared at me. "All things considered, you did okay."

I stared blankly at him. "Okay? You think I did *okay*? I just died! I died before my twenty-seven days were up, Havoc waltzed right in and ruined pretty much everything, Victoria is in the hospital, and who knows where Archer is? If he'll decide to . . ." I couldn't finish the sentence. "Death, I *failed*. That is the farthest thing from okay."

Death let out a low whistle, leaning back in his chair. "Come on, kid, did you honestly think this would be easy? That everything would be sunshine and daisies and you'd be able to top it all off with a perfect little bow?"

"Of course I didn't think that," I snapped. "I just thought—"

"This might come as a surprise to you, Hadley, but very little in life is ever easy. That's the way it's been since the dawn of time, and I'm pretty sure that's the way it's always going to be. But the thing is?" Death scooted closer in his chair, gripping my knee, forcing me to look him in the eyes. "There are things in this life that make all the other crap worth it. So you grab those moments, those people, and you run with them and you fight with everything you have to never lose them. And at the end of your life, when you look back on all the things you've done, you're going to be glad you went kicking and screaming."

It was the most I'd ever heard Death speak. I knew nothing about this . . . *man*, other than the fact that he called himself Death and he seemed content playing with my life and

Archer's like we all were in some sort of cosmic game. There was nothing about him that was human—at least not that I could see—but what he said had to have been the most human thing I'd ever heard.

"You told me you failed," Death went on. "I think you're wrong. I picked you for a lot of reasons, but I saw right through you, you know. You may not have realized it, but you were *just* as lonely as Archer was. Just as lost. Just as scared as what the future would hold for you. You simply expressed it in different ways. I didn't make a mistake picking you. And you didn't fail."

It was silent in the room for several minutes while I thought about what he said.

"Maybe you're right." My voice cracked as I spoke. "But there's just *so* much more that I could've handled better, or thought about differently, or if I'd just figured things out sooner, I could've—"

"You're sixteen, kid. You're kind of at a point in life where all you think you do is screw things up."

"Thanks."

"If you didn't have what it took, there's no way you would've been able to stand up to Havoc the way you did," Death said. "Everything that happened in the past week, all those accidents, just so happened to be some of the worst things Archer was afraid of happening. Havoc took his worst nightmares and turned them into reality."

It was so obvious Archer cared about his family above all else and would do anything to protect them. I could tell he was upset and frustrated with what was going on, but I hadn't known to what degree his deepest, darkest fears were playing out before his eyes.

"And did you notice that you happened to be included in that category too?"

I whipped my head up so quickly to look at Death I got a crick in my neck. "Sorry, *what?*"

"You were one of the first people outside Archer's family to show you cared," Death said. "You stuck with him through some of his biggest fears, and you didn't judge him. How could he not come to care about you in his own way after that? I was watching when you fell down those stairs at school, and I saw the look on his face. He was scared you'd been hurt. So don't think you aren't important to him. That you didn't make a difference. You'd be lying to yourself."

I may have made a difference, but there were still two days left before I would have known for sure if I had succeeded, and now I was never going to figure that out. I asked the question I'd been afraid to voice this whole time. "What happens if what I did wasn't enough? What if I failed?"

"There is always that chance, I suppose," Death said hesitantly.

"Then why did I die?" I asked.

"I wasn't counting on that," he admitted, looking sheepish. "And I am sorry this happened to you. Well, not too sorry, actually."

"Not *too* sorry? What is that supposed to mean?" I demanded angrily. Death was pleased I was dead? Typical.

"You weren't supposed to die," Death elaborated. "It's a specific clause in the contract, actually. See?" He took the contract from me and flipped to the last page, pointing to a short paragraph right above my sloppy signature. The language was still totally unintelligible.

"How was I supposed to know that?" I said shrilly, snatching the contract back from him, giving it a shake. "Excuse me for not being able to understand whatever these little symbols are!"

"No need to be so snippy," Death retorted. "I'd be happy to tell you." He grabbed the contract from me and skimmed through the paragraph before reading aloud, "It says, and I quote, *in the event of my demise at the hands of supernatural forces, any ties that therefore bind me to death shall not be valid.*"

"*Supernatural forces*? You mean Havoc? What does that mean?" I asked frantically.

I was dead, but somehow it felt like my heart was beating a painful rhythm against my chest.

"It's your turn to make the decision now, Hadley," Death said, tossing the contract on the table. "I made sure to put a loophole in the contract just in case something unfortunate did happen to occur. I always do. Havoc has tried to hurt enough people that I've learned it's best to have contingences, though I must admit this is the first time he's actually succeeded in killing off someone I was working with. You are dead, make no mistake, but you have two options. You can choose to stay dead, wherever that may take you, or you can go back."

"Just . . . just like that?" I said. I didn't even recognize my own voice with how squeaky it sounded. "I get to go back like nothing ever happened and the contract never existed?"

What would that mean? That everything over the past twenty-five days never actually happened? I would've never met Archer or his family or grown as close to them as I did? Would Archer be dead? If that were the case, I wasn't so sure I wanted to go back. I knew I had things to live for and was fortunate in everything given to me, but it would be a very . . . *lonely* existence without them.

"On the contrary," Death said. "The contract was very real. Your past with the Incitti family has already solidified," Death told me calmly, understanding my panic. "That won't change. That reality, the one where Archer committed suicide, ceased to be."

Relief flooded through me so sharply I nearly fell out of my chair. "When . . . when was that? When did that happen?" I asked, afraid to meet his eye.

"That first day you went to his family's coffee shop. Helping you with your homework. He realized you were trying to get to know him, and . . . he liked that. He'd never admit it, but he was desperate for someone to show they care."

It was difficult to believe that Archer had tackled this life-changing decision so early on in my twenty-seven days, but what if that was all it took? Just one small moment to show someone genuinely *cared*? A feeling of warmth spread through me at the thought, making me feel elated and weightless.

"Good," I said, and my smile was effortless. "I'm glad."

So I really had succeeded after all.

Death slapped a hand on the table. "Now let's get to it."

"Get to— We're leaving? Just like that?"

"Just like that. Unless you'd rather stay here."

Death was already on his feet, heading for the door, and I tripped over my feet and almost landed flat on my face as I tried to catch up to him. I definitely did *not* want to stay behind.

"Where are we going?" I asked nervously.

"The next step," Death answered as he swung open the door.

I paused in the doorway, my knees getting a little weak from nerves or from the fact that I was walking around in my strange nothingness body. Death made an impatient sort of noise and gently gripped my forearm to tug me forward so he could wrap an arm around my waist to lead me from the room. "We're on a bit of a tight schedule here, Hadley, if you don't mind."

"Right," I said, embarrassed at my lack of motor control. "Of course."

The door shut behind us as we stepped out of the glass room, and Death began leading me away, now to the left, back where we'd first come from. This time, however, the hallway seemed to be growing shorter and shorter, the shape of a gnarled-looking door coming into sight, one barely hanging on by its hinges.

"Tada!" Death announced, gesturing grandly at the door.

"Is this my light at the end of the tunnel?" I asked curiously. It felt a little anticlimactic at this point. I was thinking maybe I'd get pearly gates or something a little more lavish and impressive.

Death rolled his eyes, his mouth twisted in a frown of annoyance. "If there's one thing I want you to take away from this experience, it's that you should never believe everything you see in Hollywood. That, and every place has a way in and a way out."

"I'll remember that."

Death gently pressed against the door, and it swung open. I crept closer, trying to figure out what lay beyond the threshold, but I could see nothing but blackness. For all I knew, one step out there would send me plummeting down to someplace I really, *really* didn't want to end up. I didn't think Death would trick me into anything—beyond signing a life-altering contract, that was—but I didn't relish the thought of taking that first step into an uncertain future.

"Well, get to it," Death said, giving me an encouraging nudge from behind. "Just keep walking. You won't get lost, I promise."

"So, is this it, then?" I looked back to Death, still oddly afraid to move. "This is the end."

"Or the beginning," he suggested.

"There's a part of me that wants to thank you beyond belief and tell you to keep in touch," I said to him. "But then the other part just wants you to stay away from me."

Death let out a short laugh, his eyes crinkling with amusement. "You wouldn't be the first, Hadley. But don't worry. You're going to be fine on your own from now on."

"This isn't the part where we hug, is it?"

He looked horrified at the prospect. "Absolutely not. This is the part where you leave and start living your life again."

I didn't imagine Death was capable of coming up with a better send-off than that.

"You really need to work on your people skills, Death. But . . . thanks. For everything." I hoped he understood how sincerely I meant that, even if I was unable to come up with the words to tell him.

"Good luck, kid," were Death's last words before he gave me a push forward and the darkness swallowed me whole.

CHAPTER 32

Things Left Unsaid— Two Days After

The first thing I heard were voices. They began to grow louder and louder, sounding garbled until I was finally able to make out what they were saying.

". . . How long she's been out again?"

A quiet sigh. "About three days now."

There was the sound of someone clearing their throat, then silence again.

"Our hope with the medically induced coma is that her body would have an easier time healing, but I also don't want to get your hopes up, Mr. and Mrs. Jamison. Your daughter really took a beating in that car accident. Her skull was fractured, her appendix ruptured, and three of her ribs broke along with her arm."

It sounded as if someone was now . . . crying?

"So what exactly are you saying, doctor?"

"What I'm saying, Mrs. Jamison, is that there is a chance your daughter may never wake up. We will do everything we can, but we need her to fight just as hard."

"But she . . ." The voice cracked with another sob. "She *has* to wake up. She has to. She can't just . . . j-just . . ."

I tried to open my eyes, but I couldn't, as though bricks were weighing down my eyelids. It *hurt* to even try to move, but I had to stop the crying, I had to help. I *needed* to open my eyes.

I don't know how long I fought to see, but I was met with a blinding light as my eyelids finally slid open. I groaned from the pain that shot across my cheeks as I winced. There must have been something wrong with my face.

I was in a small, cramped room, on a narrow bed with scratchy sheets—a hospital bed, I quickly realized. The walls were a shade of white that seemed faded from years of patients coming in and out. There was a mess of machines surrounding the bed that were making all sorts of noises, my left arm was covered in a cast, an assortment of tubes were taped all over my right hand, and something was binding my chest, making it difficult to breathe.

Slumped over in a chair beside the bed, fast asleep, was my mother, looking disheveled and far from the fashionable, put-together woman I knew her to be. Lying on the couch underneath the window was my dad, looking just as exhausted as my mom, even while he was unconscious.

I tried to move my hand to reach out and touch my mom's arm, but that was even more difficult than opening my eyes had been.

It took several moments of telling my brain that I needed to move my mouth to be able to speak. When everything somehow managed to click into place and I could actually get a sound out, my voice sounded raspy and out of use.

"M-M-Mom . . ."

My mother's eyes flew open and she shot up like a rocket in her chair, lunging forward to grasp my hand. "Oh, *thank God,* Hadley, you're awake," she gasped. "You've been out for days, I thought— Kenneth! Kenneth, wake up!" She reached around and slapped my dad on the leg, giving him a shake. "Hadley's awake!"

My dad sat up immediately, blinking the sleep from his eyes. A look of total relief spread across his face as he looked at me. "You're awake," he said, quickly getting to his feet, coming to the bedside. "It's so good to see your eyes open, Hadley."

I was even more confused now. "Was I asleep for a long time?" I asked slowly.

My dad sighed, reaching out to gently place his hand over mine. "About four days now."

"Honey . . ." My mom squeezed my hand gently. I didn't tell her that it hurt. It seemed to be doing something to calm her down. "You were in a car accident."

It was coming back to me, piece by piece. The accident. I was hit by a car. Two, actually. And I had . . . died. Death. I'd talked with him. That much I could distinctly remember.

"I'm going to go find a nurse," my dad said quietly before slipping from the room.

"Hadley, sweetheart." My mom gave my hand another squeeze, still looking at me with concerned expression. "How do you feel?"

"I . . . don't know," I said honestly.

The feeling of numbness was slowly starting to fade, and a dull ache was beginning to creep over me. The door opened a moment later and my dad entered, closely followed by a nurse dressed in purple scrubs.

"Well, I can't tell you what a relief it is to see you awake," the nurse told me with a wide smile. "You gave us all a real fright there."

"Sorry," I said sheepishly.

The nurse started to check the mess of machines by the bed, fluttering around me like a bird, asking me how I felt and if I was in pain, what my name was, who the president was, where I went to school and what grade I was in.

I knew all of the answers to the questions, but it took me a little extra time to recall them. My brain felt like it was full of a thick, dense fog, probably thanks to whatever medication they no doubt had me on.

"Well, I'm going to call Dr. Sherman and have him get down here right away," the nurse said, turning to my mom and dad. "He'll be thrilled to see Hadley's awake."

"Yes, of course," my dad said with a nod.

The nurse frowned in thought. "Did you want to tell that boy she's awake too? He's been in here a lot, and I think he's still out in the waiting room somewhere."

That boy? "*Oh.*" It felt like my chest was ripping open as I tried to breathe. "Archer." My twenty-seven days were up. In fact, I was on day twenty-nine. I didn't need to see the numbers on my wrist to know that. "Where is he? I need to see him, I have to see him, I—"

"Hadley, I need to you calm down," the nurse said gently, examining all of the machines I was hooked up to again as they started beeping erratically. "Just take it easy, all right? It's not going to do any good if you get worked up."

"I'll go find Archer," my dad said, heading for the door. "Hang on."

The nurse said something about finding the doctor again, and followed my dad out of the room. My mom hovered beside the bed while I tried to force deep breaths in through my nose and out through my mouth. Any air I actually managed to get in my lungs burned painfully.

Then the door opened after what had felt like a lifetime of passing me by.

"Archer!"

He was standing there, his eyes wide and bloodshot, his hair a mess, looking a little worse for wear, but he was breathing and alive.

Archer was *alive*.

Sweet relief crashed over me, but the pain stayed, radiating throughout every inch of my body, and it was entirely worth it.

"Is everyone okay? Is Victoria all right? Please tell me that nothing happened to anybody, I swear I—"

Archer held up his hands to stop my rapid flow of questions. "Hadley, stop. Just breathe for a second, okay?"

"But I just . . ." I sucked in a breath, working to hold back a fresh wave of tears. One of the machines I was hooked up to was beeping erratically the more my heart pounded. "I need to know that everything is okay."

"You just woke up after being in a coma for four days, and you want to know how everyone else is doing?" Archer asked incredulously.

"Michaela, come on," my dad said to my mom, putting his hand on her arm. "Let's give them a moment."

My mom looked like she was about to start a round of protesting, but my dad murmured something that made her shut her mouth. She shot Archer a look before saying to me, "Hadley, you call right away if you need us, okay?"

"Promise," I said, desperate for them to leave so I could talk to Archer, just the two of us.

My parents left the room, my dad shutting the door quietly behind them.

I looked up at Archer, taking in every one of his features, so immensely relieved that he at least appeared to be okay that it was difficult to form a straight thought. He was watching me with a cautious expression, as if he was worried I was about to have a mental breakdown. At this point, it was a total possibility.

"You're okay," I finally managed to say, breathing shakily.

Archer frowned in confusion, moving closer to the bed. "Of course I'm okay. Why wouldn't I be? Are *you* okay?"

There were *plenty* of reasons why Archer wouldn't be okay, but I was definitely not in the mood to share my knowledge concerning that. I didn't think I ever would.

"I don't know, I was just . . . I thought you . . ." My first reaction was to shrug, and I immediately regretted it as intense pain shot through me at the attempted motion. "How . . . how is Victoria?"

"My grandmother is fine," Archer said. "The doctors say she'll pull through. Besides, she's too stubborn to die."

I wanted to laugh at that, but I forced myself not to. Laughing would probably hurt worse than shrugging had. "Good," I forced out.

Archer dropped into the chair beside the bed my mother had just vacated and slumped backward, covering his eyes with a hand.

It felt like we were both ignoring the elephant in the room.

"You know, if you ever do something to me like that again, I'm going to kill you myself."

"I— Wait, what?"

Archer moved forward in the chair, looking at me with this intense expression on his face that was alarming. "I'm not an emotional, touchy-feely kind of guy, Hadley, and I think you know that."

"I know you're not," I said. I didn't understand where he was going with this.

"They said you were dead. Do you have any idea what that was like? Sitting there and hearing doctors and nurses running around, shouting about how there was nothing they could do to save your life?" Archer had gotten to his feet sometime during his little speech and started running his fingers through his hair, just like he always did when he was agitated. Some things never changed.

"I was there." Archer dropped back into the seat beside my bed and leaned forward on his elbows, clasping his hands beneath his chin. He wouldn't meet my gaze. "We were in the waiting room, hoping to hear from somebody about my grandma, when they come rushing in with you, and you were—"

His voice cracked on that last word and trailed off into nothing. He wasn't crying, but an odd expression had taken over his face. His brows were furrowed and his mouth was twisted in a frown. I could see his fingernails digging into the heels of his palms.

"And I just keep thinking about the last thing I said to you. And, Hadley, you just . . . You were *dead* there for those few minutes. I never wanted to think about what I would do if I lost you."

"You would have been fine," I told him. He would've missed me, I know that. But I wanted to believe he would have moved on. "You know you would've been okay without me."

"No." Archer sounded furious, quick to disagree. "You don't get to decide that. You can't tell me how I feel about you, Hadley. Didn't you say the same thing to me last week? If you'd died, I would've . . ."

He looked like he might have wanted to keep speaking, but couldn't. We lapsed into an awkward silence. Honestly, I was just relieved by the fact he was actually here, and that I could see him with my own two eyes. I wasn't sure what else there was to say. Archer was right in front of me. Victoria was going to be okay, and my parents were just outside, waiting for me. I didn't know what else I could want.

"Can I ask you something?" Archer sounded calmer, not quite as agitated.

"You know you can," I told him.

"What I don't get . . ." Archer started to say, then stopped, taking a deep breath. "Why did you even bother?"

"Bother with what?" I said, confused. "Coming to the hospital?"

"With me. Why now? Why would you ever want to get to know me? I think I made it pretty clear I wasn't looking for a friend, and you just felt the need to muck that all up."

"It sounds to me like you're mad I'm your friend," I said, wanting to smile.

This somehow seemed *so* Archer. I couldn't think of anybody who would be mad they made a new friend.

"I wouldn't say I'm mad," Archer disagreed. "I'd say I'm annoyed. Annoyed because *you* are annoying."

"I'm going to assume there's a compliment in there somewhere."

"Hadley, I'm trying to be serious here."

"Okay, okay. Sorry."

He let out a frustrated groan, his head falling into his hands again. "I wasn't looking for a friend, okay? I didn't *want* a friend, and I certainly didn't want *you* to be the one that changed that. Because at first, I just kept thinking, who does this girl think she is? In what universe would she think it's okay to come waltzing into my life just to screw everything up?"

"I . . . screwed everything up?" I said, trying not to feel offended.

"Yeah, you did," Archer said. "I had every reason to be mad at the world, Hadley, and I was fine with that. I guess I even thought I deserved it. It was what I was used to. But then the moment you come along, you made me realize that . . . that I don't really want to keep living that way. But the thing is I don't know how *not* to."

It wasn't hard to make out what he was trying to say.

"So you're scared. Of me." I had to work to keep from smiling.

Archer really must have been putting himself out on a line here, because he didn't even try to deny it. "Change is scary, okay? I don't do well with change. And even if I hated pushing everyone away, I was comfortable with it because it's what I knew, and then you come and turn everything upside down, and I got scared because I didn't think I would ever actually want that change."

"But good change is okay, right?" I said hopefully.

My life had changed exponentially from the moment

Death first approached me outside that church the night of Archer's funeral. It would take time to process all of it, but I already knew that not all of it was bad. Scary? Absolutely. But bad? I didn't think so.

"I don't know," Archer said, his voice sounding strained. His foot hadn't stopped tapping out an anxious beat on the floor, and he was biting his lip, still not meeting my gaze. "*I don't know.* That's just the thing. Because . . . I look at you, and I see the person I want to be. The kind of guy who can give you everything you need. And then I remember every little screwed-up thought that's ever gone through my head, and I realize I'm never going to be worthy of a girl like you. And what terrifies me is that I even want to try in the first place."

I realized then that I'd been staring at him with my mouth hanging open like an idiot, and I quickly tried to come up with a semi-intelligent response. "When have I ever said I want you to be anything other than yourself, Archer? I'm willing to agree with you that you can be a bit of a jerk sometimes, but that's better than some Prince Charming. I wouldn't want you any other way."

"Is that . . . supposed to reassure me?" Archer said, glancing up at me with his mouth in a hard line.

"No," I said. "You said what's on your mind, and now it's my turn."

He stopped to consider this for a moment, and then gestured with a hand to continue.

"I told you I wanted to be your friend because I wanted to get to know you, and that wasn't a lie. I didn't think it would be as hard as it was to get you to warm up to me, but when you started to, I was surprised by how much I liked it. Liked *you*. You wound up being the best friend I didn't even know I wanted, and it's because of who you are. Grumpy, unsociable Archer Morales."

"Grumpy and unsociable?" Archer repeated, raising an eyebrow at me.

"Don't even try to deny it," I said, rather cheerily. "You know you're grumpy and unsociable. I'd say I'm your happy, chipper sidekick now."

His lips twitched with the barest hint of a smirk. "That's a tough burden to bear."

"Not a burden," I said. "It's give and take. All friendships are. So one day when I'm feeling moody and grouchy, as is your default setting, you'll be there to tell me to knock it off and then eat all of my fries at lunch like you always do."

"So, is this the part where we make each other friendship bracelets? Hold hands and sing Kumbaya? We could braid each other's hair, too, and paint our nails. My favorite color is red."

It was no use. I burst out laughing and immediately groaned as my midriff gave a painful spasm.

"Hadley, stop laughing!" Archer exclaimed, jumping to his feet, coming to my bedside.

"Quit making me laugh, then!" I said, somehow unable to stop even though it hurt.

"Do I need to get a nurse?" Archer asked, sounding frantic. "Seriously, stop it, you don't want to rupture your stitches or anything, and I don't—"

"Archer, I'm *fine*, okay?" I managed to catch his wrist before he could leave, despite all of the tubes taped to my hand. "Just stay."

A thoughtful look crossed Archer's face as he stared down

at me, and then he slid his hand free from my grip, reaching out to brush back a strand of my tangled hair from my face. My skin burned where he touched.

"What?" I said self-consciously.

"There's something else I realized," he said hesitantly.

"What?" I repeated, my voice rising.

"I . . ." He sucked in a breath, splotches of pink covering his cheeks. "I really . . . haveanappreciationforpenguinsnow."

I didn't comprehend what he was saying at first, but when it finally sunk in, I had to smile. It hurt, the movement pulling at the scrapes that decorated my face, but I couldn't stop. "You think I'm your penguin," I said. It was hard not to sound pleased with myself.

He didn't answer, and instead leaned down to gently press his lips against mine. The kiss lasted just a handful of seconds, but it was soft and sweet and enough to make my head spin when Archer pulled back.

"Get some rest," he said, making his way to the door. "I'll be back, though I reckon your mother has had just about enough of me."

"The nurse said you'd been in here a lot," I said, unable to keep from smiling again.

"Had to make sure you were all right, didn't I?" Archer said, clearing his throat. "You'll have to put in overtime to make up for all the hours you've missed at work."

"I'll be happy to, but can you at least wait until I'm not bedridden anymore?"

"I suppose that would be the *polite* thing to do."

"Now you're learning."

Holiday Cheer— Two Weeks After

I was going stir-crazy being stuck in the hospital. The doctor was sure I would make a full recovery, but I was being held as a precaution due to the fact that I'd had so much internal bleeding and damage done to my organs, not to mention my fractured skull.

"It's a miracle you're alive, Hadley," he'd told me, smiling sympathetically. "Just be thankful. Hang in there, okay?"

The nurses were reluctant to even let me out of bed to walk around my room or go to the bathroom on my own, but I was gradually granted more freedom to move about as I wanted.

My parents visited me every day. It was awkward at first, spending so much time together after years of drifting apart. My relationship with my mom and dad had never been perfect, but things seemed to be . . . different now. Things would get better, I hoped, but it would take time.

Other visitors came in the form of Taylor, Chelsea, and Brie. They were glad I was making a full recovery, and were only too happy to fill me in on the goings on at JFK and all the drama I'd been missing out on. It was a relief to be around that sense of normality again.

Archer was another frequent visitor of mine. More often than not, he would take up post in the chair beside my bed whenever my parents weren't present, and we would chat about his family and how the coffee shop was doing, but rarely anything about school. I did try to get him to fill me in on the things I'd been missing in my classes, but he point-blank refused, telling me that I had enough trouble with geometry as it was, and the head injuries I'd received certainly hadn't made me any better at it. I did get notes from a few of my teachers telling me that I had enough to worry about, and that homework could wait.

Much to my dismay, I wasn't given a clean bill of health in enough time for the holidays, so I was stuck in the same dumb room for Christmas. But on Christmas day, I got the best gift I could have ever asked for. My jaw dropped and a little bit of chocolate pudding landed in my lap as Archer strolled inside, followed by Regina, Rosie, and then Lauren and Carlo.

"Hiya, Hadley!" Rosie said excitedly as they circled around the bed, brightly wrapped presents and bags of food in hand.

"W-What . . ." I swallowed hard, an unexpected wave of emotion crashing over me. "What are you all doing here?"

"Well, don't look so surprised," Archer said, dropping a present at the foot of my bed.

"It is Christmas, after all," Carlo said, like it should've been obvious. "Like we'd really let you spend the day alone."

"But I'm not alone, my parents just went to—"

"We're your family too, you know," Rosie said as she pulled on the bedsheets, trying to crawl her way into bed with me.

My gaze immediately went to Archer at Rosie's words, thinking back to the last thing Archer said to me before I was hit by that car. And this was the thing about words. Said in the wrong place at the wrong time, even if they were full of doubt, words had a habit of sticking around for a long time.

"Just go with it," Archer said, attempting a smile.

"We brought desserts," Lauren said eagerly, setting one of the bags on the nightstand beside the bed. "*Zia* Regina made you cannoli!"

I immediately chucked the rest of my pudding in the trash. Who needed packaged pudding when you had cannoli?

"I remembered how much you liked it at Thanksgiving," Regina said with a laugh as I made grabby hands at the bag on the nightstand.

"You really didn't have to do this," I said, even though I'd already popped the top of the container Lauren handed me and dug in with a fork.

"*Caro*, nobody should have to be stuck in a hospital on Christmas," Regina said, sitting in the chair beside the bed.

"Now you all are too," I pointed out around a mouthful of cannoli.

"Are you kidding me? This is like heaven compared to being with the rest of the family," Carlo said, snorting. "The cops will be called if everyone keeps drinking and playing card games the way they were when we left."

"You're not wrong there," Archer agreed.

"Everyone wanted to come see you, of course," Lauren said, "but *Zia* Regina said that would probably be too much for you."

I highly doubted that, but Regina made a good point. A bunch of little kids playing sardines in a hospital room wasn't such a good idea.

"Face it, Hadley, you're one of us now," Carlo said, grinning devilishly at me. "And once you're in, there's no escaping."

"Well, aren't you going to open your presents?" Rosie asked, still trying to hoist herself up on the bed.

"Ah, I guess."

Truthfully, I wanted to keep eating desserts—calories also don't count when you've been hit by a car, Taylor and I had decided—but if they went out of their way to give me presents, I couldn't exactly say no.

My own parents had brought me a few Christmas presents in the form of a new iPad (for when being in the hospital became too unbearable, which was always) a variety of gift cards for Barney's, American Apparel, and Forever 21 totaling well over two hundred dollars, along with a bunch of Lindsor truffles. I appreciated the gesture, and was glad to have something new to amuse me other than TV, but the extravagance of the gifts was a little too noticeable. I knew my parents were just trying to make up for everything, and I hoped they'd realize soon enough that I didn't fancy things—just them.

"Open mine first!" Rosie said excitedly, now on the bed, shoving a brightly wrapped package at me.

I managed to open the present with little difficulty despite all the tubes still taped to my hand. "Whoa, a new coloring book!"

The giant fantasyland coloring book now in my hands seemed like such an appropriate gift from Rosie, I couldn't stop smiling.

"And look, a sixty-four pack of crayons!" Rosie said, shaking the crayons at me.

"Pretty sure that's more for her than you," Archer said with a chuckle, leaning up against the nightstand beside the bed.

"Who cares?" I said. "You're never too old for coloring. And besides, I've gotten bored of Candy Crush."

Rosie had already ripped open the pack of crayons and turned the coloring book to a new page, and was coloring a picture of a dragon bright pink. I would definitely be joining her later.

"This one is from us," Lauren said, handing over a present I suspected was some kind of book. "Well, my mom picked it out, but it's from all of us."

It wound up being an Italian cookbook with all sorts of recipes ranging from meatballs and Alfredo sauce to cookies and mascarpone. Written on the front page was a note that said:

> For when you can't always make it to
> family dinners.
>> *Much love from*
>> *the DiRosarios*

"This is perfect," I said, grinning. "I've been meaning to learn how to cook."

"Let's hope you're a better cook than you are a barista," Archer said under his breath, but we all heard him.

Regina scolded him with a few words in Italian that had Lauren and Carlo giggling. I settled for chucking my empty oatmeal cup at him.

My next present was from Sofia, her husband, and their kids. It was a gorgeous, hand-knitted purple scarf, along with a card wishing me a merry Christmas and hoping that I would be out of the hospital in no time.

I immediately wrapped the scarf around my shoulders and was glad it provided some relief from the chilly hospital air.

Regina's gift to me was a gorgeous silver bracelet with small pink stones set into the chain that sparkled and glinted whenever the light reflected off it.

"I got that when I spent the summer in Sicily when I was fifteen," Regina told me. "It's too small for me now, and Rosie's still a bit young for jewelry like that, so I figured you wouldn't mind looking after it for me."

"Regina, this is . . . ." I was unable to find the words to convey just how touched I was by this gift.

"I'm glad you like it," she said with a smile.

"Like it? I love it!"

"Maybe you can wear it once you're out of the hospital," Archer said after I spent a minute struggling to put the bracelet on one handed.

"Maybe," I grumbled, blowing out a sigh.

Stupid hospital.

"Is this from you, Archer?" I asked, reaching for the last present at the foot of the bed as he slipped the bracelet back in its case.

"I've been known to give presents now and then," he said with a shrug.

I knew it was another book before unwrapping it, but I wasn't expecting it to be—"*Geometry for Dummies*? Gee, thanks! This is probably the *worst* present ever!"

It still hurt to laugh, but it was impossible not to when everyone in the room cracked up laughing.

"I won't always be there to reteach you the Pythagorean theorem," Archer said, smirking at me.

"Excuse me!" I protested. "That was one time, and if you'll recall, I got an A on that last test. Just because you—"

"Hadley?"

Now standing in the doorway of the room were my parents, Chinese takeout in hand, looking baffled at my visitors gathered around my bed.

"Hey, Mom, Dad," I said, suddenly anxious.

"Who're your guests?" my dad asked, turning to look at me.

"You remember Archer," I said. "And then this is Regina, his mom—and my boss—and these are Lauren and Carlo, the cousins, and Rosie, his little sister."

"Oh, hello," my dad said while my mom remained silent, still caught off guard. "You must be the owner of the coffeehouse, then."

"I am." Regina got to her feet, extending a hand for my dad to shake. "It's such a pleasure to finally meet you."

"If we'd known you were coming, we could've picked up some more food," my dad said, placing the takeout containers on the nightstand.

"Don't worry about it," Regina said, waving a hand.

"We just wanted to surprise Hadley, that's all," Carlo said, smiling indulgently at my parents. "We all love her so much, you know."

"Your daughter is quite the hard worker," Regina added, giving me a fond smile.

I was half expecting Archer to make some comment about how I couldn't even make a latte, but instead he said, "It's never boring with Hadley around."

Given the situation, I was going to assume that was supposed to be a compliment.

"Maybe we should get going now," Regina continued,

looking to Lauren, Carlo, and Archer. "Rosie, c'mon. It's time to pack up the crayons, okay?"

I had the urge to shout at them not to leave, but it was my mom who unexpectedly said, "Why don't you at least stay for lunch? There's plenty here."

"Yeah, please stay," I said quickly, getting over my shock of my mom's friendliness. This was a nice, new side of her.

Archer slid me a look and whispered, "Don't want me to leave just yet?"

"Shut up," I grumbled, but it was difficult to keep from smiling.

Lunch went better than expected. It took a bit for my parents to warm up to the Incittis, seeing as their boisterous family was so different from our own, but soon enough they were joining in the laughter. My dad was unable to resist Rosie's adorable charm, and my mom spent a surprising amount of time talking business with Regina. I had never thought of these two important parts of my life being brought together, and I was surprised by how much I liked it. *Really* liked it.

Everyone began to pack up their things to head out once the end of visiting hours was approaching. My parents were allowed to stay, but they'd spent the night in my hospital room the night before, and I managed to convince them that it was perfectly fine to sleep in their own bed tonight.

"So," I said to Archer as Regina was trying to coerce Rosie into her jacket and Lauren and Carlo were picking up the leftovers. "When are you coming back to see me?"

Archer laughed, giving me an amused look as he pulled on his jacket. "I haven't even left you yet."

"You try spending all this time stuck in a hospital and tell me how you deal with being alone," I said.

"Yeah, no thanks," Archer said. "It's bad enough having lunch at school without you there. Your friends are insisting that they sit with me now. I swear, if I have to hear any more about how hot Liam Hemsworth is from Taylor, I'm going to lose it."

"You should be flattered," I said with a snicker. "That means they like you."

"Whatever."

It almost seemed as if he wasn't really thinking about it when he leaned down to quickly press his lips against mine—right in front of his mother and my parents.

"Um," I spluttered, my cheeks flooding with color. "I . . . guess I'll see you later, then?"

"Yeah, yeah," Archer said, smirking. "You know you will."

My mother naturally had to comment on what happened the second after Archer and his family left.

"So are you dating that boy now or what?" she said, eyebrows raised.

"I'm . . . not really sure," I admitted, a little embarrassed. "I think we're going to figure out the finer details later."

That was a conversation for another day. I didn't think either of us were in a rush to get it together. It'd happen soon enough. I was happy to wait.

CHAPTER 34

Return to Normality— Two Months After

"I thought I was ready to do this, but . . . now I'm not so sure."

I stood on the sidewalk outside JFK Prep, hand in hand with Archer, staring up at the old brick building I had somehow managed to miss in my time away.

"You could go home, you know," Archer said, glancing down at me. "The doctor said you could wait it out another week."

I hadn't been released from the hospital until well after the New Year. It was annoying and frustrating to have to take things so slowly and still rely on pain medication, but I was eager to return to school as soon as possible. I was already going to have to take summer classes to make up everything I'd missed while being in the hospital. I was ready to have my life go back to normal.

"Yeah, but this is better than being stuck in the apartment all day," I said. "I miss being around people. I even miss school."

Archer frowned and reached out to place the back of his other hand on my forehead. "Are you running a fever? Do you need some Tylenol? Because I could've sworn you said you actually *miss* school."

"Being hit by a car will do that to you, I suppose."

The warning bell rang, signaling that homeroom would start in a minute, but I wasn't exactly capable of booking it to class like before. Archer and I joined the throng of students rushing through the front doors, and while he got a few curious stares here and there and a handful of kind smiles, it felt as if no time had passed since I'd last been here at all.

"Isn't your homeroom that way?" I asked Archer, pointing in the opposite direction as he followed me to the staircase.

"Yeah, but I've been given permission to help you to all of your classes," he said, wrapping an arm around my waist to help keep me steady as we began to walk up the stairs.

"Really?"

"No. I just don't care if I'm late to class."

This made me smile.

We'd only had twenty-five days of getting to know each other before my accident, and while a little over two months had passed since then, I knew I hadn't even scratched the surface of what made Archer tick. But when I was stuck in the hospital, I'd seen an entirely different side to him. He was softer and sweeter than I would've imagined him capable. He still carried around his trademark sarcasm wherever he went, but that I didn't mind so much. He wouldn't have been Archer without it.

It seemed that despite Havoc's best efforts, Archer's life hadn't tipped back into darkness. Victoria had made a full recovery, though I thought she was even sassier now than she had been before. And the fact that his father, St. Pierre, had officially been denied his request for an appeal definitely helped to brighten Archer's mood. No more terrible accidents had occurred, and for that I was eternally grateful.

As for me and Archer . . . We still had things to work through, but it was comforting to know that we could do it together. We *were* going to do it together. There was no more question in my mind about where I stood with him.

"Here," Archer said, carefully handing me my bag full of school things. "I'll see you after homeroom."

"Thanks," I said, smiling. "Wish me luck."

Archer frowned at my wrist when I took my bag from him. "Hey, you're not wearing your beads."

He was referring to my ghost beads, the one thing on my person that managed to survive the car accident. I'd kept them on the entire time I was in the hospital, and only finally removed them yesterday. They were carefully tucked into my jewelry box where I knew they would be safe. I'd gotten used to the beads being on at all times, but I didn't need that kind of reminder anymore.

"Oh, yeah." I glanced down at my wrist, seeing smooth skin instead of dark numbers that needed to be hidden. "I, uh, accidentally left them at home."

"Bummer. They were pretty cool."

I wasn't sure if I would ever tell Archer about my deal with Death, what I did to save his life. That definitely wouldn't be an easy conversation to have, and even if he did believe me I was sure he would be totally and completely unnerved. For now, it was best to keep that part of our story secret.

But while recuperating certainly hadn't been an easy process so far, I knew without a doubt I had done the right thing.

For Archer, and for myself. I'd learned more in the past months about myself than I would've thought possible. I hadn't known at the time, but Archer had been exactly what I needed.

"Hadley!" Mrs. Anderson appeared in the doorway of my homeroom, a wide smile on her face. "It's so good to see you again! Come in, come in!"

Archer gave me a small smile before heading off down the hallway. I watched him go, still amazed at how far we had come. I honestly didn't know where life would take us—not yet, at least—but I was looking forward to finding out.

I'd already erased one dark future. I was ready for what came next.

There are so many people I want and need to thank for making *In 27 Days* possible, and to be honest, I don't even know where to begin.

First and foremost, a shout out to my parents, Sharon and Tony. You both encouraged me to follow my dream of being a writer since I was little, and if it wasn't for you, I don't know where I would be today. I love you. Another thank you should be directed to my siblings Emily, Matthew, and Kaleena, and all of my extended family and friends too numerous to name— you know who you are. I don't think I could have gotten this far without all of your love and support.

More thanks should be directed to Jillian Manning, editor extraordinaire at Blink, who found me on Wattpad and offered me the chance of a lifetime to pursue traditional publishing. You care about Archer and Hadley and their story just as much as I do, and that means the world to me.

Shannon Hassan, my amazing agent at Marsal Lyon, who took a chance on a virtually unknown author and jumped through numerous hoops to get me in the best possible place today—a thousand thanks. You are beyond fantastic.

Professor J. Morales at CSU–Pueblo, I want to thank you for all of your help as well. You've been coaching me through this whole process right from the beginning and have been cheering me on from the sidelines ever since. You can definitely look forward to amazingly positive feedback in next semester's student course evaluations.

I would also like to thank all the members of the Swanky 17's, the networking group for authors publishing their debut novels in 2017. Even though you may not have read *In 27 Days*, you still offered an incredible amount of support and encouragement during this whole process, and I am eternally grateful. You are all so very kind, and I am honored to have gotten to know you.

To Wattpad and its administrators and every reader out there, I owe you more than just a thank you and a mention in an acknowledgments page, but know that I appreciate each and every one of you, and I always will.

Lastly, the fantastic team over at Blink who helped make this book possible: I may not have met you personally or even interacted with you, but you helped make my biggest dream a reality, and I am so incredibly thankful for that.

Want a little more?

Turn the page for an interview with Alison Gervais, as well as discussion questions for *In 27 Days*!

To celebrate the release of *In 27 Days*, the Blink editors played a game of Five Questions with author Alison Gervais. Below, Alison spills some info on what went into writing the book, and her must-have meal. Enjoy!

Editors: *In 27 Days* has such a unique premise, in that the main character, Hadley, is compelled to take huge risks to save a boy she barely knows. Where did the idea for the storyline come from?

Alison: To be honest, I have no idea where the idea for this storyline came from! It sort of just fell into my head one night, and I decided to keep writing and writing to see where it would take me. I'm pretty darn happy with the results.

Editors: The book originally started on Wattpad as a story published chapter by chapter online. Did comments from readers affect the story in any way, or did you have a clear idea of how everything would play out for Hadley and Archer from the start?

Alison: Surprisingly, readers on Wattpad had a lot of fantastic input, but I think pretty early on in the story I had the general idea of where I wanted it to go.

Editors: Some of the locations in the book seem to be based on places you actually frequented, such as the church where Archer's funeral was held. How much of your own experiences show up as elements in the novel?

Alison: I actually have never been to New York City! It's a place I've always been fascinated by, with so many different cultures and such a rich history. I was, however, raised in a Catholic family, so going to church every Sunday and attending parish events were a regular occurrence—a lot like what Archer's family is involved with.

Editors: Whenever Hadley is at the coffeehouse or attending an Incitti/Morales gathering, the food sounds amazing! If Archer or one of his relatives invited you over, what culinary delight would you absolutely need to have on your plate? And is there one food in general you just can't go without?

Alison: I'm a big fan of anything pasta related, but I also adore chicken parmesan. I'd like to think that's a dish Archer's family would make frequently. In my own family, though, we have this Hungarian dish called chicken paprikash that we always make on holidays and birthdays, and that is for sure something I cannot live without!

Editors: And finally, there are a lot of fans of In 27 Days out there. What's the coolest thing you've ever been told by a fan?

Alison: I can't narrow it down to one specific experience because there's been so many over the years, and every fan is absolutely fantastic, but I've been told that reading In 27 Days helped them during rough times in their lives, that the story made them reconsider suicide, or helped them understand that suicide isn't the answer. That's one of the greatest things I think I could ever be told, not only as an author but as a person. Knowing my writing has positively affected someone is one of the best feelings in the world.

In 27 Days Discussion Questions

1. If you were Hadley, would you be willing to do whatever it took to save the life of a boy you barely knew? Why or why not?

2. Why do you think Death chose Hadley to save Archer? What strengths does Hadley have that would equip her for the task?

3. Hadley doesn't instantly fall in love with Archer, but she does fall in love with his family. What is it about Archer's family that draws Hadley in so quickly?

4. Hadley quickly learns Archer prefers to be alone. Why do you think Archer is afraid to get close to others?

5. Archer is often rude or dismissive of Hadley. If you were Hadley, how would you react? In what ways would it be hard to help someone who didn't want to be helped?

6. Even though Death sometimes gives Hadley advice, he doesn't provide many answers to her questions. Why do you think Death keeps his distance?

7. Havoc does not make an appearance until well into the story. What event do you think made him introduce himself to Hadley? Do you think he felt threatened by her as she got closer to Archer? Why?

8. What are some of the similarities between Havoc and Death? What are some of the differences?

9. Hadley's relationships with her friends and family undergo a lot of stress during those twenty-seven days. How would you feel if you were Taylor? Or if you were Hadley's parents? Do you think these relationships change for the better by the end of the book?

10. Who do you believe changed the most at the end of the story, Archer or Hadley?

Kaleena English

Watty Award-winning author Alison Gervais has been writing for as long as she can remember. In 2011, she began posting her work on Wattpad.com, and has been active on the site ever since. If she's not writing, she can be found rereading Harry Potter books, watching *Supernatural*, or trying to win the affection of her two cats, Kovu and Rocket.